AND THE WORLD LISTENED

AND THE WORLD LISTENED

The Biography of
Captain Leonard F. Plugge
1889 – 1981

A Pioneer of Commercial Radio

By Keith Wallis

with 165 illustrations

Foreword by Frank Plugge
Introduction by Professor Seán Street

KELLY PUBLICATIONS
2008

To my dear wife, Rose,
for all her patience during the years of writing this book

Also by the author

Gemstones: Understanding Identifying Buying

First published by
KELLY PUBLICATIONS
6 Redlands, Tiverton, Devon EX16 4DH UK
www.kellybooks.net
2008

ISBN 978 1 903053 23 2 (Paperback)

ISBN 978 1 903053 24 9 (Cased)

Acknowledgements

The Author would like to thank all those who have given their help and support in recording the life of Leonard Plugge, especially:

Frank Plugge – Lenny's son who has been the centre pin in the provision of family records and photographs, and personal memories of his father, usually over a pizza and a glass of wine.

Ann Plugge – Lenny's long-suffering wife, alas now gone; but the author's meetings with her are fondly remembered. A charming lady.

Mina – Lenny's sister, for her memories of their childhood.

Roland Plugge – Lenny's cousin, whose charm and wit made our meetings a pleasure.

Gerry Parnall – a cousin from the maternal side of Lenny's family, who kindly provided a comprehensive tree of the Chase line.

John Loveridge – for the details of his grandfather, Colonel Plugge, who led the Anzac assault in the Dardanelles during the 1914-18 war.

Stephen Williams – who provided a treasure trove of facts and anecdotes (and some photographs) regarding his days in Radio Normandy, Radio Paris and Radio Luxembourg. He left behind a wonderful store of memories recorded in his notes that have been incorporated in many places in the book. Tea and French Fancies will always recall his generosity.

Roy Plomley – his top floor 'workshop' overlooking the Thames, a bottle of red wine and his relaxed manner are a treasured memory. Taking Roy to lunch was an honour when he was the interviewee rather than interviewer of his guests on Desert Island Discs. My thanks to him for allowing me to quote from his autobiography.

Bob Danvers-Walker – I never thought when I listened to the Pathé News at the cinema during the war that I would be drinking coffee near the Rembrandt Hotel with voice from the newsreel. His memories of Radio Normandy were delightful.

Rosamund DuCane – Rosamund Ann (daughter of Max and Diana Stanniforth), Radio Normandy's little girl who said "Happy 'turns" to delighted children, and a few grown ups, on their birthdays. Rosamund allowed me to use several photographs and an excerpt from an illustrated letter written to her all those years ago.

Benjy McNabb – one of the early speakers on Radio Normandy, with many a tale to relate. His sister, little Flossie, who took Rosamund's place, added her side to the story.

Bill Wood – the man who introduced Lenny to wireless and remained his close friend and colleague for the rest of his life. My interviews with him provided me with an insight into the real Lenny Plugge.

Cynthia Michelle – for her recollections of Plugge as secretary in his first company, Radio Publicity International.

Joan Martin – Housekeeper at the Royal Aeronautical Society, adjacent to Plugges mansion in Hamilton Place, for her memories of Captain Plugge during the war.

April Ashley – the famous transsexual who was a close friend of Lenny, and added some amusing anecdotes for the book.

Molly Parkin – the notorious writer of erotic novels provided her personal memories, and my thanks go to her for allowing the use of excerpts from her biography.

Anne Bingham – for her hospitality and sympathetic memories of Lenny.

James Newton – a close friend of the Plugge family and source of many tales included in the book.

David Cammell – thanks go to him for the background to the making of the film, *Performance*, shot in Lowndes Square.

Christopher Musk – for his help and memories of Dickie Meyer and Isle of Man Radio.

David (Ian) Newman – probably the last surviving announcer from Radio Normandy, for his memories of the station.

Peter Taylor – for his amusing experiences during his stay at Radio Normandy.

Allen Stagg – for his immense help in providing me with details of the post-war IBC (as recording manager).

Sean Davies – for his recollections of the IBC as a recording studio, postwar.

Angela Close – office manager of the post-war IBC.

Trevor Dann – the BBC producer of *The Story of Pop,* who kick started this biography by introducing me to Roy Plomley, Bob Danvers Walker and Stephen Williams.

Bruno Le Grand – for supplying me with press cuttings and information from the French side of the story of Radio Normandy.

John Rendell – for some background about Greville.

Malcolm Baird – for his kind assistance regarding the friendship between Captain Plugge and his father.

And last, but not least:

Lynda Kelly – for her excellent work in editing my book; her advice and guidance have added greatly to the final presentation.

My thanks and appreciation go to the many others who indirectly contributed their help and enthusiasm in making this book possible.

Contents

Foreword	By Frank Plugge		8
Introduction	By Seán Street		9
Preface	By Keith Wallis		13
	1926		15
1	1889-1921	The Early Years	17
2	1922-1925	The Wireless Bug	23
3	1925-1926	Travels	33
4	1926-1927	Aether II Across Europe	43
5	1928-1930	Ships and Stunts	66
6	1931-1933	Radio Normandy Early Days	71
7	1933-1934	And The World Listened...	95
8	1934-1936	Marriage and Parliament	100
9	1936-1939	The High Life	115
10	1939-1944	War	130
11	1945-1962	Diana's Hunting Lodge	149
12	1962-1970	From Italy to Beverly Hills	168
13	1971-1979	Double Tragedy	180
14	1977-1996	The Final Years	190
	Appendix A	IBC Station Data	197
	Appendix B	IBC Post War	204
	Bibliography		205

Foreword

Twenty-five years ago, my mother rang to tell me that she had heard from a man called Keith Wallis. He told her that he had in his possession some interesting photographs and documents relating to my father, and that he would like to meet and show them to us. This was duly arranged. Keith visited us and put on a lantern slide show of grainy black and white pictures of one of my father's pioneering trips by radio-equipped car across Europe to Bucharest and back in 1926. This was my first of many meetings with Keith, since when we have had a close and interesting collaboration. I have tried to give him as much help and material as possible in the compilation of this book, since when he has become a good friend

My father was 48 when I was born, and it was not until I was six years of age that I actually got to know him. This was due to my evacuation to the USA with my mother from 1940 to 1943. Almost all of his achievements happened prior to this and although he told me of many, I was short on the details. This is where Keith has been truly amazing. His research and quest for obscure facts has been both meticulous and diligent; indeed, he would have made an excellent private detective or MI5 spy!

My father died in 1981, and although fairly well known prior to this, no book has ever been written about his life. I think that with all he achieved in many different fields of endeavour during his lifetime, he merits a biography. By his dedication and literary talent, Keith Wallis has created a fascinating read, and I together with my family owe him a debt of gratitude.

Frank Plugge

November 2007

Introduction

The United Kingdom – in contrast to many other nations – came late to legal, land-based commercial radio. LBC, followed shortly by Capital Radio and Radio Clyde, announced their somewhat muted arrival in the autumn and early winter of 1973. As a young broadcaster in the second wave of stations to go on air after that, I recall that we were not even allowed to call ourselves 'commercial'; we were part of "Independent Local Radio", in other words, public service broadcasters that happened to be funded by advertising – and at the same time, until the start of deregulation with the 1990 Broadcasting Act, almost administered out of existence by the IBA. That said, it often strikes broadcasting historians from around the world as curious that here in Britain, we were provided with Independent Television nearly twenty years before the government sanctioned its equivalent in radio. Yet this is not to say that commercial broadcasting had not embedded itself in the DNA of British electronic media years before.

The romantic swashbuckling days of offshore pirate radio in the 1960s hit a chord with a generation for whom the defiance by Radio Caroline after the Marine etc Broadcasting (Offences) Bill became law on 14 August, 1967 was a metaphor representing a spirit of freedom which, roughly coinciding as it did with the reduction in the age of voting, was political as well as cultural. The '60s 'pirates' touched a chord and the pressure they brought to bear had a direct influence on government – and broadcasting policy – within the UK. The BBC was forced to acknowledge that it had missed the mood of the time; the somewhat staid Light Programme, restrictive agreements governing the broadcast of commercially recorded music, presentation styles at odds with the mood of youthful energy that dominated so much of that extraordinary decade: 'Auntie' was out of step with a powerful part of society.

The offshore stations are what many people of the 'baby boom' years recall as the birth of UK commercial radio. Those of us slightly older recall fondly the days of 'under the covers' night-time listening to "Fabulous 208 – Radio Luxembourg, Your Station of the Stars". Here we could hear current music in shows sponsored by record companies such as Decca, Capitol and others, brought to us by presenters who became friends, such as Pete Murray, Barry Aldiss, Jack Jackson and Don Moss. We listened to *The Adventures of Dan Dare, Pilot of the Future*, and learned how to spell Keynsham – K-E-Y-N-S-H-A-M – while Horace Batchelor's lugubrious tones tried to sell us his 'Infra-Draw' football pools method. We might also – if we were slightly younger – have been keen listeners to a programme for children sponsored by Ovaltine, largely presented by children with bright enthusiasm and mostly cut-glass stage-school accents. If we had but known, this programme provided a link with a pre-war period of broadcasting when Europe-based commercial radio programmes in English challenged the paternalistic BBC for the hearts of the nation. The *League of Ovaltineys* had enchanted and entertained a previous generation as far back as the middle of the 1930s on pre-war Radio Luxembourg.

Even this could not be called the beginning of commercial radio in the UK; indeed, was not the BBC itself – as the 'British Broadcasting Company' – not commercial in its origins? Formed by a group of firms manufacturing wireless sets, its original object was to provide content which would persuade potential listeners to go out and buy radios. Beside this, through the 1920s and 1930s, there was a man who constantly pushed and chivvied the public service broadcaster, particularly after the establishment of the BBC Charter in 1927, an entrepreneur of daring and vision, who understood that the BBC, with its stern Reithian hand guarding the Sabbath, could be taken on and challenged for its right to broadcast to Britain.

Was there ever a more appropriate name for a giant of radio than Plugge? Was there ever a figure so colourful, so many-facetted – and yet so ultimately unfairly ignored by posterity, as Captain Lenny? Keith Wallis's book rectifies this gross injustice. He gives us this extraordinary story in remarkable detail, the product of years of research and unique contact with Plugge's family and archive. You do not need to be a student of radio history to be enthralled and dazzled by Captain Leonard Plugge, his flamboyant lifestyle and his huge personality. On the other hand, if radio – its past, present and future – concerns you in any way, as a student or as a broadcaster, you should know about Captain Plugge, and when you have read this book and browsed through its fascinating gallery of illustrations, trust me, you *will* know him.

One of the things one comes to understand as one grows older is that history is often cyclical; if we could only learn from the past, many of the answers to today's issues are there to guide us. This is certainly true in the world of British radio. In the 1960s, commercial radio pushed the broadcasting agenda; in the 1930s, as Mr Wallis's book shows us, the commercial imperatives of men such as Leonard Plugge likewise provided a necessary competition, which ultimately changed the face – and sound – of broadcasting in the UK. Had it not been for the war, who knows how Plugge's empire – and British radio – would have developed? What is clear is that throughout its existence, more often than it would care to admit, the BBC has been re-active rather than pro-active; Leonard Plugge was more than a businessman with a vision – he was a catalyst for change, and radio in the United Kingdom would be the poorer without him. It could be said that pre-war broadcasting was polarised by two giants: Lord John Reith for the public service sector on one hand, and Captain Leonard Plugge fighting to develop against many odds a vibrant existence for commercial interests on the other. The former has long been a household name, while the latter has been cruelly neglected. This biography restores him to his rightful place in the history of the British media.

Professor Seán Street

Director, The Centre for Broadcasting History Research, Bournemouth University

Author: *Crossing the Ether, Public Service Radio and Commercial Competition 1922-1945* (John Libbey, 2006)

Preface

The event that inspired this biography occurred many years ago with the discovery of what some might consider a pile of junk. I was at the time employed by a consulting engineer with an office in Weymouth Mews, which lay behind and formed part of a large IBC-owned building in 35 Portland Place.

Due to an increase in business, it was agreed with the landlord to extend into an unused room at the back. Builders were called in to clear it of the clutter so that we could move in. Scattered across the floor were a number of old magic lantern slides and, having an interest in projectors and everything associated with them, I carefully rescued all the unbroken ones I could find. I also took a dusty old manuscript, plus a couple of travel guides, circa 1920, and a projection screen.

After carefully cleaning the slides at home, I lost no time in setting up a homemade 'magic lantern' to view them. The pictures appeared to show the travels of a rather dapper gentleman clad in a white suit and Panama hat, and accompanied by a small group of ladies – all in a heavily laden motorcar. The manuscript described a journey through Europe in the 1920s in a car equipped with radio, and was signed by Captain Leonard F. Plugge.

However, my interest quickly waned and, with little more thought on the subject, the slides and manuscript were again relegated to storage, this time in my attic.

Many years later, I was listening to a radio programme relating to Radio Normandy. Captain Plugge was mentioned, and the name rang a bell. So, once again the slides and manuscript were brought to the light of day, but this time they were to set me on a trail of realisation and discovery.

The story to be unfolded is the outcome of several years fascinating research: it is a story of endeavour, success, humour and tragedy. Although Plugge is mentioned in many books and articles worldwide, a complete biography of him has never been written; until now. Much archival material has been lost but, fortunately, Captain Plugge subscribed over many years to a news-cuttings service, and the many scrapbooks containing these, which had survived both fire and flood, have been invaluable in the writing of this book. Being the keen photographer that he was, many 16mm films and photographs also survived these traumas. With data from BBC Caversham and the Public Record Office, it has been possible to put together the story of an amazing life.

Except by friends and family, Captain Plugge could have been virtually forgotten, which would have constituted an omission in historical records. He was a flamboyant eccentric, maybe, but a man who gave considerable pleasure to many people.

All the people approached for information, particularly his family, have given with enthusiasm. I owe a great debt of gratitude to all those who have helped and enabled me once again to present to the world, Captain Leonard F. Plugge – 'Lenny'.

Keith Wallis

1926

Dorothy let the guidebook slip to the floor of the car, the purr of the powerful engine lulling her into slumber. The other passengers also were dozing in the back seat. The heavy Packard, its tyres spitting the loose gravel to either side of the country road, rolled through the night towards the Croatian dawn. It was one-thirty in the morning; Zagreb was fifteen miles behind them and Trieste lay ahead.

The darkened buildings of Zapressio slid past. A dog, raised from its sleep by the roar of the twelve cylinders, released a half-hearted bark, more of complaint than fear.

Glancing round at his sleeping passengers, Lenny was reminded of his responsibility, and switched his attention back to the driving. The nose light on the radiator cap glowed like a miniature beacon, illuminating the little Union Jack that fluttered above it; the headlights bathed the road with a yellow glow. Seeing the bend ahead, Lenny changed down and braked to cruise round it at twenty miles an hour.

The crash echoed through the night. The bar of the unlit rail crossing sliced across the top of the bonnet, coming to rest an inch from the windscreen. A strange silence followed, broken by the rumble of an approaching train.

1
1889-1922
The Early Years

Childhood
The Royal Air Force
The Underground Group

Lenny was born Leonard Frank Plugge on the September 21st, 1889, in Camberwell, a district of south London. The only son of Frank Plugge and Mary Chase, he demonstrated his impatience to start on the road to success by being born within ten months of his parents' marriage.

Much to Lenny's later disdain, his birth certificate stated that his father was employed as a commercial traveller by Noble & Hoares, varnish manufacturers. Frank was born in Brussels of Dutch parents and did not have the ambition that his son was to show; he stayed with Noble & Hoares for fifty years. Mary was born in Dulwich, which borders on Camberwell, and was two years his senior. Lenny was two when his sister, Wilhelmina, was born in 1891. A second sister, Christina, was born in 1893.

In 1896, because of his ability to speak several languages, Frank Plugge was sent by his company to Belgium to develop sales of their products in Europe. The family moved *en masse* to share a large house in Brussels with Frank's parents. They were kindly grandparents but, as Mina recalled, as with all families living in close proximity, relations occasionally became strained.

Lenny's early childhood appears to have been a happy one, if uneventful. His father was away travelling for long periods and his mother ran the family. Mary was ambitious for her son and encouraged his multifarious interests. From an early age, he was fascinated by gadgets. When he was nine years old, he fixed up a bell in the kitchen, which he could operate with a pushbutton in the summerhouse. A ring on the bell would summon the maid to bring tea for the family. This was his first entry into the world of communications, which was to play a very significant part in his life.

Lenny was close to his sister, Mina, and they spent many hours in the large garden playing croquet. He taught her to ride a bicycle and they became keen cyclists, pedalling into the countryside whenever their mother allowed. Lenny also developed an interest in ice-skating, and he and Mina often went to the local ice rink to practise for competitions. Besides winning ice-dance awards with Mina, he became the champion of Brussels and was later to skate with Sonja Henie, the Olympic medallist and star of several Hollywood movies.

Although his mother took him to church on the tram every Sunday and he attended the local Protestant Sunday school, religion did not play a part in Lenny's later life. He was, in fact, agnostic. But perhaps the church background had its influence: he never swore and disliked his friends using bad language. Also, he rarely drank and did not smoke. This may have been because of the day when his parents were out and Mina discovered a bottle of champagne and a box of cigars. Being adventurous, the two of them decided to sample these forbidden delights. Lenny was terribly sick and never forgot the experience. Mina was unaffected: a slight knock to Lenny's pride.

The ominous rumblings of the 'war to end all wars' began to shake Europe and as the German troops massed on the borders of Belgium, Frank and Mary Plugge decided it was time to return to England.

They took up residence at 100 Buckingham Road in Brighton, a large Victorian house with ashlar facings. In October 1914, Lenny, who had been studying for a science degree at the University of Brussels, obtained a place at University College in London as a 'refugee student' where he was able to continue his studies. He moved into a flat at 4 Cavendish Square, visiting his parents as often as possible.

Lenny was a keen student and gained his degree, a BSc (Engineering) in July 1916, being awarded a Prize Certificate in Civil Engineering, with a First in Municipal Engineering. Upon graduating, he decided to apply to join the Royal Naval Air Service. But one thing worried him: his father was born in Belgium and still held Belgian nationality. Lenny felt that this fact might go against his joining the Forces. However, having discovered a cousin with the same name as his father, but born two years earlier in England, he decided to put this other Frank Plugge's details on the forms instead. The ploy worked and he was granted a commission as a temporary sub-lieutenant in the Royal Naval Volunteer Reserve.

His science degree was put to good use in the Department of Scientific Research at the Air Ministry. He spent time at Manchester University, testing light alloys and crankshaft steel for airships and aircraft. On the creation of the Air Board, he was transferred to the Technical Department and was engaged on timber testing. Subsequently he was put in charge of the Timber Testing Laboratory of the Air Ministry at Imperial College of Science in South Kensington. In February 1918, he transferred to the Royal Aircraft Factory at Farnborough where he was involved in the testing of spars and materials.

When the Royal Flying Corps and the Royal Naval Air Service were united into the Royal Air Force in April 1918, Plugge was given the rank of Captain, a title he was to use for the rest of his life. Oddly, he was terrified of flying and preferred to travel by any alternative means available.

In September, he transferred to the Design Section and, under Lieutenant Colonel Ogilvie, worked with Captain Thurston on the design of metal aircraft until August 1919, when he was posted to the Inter Allied Aeronautical Commission of Control in Berlin.

In the same year, Lenny applied for membership of the Royal Aeronautical Society. His proposer was Lieutenant Colonel Ogilvie, and he was elected Associate Fellow, becoming its youngest member. He achieved full fellowship by writing a French translation of the *Glossary of Aeronautical Terms* for the Society. This book became an official publication published by His Majesty's Stationery Office and, in a rare deviation from the norm, carried the author's name on the cover.

Being with the RAF helped his future career. At Mess dinners, he had the opportunity to meet people who would provide openings into the right social circles. No doubt, he would have regaled them with stories, including the war exploits, of his famous 'cousin', Colonel Plugge (who pronounced his name as Plugg-ee). Arthur Plugge was born in New Zealand and was a big man in all senses of the word, being six feet four tall and weighing twenty stone. He led the Auckland Battalion, New Zealand Infantry Brigade and was the first New Zealander to land in the Dardanelles ahead of his troops in April 1915. Although the action became one of the major Allied defeats of the war, the heroism of the forces involved became legendary. The beachhead, held by Arthur for ten months, became known as Plugge's Plateau. A small cemetery now marks the spot with twenty-one graves, four of which are unidentified.

Lenny established many life-long friendships at the Aeronautical Society. One such was the Master of Sempill, later Baron Sempill, who held the proud distinction of teaching the Japanese (our allies in the 1914-18 War) to operate aeroplanes from aircraft carriers. Unfortunately, this knowledge was turned against us in 1941.[1]

---

[1] When the records were released in 2002, it was claimed that Semphill, because of his work with the Japanese, was suspected of spying. However, no action was taken against him.

Another good friend was John Moore-Brabazon (later Lord Brabazon of Tara), who gave his name to the Bristol Brabazon. This 140-ton monster aircraft, the largest ever built in England at that time, took to the air in 1949 on a specially extended runway at Filton. Designed for trans-Atlantic flight, it carried 100 passengers – but only one was ever built before it was made redundant by the jet-age. Brabazon was the holder of the first ever pilot's licence. A colleague, Claude Graham White, was much annoyed by this. As one of the first Englishmen to fly, he was a prolific writer on aviation, and often made the point that when he first flew, licences were not required.

Oswald Short, the owner of Short Aviation and designer of the famous Sunderland flying boat, became a particularly close friend.

Lenny left the Royal Air Force in 1922 and surveyed the scene of post-war London. It was not a happy one; the short-lived industrial boom was declining and the rise in interest rates imposed by the Government to slow down inflation had brought investment to a standstill. Unemployment was approaching one and a half million, twelve percent of the working population. This included many men who had returned from France gassed or shell-shocked and unable to work. The 'land fit for heroes to live in' now portrayed a bleak aspect for the soldiers who had fought so hard in the First World War.

In sharp contrast to the dole queue was the world of the 'bright young things'– the flappers of the Roaring Twenties. Women, now emancipated, were in the majority. Vast numbers of the generation of young men who should have partnered them lay buried in the military cemeteries of northern France. Women, having done the work of men, were not prepared to return to the strictures of pre-war society. Ladies' fashions had become masculine in design, with tube dresses, flattened busts and cropped hair. For those with society connections, parties of every kind were popular and held in the oddest locations. One of the better-known hosts was Mrs Claude Beddington, a self-confessed helper of the under-dog and worker for lost causes. She became a well-known figure in operatic circles: between performances, whilst chatting in the foyer of the theatre, she would take the weight off her feet by resting on her shooting stick with its tapestry seat cover and the point removed to avoid damaging the carpets.

It was at one of her parties that Lenny was introduced to the Ashfield girls, Miriam and Grace, and their father, Lord Ashfield, chairman of the Underground Group of Companies. Lenny, a dedicated social climber, revelled in his newfound friendship, particularly as he admired Ashfield as the self-made man that he most certainly was. Lord Ashfield must have seen in Plugge an ambition similar to his own, as he offered him a position in the statistical department of his company. Plugge had an extremely good head for figures, which stood him in good stead in his new work of scheduling the bus services throughout London.

The Underground Group controlled most of the transport in the capital and was the forerunner of the London Transport Board. It was developed by the sheer genius of Lord Ashfield and Frank Pick, the exceptionally skilled Commercial Manager, who became Managing Director in 1928. Ashfield had gained experience in the field when he was General Manager of the electric tramways in Detroit and New Jersey. Although born in Derby, he was educated in the United States where his Detroit-born father took him as a child. On his return to England in 1907, Ashfield took up management of the Metropolitan District Railway in London, becoming Chairman and Managing Director of the Underground Group in 1919.

On his first day with the company, Lenny was put in the care of a man named Bill Wood, who was to remain a close friend. Bill was told to look after his new assistant, but at the same time warned that his charge was a friend of the top man, and any 'comments' would go straight back to Lord Ashfield's house in South Street, Mayfair. Bill need not have worried: Lenny, although ambitious, was not the type to go running to the boss with tittle-tattle.

Although the Pall Mall Place flat he found certainly offered the aspiring entrepreneur the 'good address' he wanted, it was on the fifth floor and rather small. Lenny described it as a garret; however, the rent was in keeping with his limited finances and it was a pleasant walk to the office in Broadway, past St James's Palace and across the Park.

The work of scheduling buses, although challenging, soon became mundane. Lenny, however, found Bill Wood a congenial colleague, opposite in many ways to himself. Bill was happily married and satisfied with his job, which he had already had for ten years when Lenny joined. Lenny, on the other hand, was ambitious, fond of the good life and enjoyed the company of women. Bill was to become a stabilising influence in his life.

One evening, Bill invited Lenny to his home to inspect a wireless set he had just assembled from a kit of parts. Lenny arrived as Bill was making the final connections to the batteries of the Scott-Taggart 'two-valver' and watched as his friend strung up the aerial and made the earth contact. A welcoming crackle came from the earphones when the set was turned on.

Bill adjusted the reaction and volume controls, tuned until he picked up a station and passed the headset to Lenny, who held them to his ear and listened intently. His hand gingerly moved to the tuning condenser and slowly turned it, grimacing as an oscillation pierced his ear. Bill reduced the reaction control and Lenny's face beamed as he heard the recently opened Birmingham station. He tuned again, this time to be rewarded with a Dutch voice. His friend watched as he excitedly explored the aether.

"Bill, this is wonderful!" Lenny exclaimed. "Could you possibly make one for me?"

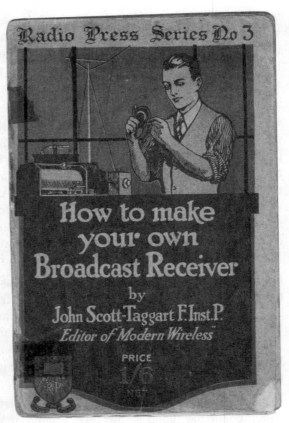

Home construction manual – 1923

"Of course. It will take a week or so." Noticing his colleague's obvious fascination, he added, "Perhaps you would like to take this one?"

"May I? I'll pay you for it – next week."

Bill enjoyed wireless construction and had other sets, so he smiled across to his wife and started to disconnect the aerial and earth, ready to dismantle the set. Lenny left with his new acquisition, hurrying along to Pall Mall Place to fix it up.

Bill Wood could not have known that this act of kindness would set his friend on a course that was not only to affect their lives, but the lives of millions.

2

1922-1925
The Wireless Bug

Formation of the British Broadcasting Company
'Which Station Was That?'
Europe tour by rail with a two-valve reflex portable (1924)
A sponsor for a commercial broadcast

Evening after evening found Plugge hunched over his little radio. The more he explored the airwaves, the more he realised how unorganised this new world was. The prime mover in the setting up of broadcasting as we know it today was commercialism. The manufacturers of wireless sets and components were aware of the numerous amateur societies up and down the country, which provided a market for their products. In 1922, the Marconi Company obtained a licence for a transmitting station at Writtle, near Chelmsford. Peter Eckersley began a series of test broadcasts, delighting his small audience of amateurs with his impressions of operatic sopranos and his announcement "Wrrrr-ittle testing – Wrrrr-ittle testing".

On November 14th of that year, the British Broadcasting Company was formed, replacing the Marconi venture. Peter Eckersley joined the BBC as Chief Engineer, but it was an imposing Scot called John Reith who was to be the main influence in the company's development.

Reith, with his engineering background, was appointed General Manager of the BBC in December 1922, with an impressive salary of £2,000 per annum. He was 34 years of age and had been looking for a job with challenge since he resigned as General Manager of Beardmores of Coatbridge earlier that year. He had little idea of what broadcasting was all about and relied on his new employees, Director of Programmes Arthur Burrows and his deputy Cecil A. Lewis, to enlighten him.

In his autobiography, Lewis remembers his first meeting with Reith:

> I stood 6 ft. 4 in., Reith was even taller. A sort of lofty detachment
> surrounded him. The gash on his cheek from a war wound added a
> certain severity to his mien. He had a pronounced Scottish accent,
> a neatly rolled umbrella and very fine hands. Those were my first
> superficial impressions of a man with whom in the early days I
> often grew intolerant and impatient for his lack of appreciation

23

and understanding of the niceties of programme building and the qualities of artists. He seemed to have no interest in or liking for any of the arts and often appeared to look on programmes as a necessary evil, produced by persons of strange character and dubious morals, utterly foreign to his strict religious background and high principles. He admitted at the outset he had no idea what it was all about; but he had one great virtue: he left us alone to get on with it.

Lewis would in time come to greatly respect this dour Scot.

Reith soon realised that his new position was one of considerable responsibility and one where his moral integrity was to be tested. He intended to take a firm grip, writing in his diary:

> I am profoundly thankful to God for His goodness in this matter. It is all His doing.

He threw himself into the running of the fledgling company, imposing his own high standards on the organisation. In November 1923, he became Managing Director.

The control of broadcasting was in the hands of the Post Office, under the eye of the Home Secretary. For the first few months, Reith had constant battles with them, most of which he won. The aggravation of a certain Captain Plugge was yet to come and, for the time being, Reith regarded him only as an important voice on the subject of international broadcasting, Plugge being heard regularly as a representative of the Radio Society of Great Britain (RSGB) on the British Broadcasting Company's London radio station, 2LO. The Underground Group of Companies had set up its own radio society, the TOT (Trams, Omnibuses and Trains) and Plugge became its leading light. As President, he was appointed to the General Committee of the Radio Society of Great Britain in 1923, becoming an active and voluble member.

Congestion of the airwaves was a subject on which Plugge and Reith could agree, and they reviewed the situation across the Atlantic with concern. In the USA, the output of many small commercial stations swamped the airwaves and there was little, if any, overall control. Private enterprise ran riot. Reith and Plugge deemed that it would not happen in the UK; strict regulations regarding power and wavelength of transmitters were applied and the BBC monopoly began.

Commercial sponsorship was allowed in limited form, but advertising on air was not. The British Broadcasting Company comprised a consortium of six radio manufacturers. Receiving licences were issued only for sets manufactured by these companies, and both licences and sets carried the BBC logo.

Lenny was spending all his spare time in his Pall Mall Place 'garret', exploring the airwaves. Bill Wood came around most evenings to help him, and the two of them would carefully log down the stations they were able to identify, noting wavelengths and signal strengths.

Plugge became increasingly attracted to the international aspect of broadcasting and was soon to become recognised as a leading authority. He realised that one of the keys to success was to get your name known and, towards this end, he became a prolific writer on the subject.

Listeners were intrigued by the number of foreign stations they were finding as they explored the airwaves. However, there was little information or guidance available to them. *The Radio Times*, first published in September 1923, devoted one page to the brief listing of continental broadcasts. Plugge began producing lists of programmes in detail, the first of which was published in *Wireless Weekly* in June 1924, and thereafter on a fortnightly basis. In July, he wrote an article entitled 'The Fascination of Continental Reception', giving advice, based on his own experience, of receiving European stations:

> If you do not mind putting up with a few atmospherics, or now and again with a little interference from some coastal station transmitting on spark or C.W. using a similar wave, and are prepared to overlook an occasional distorted note, or one which is not quite as clear as Big Ben sounds when in sight of the 2LO aerial, then to you the lure of foreign lands will no doubt have some attractions.

> If you are a traveller, in imagination or fact, have visited the Continent, or intend doing so, if you are interested in languages, the thoughts and methods of other countries, their customs and literature, then Foreign Station reception will have its fascination to you – the fascination of listening to someone speaking to you across the sea that makes us an island, speaking from the other side of the water, hundreds of miles away. Many such people are at your disposal for the turning of a dial, and if you are an enthusiast you will not be discouraged by failures and difficulties, but by perseverance will endeavour to achieve better results.

Charts were included giving the day and time of broadcasts from most of the major European stations. These differentiated between telephonic (speech) and spark gap transmissions, the latter being used for time signals. By July 1924, *Modern Wireless* was publishing more detailed

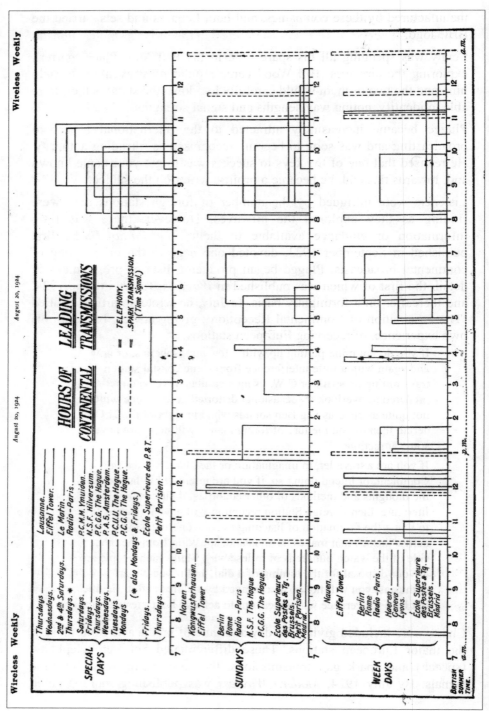

New chart of broadcasts – August 20, 1924

listings, prepared by Plugge. In November, separate lists of American stations were added. Lenny took an interest in the broadcasting stations in the USA, and had published articles on the Pittsburgh station KDKA, well known as the first commercial radio station in the States.

Whilst complimenting the BBC on its service in his articles, he pointed out its failing to produce a morning news bulletin. In fact, the BBC was banned from broadcasting news until after seven o'clock in the evening. This was due to the Press Association's insistence that newspaper sales would suffer if the news were broadcast earlier. The powerful continental stations were not under the same stricture, and produced regular news bulletins throughout the day. They also mastered outside broadcasts of sporting events, yet to be undertaken in the UK.

At the age of thirty-four, Lenny felt the need for first-hand experience of the stations to which he had spent so many hours listening. He also wanted to experiment with reception of British transmissions abroad. Consequently, in the summer of 1924, he embarked on the first of his many trips around Europe. He acquired a two-valve reflex portable, which he packed together with its batteries into a strong leather case, in preparation for the trip.[1] Lenny came to appreciate the difficulties of carrying a radio through Europe in the twenties. Permits were required and time had to be spent obtaining these from the embassy of each country to be visited. France was particularly strict and would not allow the use of foreign-made equipment within its borders.

Eventually, all was ready and Lenny set off for Newhaven, bound for Dieppe and points south, but as soon as he boarded the train in France, his precious wireless was confiscated and placed in the hands of the guard until arriving in Zurich. Once installed in his hotel, he asked the permission of the manager to set up his wireless in the dining room. The manager was pleased to allow this, but only after all the guests had finished eating. With a hundred feet of aerial wire slung up to the picture rail and the earth attached to a convenient radiator, he started turning the dial. Within fifty seconds, he heard the sound of de Groot's Orchestra from the Piccadilly Hotel being broadcast from England. Seeing his delight, the manager asked if he might listen. From then on, the earphones were passed from head to head; even the hotel doctor was called to join them.

The sensitivity of receivers in 1924 left a lot to be desired and the running and fixing of the aerial was of great importance. Between a hundred and a

---

[1] The set consisted of two dull emitter valves, and four bell type dry batteries, two in series and two in parallel. A bank of six dry cell batteries, giving the necessary 30 volts, supplied the high tension.

hundred and fifty feet of wire was not unusual, and Plugge had some hair-raising experiences on hotel balconies, in an effort to obtain the best reception. As a committee member of the RSGB, he was warmly welcomed at many of the broadcasting stations he visited, and was several times invited to speak over the air, his fluency in French and German putting him in good stead.

His extensive rail trip took him to Innsbruck, Belzano, Cortina, Venice, Milan, Genoa, Bordighera, Mentone, Monte Carlo, Nice, Cannes, Turin and Geneva. Throughout the journey, he made copious notes regarding not only reception but also technical details of all the stations he visited. These notes were to provide material for a series of articles he was to have published all over the world, describing the workings of most of the major European broadcasting stations. From translations in languages as various as Serbo-Croat and Japanese, few countries were not to know the name of Captain Leonard Plugge, intrepid traveller and expert on continental broadcasting.[1]

Prior to his leaving, Lenny's mother had been ill and while he was away she died at her home in Brighton. He never forgave himself for not being with her. He had always been very close to her, closer than to his father who had spent so much time away from the family on business.

It was apparent from his experiences in Europe that the Continent had its own special problems, which were soon to affect the UK. Each country in Europe was broadcasting in its own language, with complete disregard for adjacent states. By the beginning of 1925, there were forty stations operating. Some listeners were unable to enjoy their local programmes due to interference from a stronger neighbouring station transmitting on a similar frequency. It was obvious that an international agreement was necessary, and Plugge took every opportunity to encourage its introduction. Coupled with this, he strongly urged that call signs be allocated to all stations, and that they be given out at regular intervals during a broadcast. Lenny, as a listener, knew the frustration of tuning into a programme and having to wait an hour or more to discover its identity. He made this point very clearly during his broadcasts on 2LO in January and February 1925. 'Which Station Was That?' was the lead article in the second issue of the BBC's *Radio Supplement* in July. Although unaccredited, the programme listings can be attributed to Plugge, as they are identical to those he edited in the *Wireless Weekly* supplement in March

---

[1] The extent of his coverage in the press during his career was impressive. His name appeared in over 260 newspapers and magazines in the UK. In Europe, the figure was 155, over 40 in the Americas, and 50 for the rest of the world. The world certainly knew the name of Captain Plugge.

entitled *The Foreign Radio Times*. This gave the week's programmes from Paris, Zurich, Berlin, Hamburg, Konigsberg, Leipzig, New York (Schenectady), Pittsburgh, Kansas City, Los Angeles and Zion (Illinois). The listings in *The Radio Supplement* were extended to give details of Vienna, Brussels, Prague, Munich, Hilversum, Rome, Oslo, Barcelona, Lyons, Graz (Austria) and Canadian stations Monckton, Montreal, Winnipeg and Ottawa. The first issue also included Plugge's well-circulated article 'A Clear Band of Ether: A Plea' credited to him. Most of the first issue was Plugge's work, so perhaps the BBC felt it was not politic to put his name on everything. *The Radio Supplement* continued to publish his articles as well as his programme listings.

The points Plugge made in these and subsequent articles did not fall on deaf ears. The final paragraph of 'A Clean Band of Ether' sums up the situation where telephony (speech and music) was clashing with telegraphy (Morse code):

> Telephony has a right to live, has to live and will live. A place
> must be found for it: it is entitled to a clean piece of ether of its
> own. Let it then, have a definite waveband allocated to it – a band
> which will be able to contain the reasonable number of stations
> which it is expected will be in commission within the next two or
> three years. No Morse transmitting station should be allowed to
> come within this band. It will be the home of telephony: telephony
> will be within its own domain. All this is not impossible.
> Authorities should move. And when in the daylight of the future
> this telephony band will be finally adopted, and when the listener,
> educated to the disadvantages of oscillating, will be equipped with
> the supersonics of today, he will be faced with the enviable
> situation of being able to receive any such station as he may desire
> to bring in by a few movements of a pair of dials.

Action came quickly: the BBC convened a conference in London of all the leading European broadcasting authorities to discuss cooperation in the development of international radio. In April of 1925, BBC Director of Programmes Arthur Burrows took up the post of Secretary with the International Broadcasting Bureau in Geneva.

The problem of interference was brought home to listeners on the south coast of England in the spring of 1925. They began to experience breakthrough of foreign record programmes on broadcasts from the BBC station in Bournemouth (6BM) which had opened in October 1923 with a power of 3 kilowatts. Manchester and Oslo were having similar trouble. Direction-finding equipment was erected on rooftops in London and the southern counties, but the location of the offending source proved elusive. The newspapers carried the story of the foreign 'intruder' of our airwaves, and it was decided that Radio Paris was the culprit. Radio Paris (originally Radiola) was the first broadcasting station in Europe and was carrying out experimental transmissions on 373 metres, close to the wavelength of 385 metres used by Bournemouth.

Plugge carried out his own investigations and eventually discovered the true source. It was a private company, manufacturing medical and wireless apparatus, operating in the Boulevard Pereire in Paris. Its amateur station was transmitting on 380 metres, but due to poor control, its frequency tended to drift. When approached, the manager of the company said he appreciated that his transmissions may be interfering with the BBC broadcasts, but there was nothing he could do; the wavelength had been allocated by the state. The company had, in fact, sent agents throughout Europe and even to Egypt to report on its transmissions, and all reports were very good. The intention was to produce regular broadcasts, with "excellent concerts" being promised, much to the concern of the BBC and its listeners. However, no further problems were reported, so one may assume that the company managed to stabilise its wandering frequency. The episode helped Plugge to keep his name in the public eye.

Plugge's entrance into the developing world of broadcasting, and the impact he made over a very short period, can only be described as meteoric. From joining the Underground Group of Companies in 1923, here he was, two years later, being referred to as the leading authority on Continental broadcasting. Still in full-time employment, his involvement in the field of wireless was all in his spare time. He was on the RSGB committee, had published innumerable articles and station listings, and had visited many of the major stations in Europe and broadcast from several.

Yet he was just beginning. His driving ambition, fuelled by a lack of cash, led him to consider ways to turn his interest towards a profitable reward. An idea for expanding the entertainment available to UK audiences was in his mind. Under the strictures of the Post Office and the BBC, development in the UK was out of the question, but a potential audience certainly existed in this country for an alternative English-speaking programme. Without doubt, its European counterparts held the British Broadcasting Company under John Reith in great respect, but the presentation was formal and aimed at improving the listener's mind. Wireless was still to some extent a novelty in many homes, its sophistication going no further than a crystal set with earphones, often placed in a pudding basin so that the family could cluster around to hear the amplified voices from the air. However, valve receivers with loudspeakers were becoming more common and, as indicated by the publication of foreign station listings, people were prepared to look further afield for their entertainment.

Lenny looked towards France, in particular the Eiffel Tower station, as a vehicle for his first experimental commercial transmission, aimed at southern England. The Eiffel Tower, originally built for the Paris Exhibition of 1889, was due to have been demolished in the latter days of 1914. However, at the outbreak of the Great War, it was commandeered by the French military authority for use as a radio transmitting aerial. The company that owned the Tower were placated to some extent by a promise that they would be allowed to retain the possession of it for as many years after the war ended as months that the war lasted. In 1925, the transmitter was still controlled by the military and its chief function was that of transatlantic and trans-continental telegraphic work, although the studio was loaned for one hour a day to the Societé des Amis des Concert Artistiques de la Tour Eiffel. The director of the Societé, Monsieur Privat, organised afternoon programmes of music interspersed with comment on current affairs by leading authorities of the day. All the performers were volunteers who gave their services free. The transmissions were supported by subscriptions from the members of the Societé, but these were not always renewed, so alternative means of financing were sought. Another association was set up called Radio Popularisation or 'La RP' for short, which sold wireless sets and components at a cheap rate to members of the Societé. Consequently, regular advertisements were broadcast during the afternoon concerts, mostly for radio valves. A three-valve receiver called the Radio-Meccano-Phone was also offered, the name being copied from the famous model construction kit.

Radio Paris had a similar money-raising arrangement but with the manufacturers of wireless equipment requiring them to subscribe a proportion of their profits for the upkeep of the station. These manufacturers were then entitled to mark their goods with the initials GDER (Groupement pour le Developpement des Emissions Radiophoniques), indicating that they were supporting Radio Paris. Participating manufacturers had their names published and broadcast. Broadcasting was not yet monopolised in France, hence no licence fees were imposed and stations had to provide their own finance.

Lenny had already met Monsieur Privat during his previous visit in December 1924, and had given a short talk on the air, so he felt that his proposed experiment might be acceptable. He had also discussed the question of making the broadcasts from the Eiffel Tower station of more interest to UK audiences, by having an occasional announcement in English. Monsieur Privat agreed to think about it.

The next obstacle to overcome was the finding of a suitable sponsor, a well-known company who would be willing to back him. Through his many contacts, he eventually obtained an introduction to the publicity manager of Selfridges. This famous London department store was opened in 1909 by the American born Harry Gordon Selfridge and was renowned for its modern approach to retailing. Selfridge brought with him the secrets of success he had learned as a partner of the Marshall Field store in Chicago, where he amassed a fortune when he sold his shares in the company.

In 1925, wireless was the 'in thing', and the Oxford Street store had been in the forefront of introducing the latest ideas and inventions to the public. Its rooftop aerials for 2LO had begun transmitting in April. When the newspapers refused to publicise BBC programmes, Selfridge assisted by allowing the broadcasters to use his advertising space.

It was during this period that the Baird Televisor was being demonstrated on the first floor, giving flickering pictures of a winking mask, to the amazement of the shoppers. Although the transmission was only from one room to another, Selfridge thought it was worth paying John Logie Baird £25 a week for three demonstrations a day and his personal attendance to answer questions. Plugge had a great interest in the experiments with television, and discussed the subject with Baird many times. The two formed a friendship that was to last until Baird's death.

Plugge had found his sponsor: Selfridges was prepared to back his experimental commercial broadcast, advertising its ladies' fashions. The groundwork was laid, now to put it into operation.

Gordon Selfridge had sponsored the abortive Channel Tunnel in 1914; his association with Plugge was to be more successful.

A young Lenny in RNVR uniform

Frank Plugge Senior – Lenny's father

In full RAF uniform

Colonel Arthur Plugge

Lord Ashfield and daughter

Frank Pick

Bill Wood

C.A. Lewis

wireless set in a leather case that Plugge
d on his train tours of Europe in 1924

John Reith

two-valve reflex receiver ready for use

Peter Eckersley

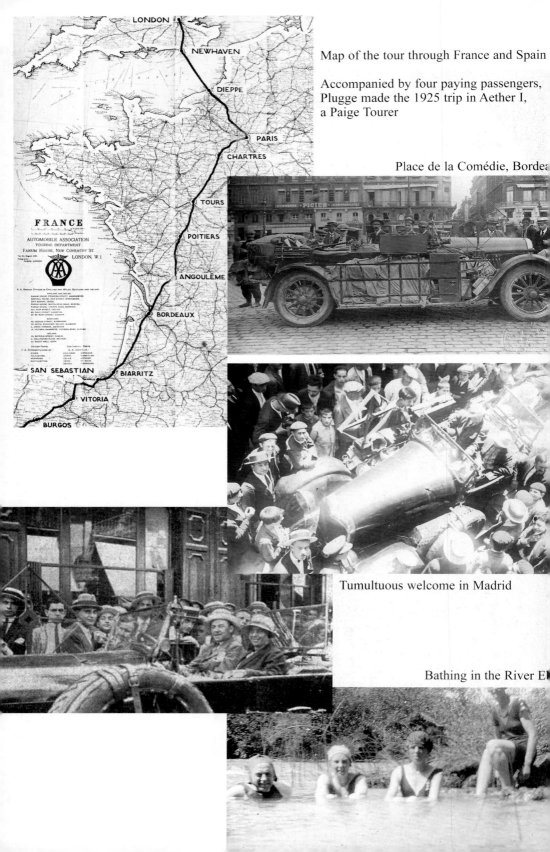

Map of the tour through France and Spain

Accompanied by four paying passengers, Plugge made the 1925 trip in Aether I, a Paige Tourer

Place de la Comédie, Bordea

Tumultuous welcome in Madrid

Bathing in the River E

1 PESETA   Año IV. -Julio, 1926.

Aether 1 at Radio Lisbona – pictured here on the cover of *Radio Sport* – July 1926
Captain Plugge's 1925 tour was well reported in many magazines and newspapers

Diagram of the
Western Electric receiver
used by Plugge on his 1925 tour

Front panel of the receiver

Plugge ready to test the railway
track during the 1926 General Strike

The train key
awarded to Plugge for his services

Aether II in
London before
the ambitious
1926 tour

The wireless
equipment on
Aether II

Map of
the tour

A bobby takes an interest

Dover: no drive-on ferries in 1926
The Packard is hoisted aboard

Plugge broadcasting from
the Nuremburg radio station

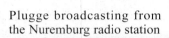

Back to the microphone,
this time in Vienna

Broadcasting from Budapest

Stuck in the mud
The road from Belgrade to Nish

Serbian customs post

The ladies lend a
hand to move a barrier

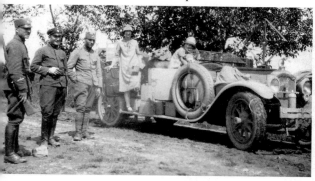

Filling up in Zagreb

Back in Paris, safe and sound

Aether III – a fawn and black Standard YR51

Map of the
1927 tour
with two cars

Connell and Plugge
reviewing the new
receiver

Offloading the car in Dunkirk

The loudspeaker mounted in the roof

Aether III

The dashboard

Tarragona,
outside Hotel de l'Europe

Filling up in Malaga

Aether III

An inquisitive customs
officer at Elvas

3

1925-1926
Travels

France and Spain tour with a Paige Tourer, Aether I (1925)
Plugge on Road Markings
The General Strike
Rail trip through Scandinavia
Radio International Publicity Services Limited

Lenny decided he would combine his proposed sponsored broadcast from the Eiffel Tower with another tour of Europe. This time, however, he would go by car. Not any old car, but one fitted with wireless, so that he could monitor broadcasts throughout his six-week journey.

The idea of a car with radio was not original. The Marconi Company had fitted a Daimler with a radio for the 1922 Olympia Motor Show. This car was also shown at the Glasgow Show the following January. The Post Office licensed a special transmitter so that it could be demonstrated. George Frost, the President of Lane High School Radio Club in Chicago, had fitted a Ford model T with a radio in May 1922. In February 1923, C.H. Gardner had experimented with radio transmission from a racing car when attempting a speed record at Brooklands. He also tried using a portable radio on trains in England the same year, but no one had taken up the idea commercially. Car radios were first used by police in 1922 by fitting two ex-RAF Crossley tenders with roof-mounted aerials. Initially, transmissions were from a few police vehicles to a base in Scotland Yard, and only Morse code was used. Patrol cars would not be fitted with radios until 1932.[1]

The car Plugge chose for this trip was a two-year-old Paige Tourer with a 25-horsepower engine developing seventy brake horsepower. The registration number was V7700 and, although of American manufacture, it had a right-hand drive. This car was a far cry from the little chain-drive FN in which he learned to drive in Belgium. Large, robust and impressive, the Paige was ideally suited to touring on the Continent. And Lenny liked nothing better than to be the focus of attention.

---

[1] See *New Shell Book of Firsts.*

Special additions had to be made for the car to carry all the additional equipment required for the trip. With the help of his good friend, Bill Wood, Lenny constructed a wooden platform along the offside, and the radio was mounted adjacent to the driver's door at a height that meant the controls could be operated whilst driving. This large receiver, a type 44002 made by Western Electric in the United States, was housed in a leather case with a removable front for access, which could be replaced for protection in bad weather.

A fifteen-inch frame aerial was mounted on a rotating base, forward of the windscreen, again on the offside, so its position could be adjusted on the move. A set of earphones were fitted in front of each of the five seats. And the car was christened 'Aether I'.[1]

Lenny was not going alone. He arranged, through Mimms travel agents in Victoria, to be accompanied by paying passengers. These four women were schoolteachers, all keen to tour the Continent by car, which in the nineteen-twenties would have been considered quite an adventure. The opportunity of seeing new places in the company of a dashing young man must have been rather attractive.

Lengthy arrangements needed to be made, particularly regarding the use of the radio. Fortunately, France had relaxed its regulations covering the use of foreign equipment within its borders, but many forms still had to be filled in. The Automobile Association provided him with maps and reports on the state of the roads.

Eventually, in August of 1925, all was ready and the party set off, bound for the Newhaven-Dieppe ferry. Lenny was sporting his new white Panama and the ladies wore their best cloche hats. On arrival at the port, Aether I was unceremoniously slung in chains and hoisted onto the ferry.

The French customs at Dieppe eyed the bouncy young man and his companions with suspicion; such a party was not a common sight, particularly in a car equipped with a large wireless set. Their papers were laboriously checked and rechecked, but the officials could find no fault. At last, they were able to drive away from the customs shed and point Aether I in the direction of Rouen.

They wasted no time in turning on the receiver and, with the sound of 2LO in their ears, they cruised the long straight roads of northern France,

---

[1] Aether is an alternative spelling for ether, but the former version is generally used when referring to myth or legend. Plugge obviously considered this spelling more appropriate to use in naming his cars. Collins Dictionary includes the following definition: Greek Myth. the upper regions of the atmosphere; clear sky or heaven.

heading south. The passengers had already been given their jobs. One was to monitor the supply of provisions, one took care of navigating, and another was charged with keeping notes on the radio stations they received and the quality of reception.

The first thing they noticed was sudden fading, which could sometimes be identified as being caused by screening of the signal, but often the reason was obscure. It soon became apparent that there were problems with receiving on the move, engine interference being the major one when the magneto caused a constant background noise. Reception was impossible when the lighting dynamo was charging and so they disconnected it and used the main battery for the lights. The receiver itself was powered by batteries that were to last the whole trip. They noted that for future trips the engine's electrics would need a certain amount of screening. They also discovered that the radio was a good diagnostic tool for the condition of the engine, as any misfiring could be heard through the earphones.

The high customs duties in France meant that a deposit of £600 was required to enable Plugge to bring his £1,000 car into the country, even as a visitor. Apart from the 45 per cent duty, a luxury tax was also levied on many goods.

The sight of this remarkable limousine, its sides loaded with baggage and strange looking equipment, caused quite a stir in the small villages and towns. Lenny delighted in stopping to demonstrate his radio to the French people who crowded around the car. The earphones were passed around, the strains of the Savoy Band from Daventry assailing unaccustomed ears. Surprisingly, when a French station was tuned in, a look of amazement would show on their faces as they heard their native language.

Lenny kept the wireless, aerial and battery box safely in his hotel bedroom at night, where he listened until the stations closed down.

The French government wanted to encourage the use of radio and to this end did not charge a licence fee, and only a franc for the registration of a set. Ready-made receivers were expensive, and amateur radio enthusiasts enjoyed building their own sets from parts that were in copious supply in the shops. The aim was to build a set with the fewest possible components, and prove that even distant stations could be received with the minimum of outlay. British parts, particularly loudspeakers, were highly regarded but beyond their means, due to the enormous customs duties and unhelpful rate of exchange. On reaching Spain, Lenny encountered the first major problem, which he described in an article, published in *The South African Wireless Weekly* in August 1926:

> The customs officials strongly objected to my using [the wireless] in their country without my previously having taken out a license and made a declaration that I was a Spanish subject and several other formalities which I did not quite understand. It is not necessary to enter into all the words that were exchanged during the two hours detention – suffice it to say that after these two hours we were gaily listening to the Savoy Hotel afternoon dance music from London and enjoying the bright Spanish sunshine, the warm Spanish breeze and the beautiful Spanish scenery. Spain is overrun with Guardia Civil armed to the teeth with rifles, pistols, revolvers and daggers, who resemble pigeons both by the colour of their coats and their distinctive walk, and secondly because they were always seen in pairs.
>
> The Guardia Civil were men who would stop the car from time to time and very many more times than we would have wished, thoroughly examining our papers in all cases.

Due to the many articles he had published, Captain Plugge discovered that he was something of a celebrity. This was particularly apparent when he arrived in Bilbao. *Modern Wireless*, *Wireless Weekly* and *The Wireless Constructor* were for sale on the newsstands, and the local amateurs avidly followed each new circuit that was published.

Plugge visited the broadcasting stations in San Sebastian and Bilbao. In Durango, he found that radio was still a novelty:

> My wireless set caused a tremendous amount of interest among the crowds who watched the unloading of the car and also among the staff of the hotel. The result was that I was kept up quite late in my bedroom that contained no less than four chambermaids, the hotel proprietor, his wife and their two daughters, who listened to the Daventry Station relaying the Covent Garden Opera from London. The amazement on their faces was worth gold to see. From here I tuned in several other stations, the Bilbao one being naturally the best. Union Radio Madrid also came in very well indeed and seemed to interest my crowd of visitors more than the British station. Strangely enough this transmission appeared to be more extraordinary to them, no doubt because they understood better what was being said.

Madrid hosted two stations, Radio Iberia and Union Radio, the latter having been recently inaugurated in the presence of King Alfonso. The station had a van equipped with four loudspeakers, which toured the city and its suburbs, bringing transmissions to those who could not afford a receiver. Local wireless dealers also took their wares to the people: salesmen gave demonstrations in the cafes, carrying a superhet from table to table. Plugge's visit to Union Radio laid the foundations for the future development of a commercial broadcasting network.

Although this tour was a serious experiment for Plugge, he had to consider his fare-paying passengers: the four schoolteachers in the cloche hats. They spent a lot of time exploring the sights of the towns, and a comprehensive pictorial record was kept; over a hundred photographs were taken. Many of these were made into lanternslides on his return, for use in the lectures he gave. To quote from an article describing the journey:

> It is doubtless interesting to do a thing for the first time and long
> distance continental touring by car equipped with wireless had
> probably not been attempted before this trip with a 25-70
> horsepower Paige car and a Western Electric seven-valve
> supersonic heterodyne receiving set.

Heading north on the return journey, Lenny proudly drove his Paige through town after town, his Panama set at a jaunty angle, delighting the inhabitants. His passengers waved imperiously, revelling in the sensation they were making, unaware of the part they were playing in the history of commercial broadcasting.

They reached Paris in late August and Lenny went straight to the Eiffel Tower station to meet with his old friend Monsieur Privat to discuss arrangements for the Selfridges broadcast. The day of the momentous event soon arrived. On the 29th of August 1925, an English voice gave the first commercial broadcast aimed at a British audience: Captain Plugge extolled the virtues of the fashions available at the Selfridges store in Oxford Street. Reports on the reception were requested from listeners, and comments on this auspicious transmission were received from three people, perhaps the first of the many who were to become fans of the English broadcasts from across the channel.

To ensure that his European tour was noticed, Plugge published articles in *Christian Science Monitor* in Boston, *L'Auto Italiana*, *Auto* in Budapest, *La Vie Automobile* in Paris, *Radio Amateur* in Vienna, *Radio Sport* in Madrid, *T.S.F.* in Lisbon, *Motor* in Copenhagen, *Telegraph & Telephone* in Belgrade, *Radio Express* in the Hague, and many others. The BBC's *Radio Supplement* also carried the article.

Not satisfied with just writing, Lenny talked about radio at every possible opportunity. He flew to Paris on November 27th, where he broadcast from the Eiffel Tower station about 'Recent Developments in British Broadcasting'. He then took the train to Brussels, chatted over the air at Radio Belge, and returned by train to Paris before flying back to England on the 28th. On December 5th, on 2LO (following up on his two previous broadcasts on the 'International Value of Broadcasting' and 'Supersonic Reception' earlier that year), he broadcast about his European trip. Becoming a circuit speaker with the Selborne Society allowed him to spread his thoughts on broadcasting to an even wider audience.

The French Government was becoming concerned about the commercial broadcasting (in French) being carried out by the three stations: Eiffel Tower, Radio Paris and PTT (Posté, Télégraphés et Téléphonés). The main culprit was Radio Paris, which devoted as much as forty minutes an evening to commercials, with the PTT doing a bit less. The Eiffel Tower did very little, yet it was coming in for all the criticism while the other two were ignored, which tended to give the impression that there was a political motive. Privat's control of the output of the station was controversial due to its concentration on the freedom of speech by eminent artists and intellectuals of the day. These took part in the presentation of special news items, termed the 'spoken newspaper'. The Government was unhappy about these broadcasts, and were further aggravated by the possible influence of Plugge's pressing for commercials aimed at a UK audience. This argument was to continue for the next few years.

*

As well as wireless, Leonard Plugge took an active interest in road safety. In March 1926, he published an article in *Auto* (the forerunner of *Autocar*), giving his suggestions for the improvement of road markings. This article subsequently appeared in motoring magazines all over the world. He wrote:

> With the new regulations which are now in force in the
> metropolitan area of London, signals for the direction of traffic
> imposed on the road surfaces are becoming more and more
> prevalent...

He discussed various methods that had been tried in other areas to overcome the obliteration of white road markings and ways of keeping the markings visible in bad weather. He then described an entirely new idea:

> The more important question is that of legibility. This is intimately
> connected with perspective and appears to have been overlooked
> both by those who have applied the signs to street surfaces in

38

The centre lettering or sign (numbers 2, 5 and 8) is the way the authorities print them on the surface of the road, with the result that the driver of an oncoming car gets only a very indistinct foreshortened sight of them (as numbers 3, 6 and 9). Captain Plugge suggests that the words  and signs should be printed as in the top line so that owing to the foreshortening they would appear to the driver as in the middle line.

London and the highways of many of the counties. The signs at present used, be they in the form of letters or of arrows, have, in fact been applied in such a way as to give their true reading only when viewed immediately from above, a position which the driver in the vehicle never occupies. Many drivers on being proceeded against for not conforming to signs of this description have stated in their defence that they were unable to read the signs, or that it was too late to change their course in accordance with the indications. These remarks may easily be verified. If the letters are merely printed as we see them today at Parliament Square and at Aldwych, it is practically impossible for the driver to grasp their significance until he is close upon them and even then he would need to exercise some ingenuity. Signals far from presenting difficulty should be so displayed as to force themselves on the mind of the party for whom they are intended. A motor vehicle driver is already harassed by the numerous controls, which require his constant attention, and any signal, which is so arranged as to distract him unduly, only increases danger instead of minimising it.

The accompanying diagrams based on a close investigation, show the usual type of printed letter employed, together with an illustration of their appearance to a driver when he is sitting at the wheel of an ordinary standard car some 20 yards away from the sign. From these diagrams it will be seen how distorted the letters appear to him. If the signs are to prove of value at all, it is essential that they should be so proportioned as to appear clearly and without distortion, to drivers of oncoming vehicles at a reasonable distance from the controlled area. To be of any real value signs should look normal when viewed from the wheel. They would then convey the required signal to the driver in sufficient time to warn him of the necessary course of action to take. The designs in the upper portion of the illustration, which have been mathematically distorted for the purpose, furnish a clear example of what is required. If these are exhibited on the ground in the manner suggested in perspective, they will appear to be normal when observed by a driver from a 'working' position.

The permanent adoption of the distortion method of signalling and traffic control will be to the advantage to all those concerned with road transport.

Plugge's idea was taken up by local authorities and is the norm today.

By 1926, the post-war depression had deepened, culminating in the General Strike in May of that year. The discontent of the coal miners, backed by the trade unions, eventually brought out the railway men, transport workers and the newspapers. The lack of printed news media put the propagation of information firmly on the shoulders of the British Broadcasting Company. John Reith was determined to steer a middle path and not to allow the BBC to become a government organ. A strong faction in the Government, lead by Winston Churchill, put considerable pressure upon the Company. The Cabinet, however, was split and Reith kept his independence. The strike gave radio an unexpected boost. With no newspapers other than the Government's official organ, *The British Gazette*, people foresaw the need to be kept informed through the wireless. The stocks of receivers were soon exhausted.

During the strike, some from the middle and upper classes enjoyed the chance to drive buses and trains, and to distribute Churchill's *British Gazette* by car. The strikers were hard hit, the miners hardest of all. They too had a newssheet, *The British Worker*, which Hugh Gaitskell, down from Oxford, helped to distribute. Leonard Plugge drove an underground train.

When the strikers walked out from their jobs on the tube, it was necessary for someone to take a train through to check the safety of the lines. Lenny was ready; he tested the three principal lines, the Piccadilly, Hampstead and Central. One week on each proved the lines were safe. On some days, he wore his Royal Naval Volunteer Reserve (RNVR) uniform, and was cheered by the passengers. He had his wireless with him in the cab, but the receiver did not work, the screening of the tunnel being just too much for this well-travelled set.

Lenny was presented with a spanner inscribed, 'A souvenir from the Superintendent of the line to Captain L.F. Plugge who drove the first train on the Underground Railways during the General Strike. May 1926'.

The strike lasted nine days. In the following year, the Government passed the Trades Dispute Act making general strikes illegal. Some years later, Plugge and Gaitskell were again to appear on opposite sides of the fence.

*

Lenny began to plan another European trip to experiment with reception on railways, this time through Scandinavia. With his Western Electric receiver plus batteries and a frame aerial neatly packed in three leather cases, he left London once more. This time he had fitted a small flap to the bottom of the aerial case so that he could use it without taking it out. As can be imagined, this equipment was bulky and heavy. The portable sets available at the time were not suitable for use on trains, due to their limited range of about ten miles. Fellow passengers must have been amazed to see Plugge set up the fifteen-inch frame aerial on the table under the window, balancing the receiver on his lap while he adjusted the controls.

During his visit to Sweden, he was entertained at the Stockholm and Malmo transmitters, which had been opened only at the beginning of 1924, each with a power output of 2 kilowatts. They were Government controlled and became known to the foreign listener by the station signal, a Swedish folk song played on the celeste. Technical development was in the hands of the Post Office, and a licence fee of eleven shillings was charged, half going to the Government and the other half to Radiotjanst Aktiebolaget, the broadcasting company. The third station in the chain was at Gothenburg.

In Denmark, Plugge visited other recently opened radio stations at Copenhagen and Ryvang. Copenhagen was built by M.P. Pederson Engineering Company and was opened in 1924. It was financed originally by amateurs and the radio industry, but was taken over by the state in the spring of 1925. Its power was only 500 watts, as opposed to that of Ryvang, which was owned by the military and had a power of 1.5 kilowatts. The Post Office operated a station at Lyngby, giving weather forecasts and agricultural news.

In an article published following this trip, Plugge compared the reception on the different lines on which he travelled. He found that the best reception was on long wave, as interference from the train's dynamos cut out all short waves. It would appear that, despite the comparatively crude equipment of the day, he was easily able to receive the UK stations.

He also considered the possibility of two-way reception on trains, so that the businessman could be in contact with the office whilst travelling. He was later to develop the idea of two-way radio for use in police cars.

On this and previous trips, Plugge travelled 16,000 miles by train. The results proved that it was quite feasible to get adequate reception whilst travelling on the railway, provided the correct equipment was used. He welcomed the news that the Canadian National Railways had installed receivers in its trains for the pleasure of passengers. The CNR had set up transmitters mostly of 500 watts output, to cover Canada, and aerials were attached to the observation cars of its main-line trains. An operator travelled with the train, and the passengers were provided with earphones. Occasionally, loudspeakers were used.

In the Spring of 1926, the Cornish Riviera Express was fitted with radio for the entertainment of the passengers, and offered a choice of loudspeaker or headphones.

By now, Lenny Plugge had created a considerable workload for himself. The mass of programme data from the many Continental stations had to be prepared and issued to magazines, including the BBC's *Radio Supplement*, which gave details of foreign broadcasts. Plugge decided to set up his own company and run it in the evenings, to handle the business – for a business it had become. He held the rights to the publication of this information in the UK, something he had set up during his visits to the stations.

With the help of an old university friend, George Shanks, Plugge set up Radio International Publicity Services Limited. The company was located at 23 Devonshire Street, London, where the daily round of issuing press bulletins and programme details (many requiring translation) was in the capable hands of a Mrs Oldacre assisted by a small group of translators and typists. Cynthia Michelle (then Miss Cross) remembers how Captain Plugge would come into the office after finishing at the Underground Group, always immaculate, his winning ways charming the office staff:

> After all these years, I remember how happy I was in my two and
> a half years with Captain Plugge's company. My job was that of
> an audio typist and most of my time was spent typing reports that
> Captain Plugge had put onto his Dictaphone machine.[1]

Plugge was fascinated by anything new. His Dictaphone was one of his favourite acquisitions, which he was to install alongside his radio receiver on his next tour – this time in Aether II.

---

[1] Cynthia Michelle in an iInterview with the author – June 7th, 1989.

4

1926-1927
Aether II Across Europe

Europe and the Balkans with Aether II (1926)

France and Spain with Aethers II and III (1927)

The forthcoming tour was a far more ambitious affair than the previous. Equipped this time with a transmitter as well a receiver, the plan was to travel across Europe, through the Balkans to Constantinople (now Istanbul). This historic trip would cover some 4,500 miles and was to take one month.

Aether II – a 12-cylinder, 120-horsepower, seven-seater Packard – was four years old, painted 'Desert Sand' with red wheels, all in a special Carmaloid finish.[1]

Plugge approached several companies to act as sponsors. Dunlop Cord tyres were fitted, Exide batteries were installed, and Mobil supplied the oil. All these manufacturers were to be 'plugged' in the frequent reports to be issued. The Packard, like the Paige, was specially fitted with a rack along the driver side on which the receiver, transmitter and Dictaphone were mounted, all of which were operable by the driver whilst the car was in motion. The Dictaphone had a polished speaking tube, reminiscent of those used by passengers in the large limousines of the time to talk to the chauffeur. A cone loudspeaker was mounted towards the rear of the car and a frame aerial towards the front. The space under this equipment was used to store the passengers' luggage. Access to the driver's side of the car was impossible, and even the other side was crammed with seven petrol and four oil cans, together with a spare tyre. A little Union Jack topped the radiator cap which, apart from the usual thermometer, was fitted with a lamp that shone white light upwards to illuminate the flag, white downwards to show the thermometer-reading, while in front it glowed green to starboard and red to port. The headlamps had protective mesh over the glass. Being an open tourer, it had an adjustable windscreen to protect the rear seats. The space in front of the seats was a clutter of picnic baskets, bags and anything else that would not fit on the outside.

---

[1] Carmaloid was a patent finish similar to modern cellulose.

Plugge's choice of receiver was once again the Western Electric superhet. The transmitter was of the same make, containing two valves capable of producing an output of 10 watts. The frame aerial was the same as before, as were the earphones, but a 15-inch diameter Western Electric Kone speaker supplemented them. This was mainly so that Plugge could demonstrate the radio to the people who crowded around Aether II during their frequent stops. To assist the local customs officers, a small metal plate was fitted to the side of the Packard giving full particulars of the car.

This time, five women were to go on the expedition and, as before, each had a particular part to play. Ethel, the navigator, prepared the route beforehand with the help of maps and books. The information available for the Balkans was given in a handbook produced by the Geographical Section of the Naval Intelligence Division of the Admiralty published in 1920. This included itineraries and details of the state of the roads, together with some historical background, plus useful words and phrases. The latter were essential for an area where few people spoke English. A navigating book was completed and used throughout the trip.

Mildred and Myfanwy were nominated as the 'housekeepers' and were to do all the shopping and keep the accounts. Florence was the diarist and kept a written record of the journey. Lenny intended using the Dictaphone to keep a verbal record, but felt that a written account was also necessary in case any of the fragile cylinders were damaged. In addition, Florence was given charge of the Baedeker travel books so that she could act as guide to the many towns visited.

The official documents, passports and names of contacts were put in the capable hands of Dorothy, who had helped obtain many of the necessary permits from the Embassies. Unfortunately, none of the women was able to drive, so Lenny would have no opportunity to relax en route throughout the next thirty days, the planned duration of the trip.

Plugge had arranged with Monsieur Privat in Paris to broadcast progress reports on his tour from the Eiffel Tower station at 7.30 each evening. Using his portable transmitter direct to Paris, he would send these over the air. Another well-known amateur and friend, Gerald Marcuse,[1] was to listen out for the transmissions from his London base. Cables were also sent to the London office of Radio International Publicity Services, so that Mrs Oldacre could ensure coverage of the trip in the national press. A complete schedule had been sent to all the various radio stations he was to visit, advising them of anticipated dates and times of arrival. Optimistic, maybe, but Plugge's planning was very efficient.

---

[1] Gerald Marcuse was particularly well known for his work on *Empire Broadcasting* in 1927.

Plugge's own journal best sums up his attitude to this journey:

> The world has now reached a stage in its history when the 'conquest of Space' is the order of the day. Week by week new advances are made, fresh ground is won and old positions consolidated. The campaign continues unabated and the more ground we gain the more determined do our efforts become to subject space to the will and control of man. The prospects are entrancing; the possibilities immense; and the prize is the universal comity of nations. Free intercourse between peoples; easy access to all countries; the power not only to converse with, but to visit people in every quarter of the globe; to enjoy what each has to face; to understand the point of view which each has in mind; to break down the narrow confines of boundary and of frontier – this is what is offered by the conquest of space.
>
> The visionary may look into the future and picture a world in which all communication is made by radio and all transport is effected through the air. But for the moment it would be well to confine our aspirations to matters of more immediate and more practical attainment. In wireless we have ready to our hand, the means of making our voice travel unhampered by the restrictions of Space. The prospect of free intercourse is almost achieved. But it is not enough. We desire to travel ourselves; and much can be done with the means of transport at our disposal, which, if allied with radio, can go far along the road to the elimination of Space.
>
> Not long ago I excited the not very credulous interest of my friends by announcing my intention of motoring in a radio equipped car from London to the Black Sea and back again to London in thirty days. It was impressed upon me – *inter alia et ad infinitum* – that though I might get as far as Belgrade, there would be small hope of proceeding further and that if I were so unwise as to attempt to proceed further, I should be condemning the car to a lingering death in the mud of the Balkans and that I myself would return to London by a train a disillusioned and a not very dignified man. These gloomy prognostications were somewhat enhanced when I admitted that my project included the company of five ladies, not one of whom was able to drive a motor so as to give me any assistance at the wheel. However, I believed this to be possible and with the assistance of the friends who were to accompany me, the preparations were begun.

With these ideals in mind and the Union Jack mounted on the radiator cap, illuminated by its special little light, Aether II was ready.

Once again, a heavily laden motor car with a complement of fashionably dressed ladies in the charge of a dapper English gentleman was to bemuse the customs officials, but this time at Ostend. After an overnight stop at Bruges, which included a demonstration outside the old belfry, the group headed for Brussels, arriving at the Hotel Metropole at 11.30 in the evening of August 1st, 1926.

The shock absorbers already needed topping up with compressed air, so this was one of the first jobs to be done on arrival. The cone loudspeaker was showing signs of damage due to careless handling in the garage and the inquisitive fingers of the spectators who clustered around the car. Fortunately, Lenny was able to make good the damage with paper and glue, with no apparent loss of quality.

After an interview with the press and a brief discussion with the director of Radio Belge, Monsieur Van Soust, they headed for Germany. The border guard at the Belgian exit frontier at Aachen refused to accept the information on Plugge's little metal plate on the side of the car and insisted in checking every detail to ensure that they were in strict agreement with the facts.

Cologne was the next overnight stop. They attended early morning mass at the cathedral before leaving for Nuremburg, where Plugge was to give a talk on the air at 8 pm that evening. They made a brief visit to the Frankfurt radio station and sent a telegram to Nuremburg informing them that they would be late. At nine o'clock, they were still sixty miles from their destination. Lenny, whilst driving, was tuning in to both the Nuremberg and Munich stations to ensure that his telegram message advising of his late arrival had been received. Although he was to speak at Nuremberg, Munich was also to transmit his talk by relay. He was relieved when he heard the Nuremberg announcer reading out his message over the air.

The plan to complete the return journey to Constantinople was already looking a tough task. They eventually rolled to a stop in front of the Rotehahn Hotel, Nuremburg, at 10.50 pm. The ancient town of Nuremburg was in darkness. Having quickly checked-in, they set off to find the broadcasting station, which turned out to be easier said than done. When they did find it, the station had just closed down. The director was about to leave but, on seeing them, he went straight back and gave instructions for the generators to be restarted, advising listeners that all was well and the famous Captain had arrived. The director of the Munich station, Dr Von Westerman, had travelled to Nuremburg to greet Plugge and discuss with him his ideas for putting plays on the radio, including Shakespeare.

The next day, after a quick tour of the old town with the Mobil Oil representative, they set off once more for the long haul to Czechoslovakia. Before setting out on the road to Prague, the tank was filled with twelve gallons of petrol at the exorbitant cost of 38 shillings. They travelled through the picturesque villages of Southern Bavaria, the tanned and barefoot inhabitants busying themselves with their crops of sugar beet and hops. Several times, progress was hampered by a leisurely procession of geese making their way along the road in front of them. Having passed through Hirshau, Essenbach and Wernburg, they reached Lohma on the Czech frontier at eight o'clock in the evening. They were quickly cleared at the German customs and then skidded their way along an appalling road to the Czech border post. Whilst Lenny was inside sorting out the passports, his passengers amused the locals by talking into the Dictaphone, describing the scene for future reference. An official eventually climbed into the car and attached a string to the steering wheel to show that it had cleared customs, which allowed them to set off again into the night. Soon, Lenny began to encounter the mud that was to cause so much trouble throughout their travels in southern Europe. The roads were not yet adapted to the needs of the motorcar, the usual traffic being horse and cart. Worse was to come.

At midnight, they pulled up on the side of the road to tune the radio into London. The music of the Savoy Orpheans floated over the countryside, closely followed by the chimes of Big Ben. In true English style, they corrected their watches.

Arriving at Pilsen, they found that Monday night was dance night at the Central Hotel. After a quick wash and brush-up, they surprised the locals by foxtrotting around the floor. A meal, with a glass of Pilsen beer for each of the women, completed the evening. Lenny retired to bed, but was concerned about Aether II being left unguarded outside the hotel. After much consideration, he decided to sleep in it.

Despite having had a late night, the party rose early to travel the fifty miles to Prague. Now driving on the left-hand side of the road – the rule for Czechoslovakia in the twenties – they left the smoking chimneys of Pilsen behind them. The roads seemed even worse than the day before. The numerous potholes were casually filled with tufts of grass, allowing the carts to roll them in. To help with the upkeep of the roads, small tolls were imposed at the towns they passed through.

The party arrived in Prague at 11.30 in the morning and took a late breakfast at the Palace de Prague Hotel. Lenny was met by engineer

Svoboda who accompanied him on a visit to the Radio Journal Broadcasting Station. Meanwhile, the women explored the city with its many castles and palaces. On the steps of the Royal Palace, they admired the magnificent view of Prague and wrote postcards to send home.

Lenny was involved in discussing the problems of broadcasting with Svoboda. The station, which was located at Strasnice, was equipped with a 5-kilowatt Western Electric transmitter and was run by the Post Office. Twenty-two outside halls were connected by landline, as was the Prague Observatory which provided time signals. Each month, the local postman collected the one-shilling licence fee from the 220,000 listeners. Prague also controlled the other two Czech stations at Brunn and Bratislava.

Brunn, in fact, was the next stop on the journey and Plugge was to give a short talk. After an overnight stay in the small village of Cechtic, they travelled on to Brunn, known locally as Brno. Captain Antony Slavik, who operated the Marconi transmitter, welcomed them and explained the keen interest in wireless in his country. Most receivers were homemade from British components.

As he could not speak the local tongue, Plugge gave his talk in German although it was an unpopular language in Czechoslovakia due to the long occupation by the Austrians.

Vienna was the next stop on the itinerary. After taking two hours to clear Czech customs, the six travellers found themselves in Austria in the late evening. Struggling to avoid the many unlit market carts that cluttered the road, they comforted themselves by tuning the wireless to Radio Vienna. The strains of *Vienna, City of My Dreams* greeted them. Later, as they crossed the high bridge over the Danube, the orchestra played *The Blue Danube*, as if to welcome the 'wireless car'. The Hotel Bristol was a sharp contrast to the village inn where they had stayed the previous evening, and the group wasted no time in taking advantage of the comforts offered.

The bad roads in Czechoslovakia had had a detrimental effect on the car: the radiator had started to leak badly and one of the luggage racks had broken. As there was no Packard agent in the city, Lenny sought the help of the Buick representative. The radiator and the rack could not be repaired but the battery, which had been under a heavy strain with all the night driving, was recharged.

The women spent the day touring Vienna and in the evening accompanied Lenny to the broadcasting studio. Draped in green velvet, the studios were the most impressive they had seen. The directors and staff greeted Captain Plugge with great ceremony and kissed the ladies' hands. Lenny positioned himself behind yet another microphone, and gave his talk. He spoke first in German and then in English, describing his tour to date and sending greetings to all the listeners. The women looked on proudly as their 'chauffeur' piped out his message in the rapid high-pitched voice they had come to know so well.

The group was pleased to find that letters they were expecting and spare Dictaphone reels had arrived.

The next day, Dorothy and Lenny visited the Rosenhugel high-powered transmitter together with Dr Schwaiger, the Station Director. The rest of the party continued their sightseeing.

At four the following morning, they headed out of Vienna towards the Hungarian frontier. Because of the leak in the radiator, they had taken a supply of water in the spare petrol cans, and had to stop every three-quarters of an hour to top up.

Customs guards could be very frustrating, and those at the crossing from Austria into Hungary were no exception, as Lenny describes in his journal:

At Nickelsdorf, which we reached about 7.30 am, the Austrian Customs Officers inspected our papers, passports and the car and after about half an hour we were allowed to proceed. Not far, however. We soon saw in the distance an armed Hungarian soldier standing in the middle of the road with upraised hand, looking very important indeed. His rifle was loaded, too! As soon as our passports and papers were handed over, he entered the tiny hut by the roadside and removed the deadly medicine for breakers of Douane regulations. No doubt had I refused to stop I should have been shot!

Soon several khaki clad figures were more than interested in us and our car and they proved to be exceedingly genial fellows, posing splendidly for our cameras. We were glad that we had undertaken our journey in daylight, rather than the night before, as this passing through customs, both out of Austria and into Hungary was most interesting and we were pleased to get pictures. So often we passed interesting places and persons when, owing to lack of light, photography was out of the question. The uniforms of the Customs officers here were very attractive. They seemed to affect rather highly coloured collars and the hats were very smart. There was much clicking of heels and the men were very military in bearing and seemed well trained and efficient. The precision and smartness impressed us very much. Many of the men had marked Slavonic features. They were all very pleased to pose for their photographs and one came forward, fixed his bayonet and stood to attention just behind his companion beside the car, in order to provide us with an interesting picture.

After the passports had been examined in the little hut, we were told that we should have to go on to another place where the details and papers of the car would be better understood. We were getting beyond the area of frequent cars and into countries where the chief customs business is transacted either on the railway or the river. So an armed guard mounted the footboard and rode with us to the railway station at Haggeshalmi, where the papers were again examined. Here the officials had received a telegram from Budapest and knew a great deal about our coming. There was no difficulty, therefore, although they considered it necessary to go into all the details, thus causing annoying delay.

This was only a taster of the delays that they were to experience with the customs authorities as they travelled towards the Balkans. Across the border, the countryside became boring, with mile after mile of maize fields. The monotony was broken only by the mud houses and the colourful headscarves of the women and children.

In Budapest, they were fortunate to find a garage next to their hotel, where the mechanics were prepared to work all night to fix the leaking radiator, change the oil and give the Packard a much-needed wash. It was noticed that the nearside rear wheel was very close to the underside of the mudguard; apparently, the pneumatic damper had developed a leak. Closer inspection revealed a crack in the casing, so a longer stay in Budapest was now inevitable. Lenny remained at the garage to supervise the welding. The first effort was unsuccessful but eventually all was well and the damper was pumped up once more with compressed air.

As well as the unusual car, the appearance of five smartly dressed English women caused a great deal of interest. And there was the odd occasion when an unscrupulous individual would try to take advantage. An example is included in Florence's diary, when they were sightseeing in Budapest:

We decided to return to the Pest side of the river and visit the Houses of Parliament, so we took a taxi. The driver was a strange rough-looking individual and we suspected, from the look in his eye that he might, on occasion, desert the path of rectitude. On alighting, we knew it! He demanded payment in fluent Magyar (or Greek for all we knew) and when we showed him our money he pointed to 250,000 korona. Now we had just changed a £1 note for 350,000 korona and we did not feel like giving most of it away for a five-minute taxi ride, so we argued. He would not give way. We offered him 25,000. Nothing doing! We asked him to write

down his demand, which he did thus – 250000 – a small cipher at
the end. Deadlock! Then I spied a policeman across the square and
ran to him for help; as a general rule we found the Hungarians
very friendly and helpful. He came over at once, examined the
taximeter and took from my outstretched handful of money 25,000
korona. The taxi man bowed and smiled his thanks and fury and
we walked triumphantly away towards the Parliament Houses.

Before they could continue their journey, they had to go to the British
Embassy to arrange for the issue of visas for Serbia. Captain Plugge made
another broadcast and there was more sightseeing for the passengers. Then
it was time for dinner on Margaret Island, the popular entertainment centre
and playground of Budapest, before moving on. Unfortunately, they took
the wrong road and realised it only after they had travelled fifty miles
along the left bank of the Danube. The only bridges had been in Budapest
and by the time they arrived in Zolt, it had become imperative that they
find a means of crossing the swollen river. Eventually they found a barge
large enough to take Aether II, and a motorboat towed them across. Lenny
takes up the story:

We drew in, however to a small landing stage some distance from
the village and as we approached it I looked at it in dismay; it
looked unclimbable by a car not already on the move. Frail
looking boards had to be placed between the ferry boat and the
shore and opposite lay a sharp turn to the left, a very steep incline
on a narrow rough track, another sharp turn to the right and then
left again to the top! However it was useless to hesitate. While the
men were fixing the ferry and the planks, the girls ran up the track
to discover its exact nature and came back to cheer me with the
news that beyond the turn at the top all would be well. Then they
all armed themselves with huge stones, ready to place them behind
the wheels should the engine stop and when all was ready I started
up and 'went at it', hoping for the best. Luckily, my first attempt
was successful; but I should not advise any motorist who takes his
car over any of the Danube ferries. The girls abandoned their
loads of rocks and sped after me and soon we were all aboard and
making for Dunfoldvar.

In Dunfoldvar, it was market day, with peasant women in national dress
squatting under large umbrellas selling fruit weighed out in hand-held
balances. The travellers could not resist buying some of the local cakes to
eat on the way. From Dunfoldvar, they picked up the main road out of
Budapest, the one they should have taken when they left the city.

Beyond Budapest, it became apparent that the roads were definitely not suitable for a motorcar. The Danube floods earlier in the year had caused widespread damage and many of the roads had been washed away. The next large town was Paks with its acacia-lined avenues. Here, Lenny had his first experience of buying his petrol by weight.

The publicity generated by the trip surpassed even Plugge's expectations. Throughout the journey, news of the approaching English Captain and his wireless car preceded him. The party's progress was reported in the local papers along the way. Crowds met them in many of the towns, keen to hear the demonstrations that were proudly put on for them. Wireless was still very much a novelty and many in the crowd were hearing it for the first time. The few who possessed a receiver listened to the Captain's regular broadcasts from the local stations with curiosity and admiration.

However, the roads were not getting any better. Due to the Danube floods, Lenny and company had to take many detours, often through tracks thick with mud. Progress was slow and the last few miles into Mohács, on the border with Serbia, were a veritable nightmare. The nightmare worsened when they arrived in the village. Lenny recounts what happened:

> On this particular frontier I found exceedingly bad arrangements
> with regard to Customs. It appears that in this small town of
> Mohács it is necessary before leaving the country to register at the
> police station and have the luggage examined. But on the road in
> the village there is no indication that such a procedure should be
> taken and we were looking out for the actual frontier village,
> Udvar, which is 20 kilometres from here. It was badly indicated in
> the Michelin Guide, which put it at some 20 miles north of where
> I now was, so as we came through Mohács at about 5 o'clock I
> enquired from any person that looked official, soldier or
> policeman, where the Customs were, but always got an answer to
> proceed straight ahead, with the result that on very bad roads we
> went further and further and at last, 11 miles beyond Mohács, we
> arrived at Udvar.

> Here we found some Hungarians on guard and I was brought to
> see the Captain in charge. He coolly informed me that I would
> have to return all the way to Mohács, on the very bad roads I had
> just been covering, in order to have the signature of the police
> before leaving the country. Think of it! Raining fast – everyone
> very wet and cold – another 22 miles through that dreadful mud.
> Apparently it was quite a usual practice that this should occur, but
> it appears to serve no purpose except the annoying and hampering
> of foreigners. The Captain in charge, a man called Sneider, was
> personally very kind. He was evidently the victim of the system!

He telephoned through to Mohács to try and see if they would allow me to proceed, as my presence there was well known, photographs having appeared in the local press throughout the country. Indeed, several of the many people who came and spoke to me had in their pockets copies of the paper in which the photographs of the car appeared. But the authorities were adamant. I had a long argument with the Captain – threatened to abandon my trip altogether – it was of no avail. I saw that I should be compelled to go back to Mohács for this police procedure. The Captain delegated one of his soldiers to go with me, but he proved to be more hindrance than help. He spoke nothing but Hungarian and seemed very stupid.

After a very slow run through the greasy mud, we were again in the streets of Mohács and after several false directions we finally found ourselves outside the Customs House. It is on the quay by the Danube, as the Customs work consists principally in checking the traffic up and down the river. The officer here had been asked by telephone to await our coming, but when we arrived, in the wet, cold and darkness, we found the place locked and deserted – he had gone home. Another soldier offered to come with us to find him, but neither he nor our first escort seemed to know quite what to do, they seemed to be scared. They went into a sort of public house and were there informed that the Captain had gone to bed and were not inclined to go and ring at his door, or do anything, as far as I could gather; and not being able to speak Hungarian I could not tell them to take me to the house. When I realised the deadlock I ordered them both off the car – one of them insisted on staying and I had to push him off the running board, and decided to try and arrange matters on my own.

I went back to the hotel we had noticed in the village and fixed up for rooms for the party and there I came across a man who could speak German. He eventually managed to find somebody who knew where the Captain lived. It was already nine o'clock when at last we were brought to the Captain's private address. This was a large house in which several apartments were rented and the woman in charge of the house did not want us to go in. It took some twenty minutes conversation, together with the man who spoke some German, to get her to allow us to enter the building. When at last I was admitted, she showed me where the apartments of the Captain were, but I gathered that if I went and knocked it was entirely my responsibility! I dared it, however, and at last he came to the door in pyjamas and a coat. Fortunately he spoke several languages (including Russian) and we could communicate in German. It was difficult even now to get him to do anything.

I had to tell him I intended to proceed to Belgrade that night in order to move him at all. He said he had waited some time for me, but thought probably I had had a breakdown and that was why he had returned home. He would stamp our papers immediately had he got the stamp, but it was necessary for him to go to the office in order to get it. I persuaded him to dress, gave him a lift in the car and eventually arrived back at the offices beside the Danube.

There was a Danube sailor on guard for half the building, but the other half, in which his offices were, was closed and locked and my Captain explained that he had not got the key.

"Shall I take you home again to fetch the key?" I asked.

"I have not got a key at home," he replied, "There is only one key. We cannot afford more than one key in Hungary, because we are so poor."

"Who has the key, then?" I naturally enquired.

"Oh, the man in charge of the Custom House (caretaker?) but I do not know where he lives."

"But how extraordinary!" I remarked, "that you do not know where your subordinate lives."

"Yes, it does seem strange," he replied, "but I have been here four years and they change about every month. I have no idea where this one lives."

So I asked him if we could get through any of the windows and we tried, but without success and he finally decided he could not get the stamp that night.

Then I suggested that it might not be necessary to have the stamp if he gave me a letter to Captain Sneider in the next village, explaining matters; surely with his signature that ought to be sufficient! After a long discussion he consented to write a letter saying that he had actually seen the car and then I thought that for the time being our troubles were over. Optimist! I handed him our passports to sign and then for the first time I learned that it was necessary for me to have them stamped at the Police Station! Up till now there had been no indication of such a thing.

"Well," I said, "we must have this done now, in order to let me leave without further delay."

But the Police Station was closed now, as by this time it was a quarter to eleven.

"Shall we go round to the Police Station and—"

He thought it would be better to stay where we were and telephone.

"Don't telephone!" I implored him, "If you do we will never get anywhere. Let us go round and see, then possibly we may be able to do something."

We got in the car and went round to the Police Station. There we found everything in darkness, but after ringing and making a noise we managed to get a policeman, who came down, also undressed. After some long persuasion to put on his uniform, a performance which lasted some twenty minutes, it transpired that another official, a civilian, who arranged about the passports, was living in a different part of the village and perhaps if we went to see him, he might come round and sign the passports. Into the car we got again and went round to this man's house. Here again we managed to wake him up – he was also in bed and after some long discussion he agreed to come round to the Police Station. Another twenty minutes delay and we took him there, he stamped the passports and a quarter before midnight we were at last free to proceed towards Serbia.

This episode demonstrates one of Lenny's favourite techniques. He called it 'warming up' and he used it regularly throughout his life. He would never take 'no' for an answer and would use his guile to try to get around officialdom in whatever shape or form it came, whether a government department or a parking attendant. Sometimes, an old white fiver in the right hand with the instruction, "Distribute this and get busy!" did the trick.

After staying the night at the hotel in Mohács, they proceeded on to Semlin. The 11th of August found them struggling through foot-deep mud on the approach to Belgrade. The radiator honeycomb kept blocking with mud; Lenny persuaded one of the women to walk along the side of the moving car and, with a hatpin, dig out the mud from the radiator so that the engine would not overheat. He dared not stop, as the car would have become stuck. They eventually made it to Semlin, bedraggled and covered with mud. A ferry took them across the River Save and they arrived in Belgrade.

The capital still showed obvious signs of the bombardment it had suffered from the Hungarians during the Great War and the earlier Balkan conflicts. There were shell holes in the cobbled streets and the houses in several of the roads were boarded up. As there was no radio station in Serbia, the 4,000 listeners tuned into Budapest, Prague, Rome and Toulouse, at a cost of 25 shillings a year.

The news regarding the future progress of the trip was not good. The British Ambassador told Plugge that the Turkish authorities would not allow him to take a radio into their country, and the Bulgarian Ministry warned that he would not get a car through the Dragoman Pass. To add to this, a man at the hotel told them that they were going to their certain doom. It was also Friday the thirteenth!

'Mad dogs and Englishmen' had a ring of truth in Lenny Plugge's case as, unheedingly, they set out to cover the next stage of their itinerary. A few miles from Belgrade, the car started to slip and slide over a three-inch layer of mud covering the road. The mud became deeper and deeper. Lenny tried to select a different gear to give him that extra bit of traction, but the Packard sank up to its axles and gave up. Fortunately, a farm cart stopped and the farmer, after some persuasion, hooked up his bullocks to the rear of the heavy tourer and unceremoniously towed it backward to Belgrade. But Lenny and his companions were not to be beaten. He had with him some chains for the rear wheels, which were fitted at the local garage. They set off again.

This time they managed to get past the danger spot. However, a few yards further on, Aether II again expired in the soft brown mud. A considerable time elapsed before some men appeared with a horse drawn cart to find this large, strangely equipped motorcar in which sat, dejectedly, five ladies with cloche hats and fur trimmed coats, the driver in white suit and Panama turned up at the front. The men overcame their surprise and were soon harnessing their horses to the front of the vehicle. While the horses pulled, Lenny revved the powerful engine and everyone, including the women, pushed. Slowly, they edged forward, sliding from one side to the other to avoid the worst of the potholes and eventually ended up on a bank on the side of the road. At this point, the helpers apologised for having to leave to get home before dark. Lenny managed to obtain a promise that they would return in the morning with oxen. After preparing a makeshift meal from their emergency supplies, the not-so-happy band of travellers settled down for the night.

Dawn broke and the bullocks arrived. Aether II had sunk even deeper over night. The rear wheels were eventually levered up using strong poles with stones placed under them. The four bullocks attached to the front gradually pulled them free. Slowly but surely they dragged the car, its running boards level with the mud, until they were on firm ground.

By Sunday night, the travellers had reached the Bulgarian frontier where they were given a military escort. As private individuals were not allowed to operate a wireless in Bulgaria, this escort was to accompany them throughout the country.

Having made it to the start of the Dragoman Pass before nightfall, they settled down to sleep amidst the rough moorland of the pass with the rugged mountains on either side. Lenny recorded the scene:

> Deciding that the domestic duties should be left till the morning, the girls just cleared away the meal and then we all sat in the car and I tuned to Daventry. Sunday night! The strains of *The Lost Chord* came through in that still cold air as clearly as if we were in our own homes sitting in armchairs and listening to music a few yards from us. Yet here we were nearly two thousand miles from England. A little later Gounod's *There is a Green Hill* was heard. Almost shut in on both sides by mountains as we were, the effect of the music in the wonderful silence of the Pass was indescribable. Extensive as had been my researches into the possibilities of wireless reception, I confess that I had hardly expected to get such a clear result from the loudspeaker in a position so screened by mountains.

Their personal soldier acted as sentry while they slept.

Upon waking in the morning, they found two more soldiers had joined them, this time on horseback. One was an officer who kindly offered to precede them to pick out the best route. They followed the riverbed that ran through the pass, but again they became stuck, this time in soft wet sand. Once more, bullocks came to the rescue and pulled them across the sand and rough rocks. Amazingly, they never had a puncture at any time on their tour – a good advertisement for Dunlop.

At Sofia, they were welcomed by the English colony, attended by the Chief of Police and the Home Secretary, as well as Aviation and Military representatives. All were rewarded by a demonstration of the wireless. Permission was also given for a public hearing, which was held in a hilly region just outside the city. It was well attended and the chimes of Big Ben echoed over the assembled throng.

Time was now rapidly running out. They were well behind schedule, and the sad decision had to be made to head homewards. To be only two hundred miles from the Black Sea was frustrating, but they all had to get back to London. Ethel was particularly concerned because her holiday time had expired. Since it was agreed that they would return via Romania, she decided to catch the train when they reached Bucharest.

They left Sofia at four in the morning and spent the night in Tirnova, the ancient capital of Bulgaria. They continued next day and arrived in Rustchuk at 3.30 pm. From here, they took the ferry across the Danube and, four hours later, entered Bucharest where Ethel had to leave and return to London. Sadly, they hurried her to the railway station to catch the Orient Express. They now had to negotiate the long road back without their navigator.

Of the many things to be done before leaving, the most important was a complete overhaul of the car. This took two days, which gave them time to explore the capital. Lenny had his usual duty calls to make, and was pleasantly surprised to find that the Packard agent was a man who had been with him at University College in London, before the war. Captain Plugge was to give his usual demonstration at midnight the day before they left, and describes the evening in his journal:

> Well, our route decided on and the car finished, there was little left to do in Bucharest. We agreed that after the midnight wireless demonstration we would pack and load up the car and if possible travel through the remainder of the night.
>
> Having dressed for dinner, we decided that it would be pleasant to take that meal in the gardens of the restaurant in the Chaussee that the girls had visited the previous evening. This necessitated driving through the square where the wireless concert was to be given. Imagine our great surprise when on arriving there we saw a goodly number of people already assembled and along one side a contingent of soldiers! However, our meal was an essential item, so I drove on, to find the restaurant gardens a dazzling picture of merry diners and flitting waiters, enlivened by the music of a capable orchestra. Numbers of cars were drawn up in the space outside the gardens and naturally the Packard made a great sensation among the motorists.
>
> The friendly English-speaking waiter at once recognised the girls and found us a table on a dais quite close to the dancing floor. Again, as ever on this holiday, it was necessary to be as quick as we could, but the pauses, which always occur between the courses of a meal, gave me an opportunity to enjoy a dance with Myfanwy.
>
> But before the meal was over I received an S.O.S. from M. Bebis, requesting me to come as quickly as I could to the square, for the people were getting clamorous in their anxiety to hear the radio. Off we went back to the crowd. I drove slowly towards the assembly and as the people realised our approach, our coming was heralded by great cheers and then a sudden rush nearly

overwhelmed us. A real mob beset us on all sides – they jumped on the running boards, climbed on the luggage carriers, took a grasp or a footing wherever they could, till we trembled for fear that all the apparatus on the car would be ruined. Just as we were giving it all up as lost, however, a sturdy line of soldiers appeared and joining hands made a strong cordon round the car, driving the crowd back on all sides. I perforce stopped the car, so the military were able to widen their circle and we had space and leisure to breathe once more. What an experience! One more of the thrills of the holiday!

English people in the capital of Romania at eleven o'clock on a Saturday night, in the midst of a dense throng of excited men and women, but protected from the violence of their friendly demonstrations by at least a platoon of their own soldiers! The police were nowhere in evidence; the controlling of crowds is apparently done always by the power of the army.

I was requested not to begin the wireless demonstration until the arrival of the Officer Commanding the military guard, so in spite of our hurry, there was a delay of twenty minutes before the people were rewarded for their eagerness, interest and patience! Then I gave them the programmes from the various European stations, a 'Dunlop' official telling the people in the Romanian language what transmissions they were hearing. Just before 1 am. E.E. time, midnight English Summer time, I tuned in to London, and there, 1300 miles away from our beloved capital, the sonorous booms of Big Ben echoed in the stillness of that glorious summer night. Instinctively one glances up expecting to see the familiar clock face of Parliament Square.

After leaving Bucharest, things did not go well. At one point, the travellers stopped to placate some local peasants whose goose they had just run over, after which the car would not pull away. The cardan shaft (propeller shaft) had at last given up the ghost. The atrocious roads had taken their toll and cracked the casing. Fortunately, they managed to get a tow into Zagreb from a large limousine; as neither vehicle had a towrope, they had to use the tyre chains which, despite breaking several times, hauled them to the garage in Zagreb. Unprepossessing though it was, once the mechanics got started, Lenny was happy that they would successfully complete the complex repair. It would not be a quick job so they spent some time exploring the town.

Lenny took the opportunity to visit the Radio Klub Zagreb station. He was quite impressed with what he saw, and was asked to broadcast a short speech to the listeners. He was also allowed to connect his transmitter to

59

the station's aerial. The results were excellent, but due to a momentary lapse of concentration, Lenny received a nasty shock when he made the connection. His fingers were quite badly burned.

The repair to the car was completed the following day, and eventually the five of them left at one the following morning. They swept out of Zagreb in the direction of Trieste. Lenny felt tired and reprimanded himself for not waiting until dawn to start the next stage of the journey, but the necessary repairs to the cardan shaft had put them behind schedule. His burned, bandaged fingers ached abominably. However, bearing in mind the length and difficulty of their journey, he considered they had been remarkably fortunate not to have suffered worse injuries.

Dorothy let the guidebook slip to the floor of the car, the purr of the powerful engine lulling her into slumber. The other passengers also were dozing in the back seat. The heavy Packard, its tyres spitting the loose gravel to either side of the country road, rolled through the night towards the Croatian dawn. It was one-thirty in the morning; Zagreb was fifteen miles behind them and Trieste lay ahead.

The darkened buildings of Zapressio slid past. A dog, raised from its sleep by the roar of the twelve cylinders, released a half-hearted bark, more of complaint than fear.

Glancing round at his sleeping passengers, Lenny was reminded of his responsibility, and switched his attention back to the driving. The nose light on the radiator cap glowed like a miniature beacon, illuminating the little Union Jack that fluttered above it; the headlights bathed the road with a yellow glow. Seeing the bend ahead, Lenny changed down and braked to cruise round it at twenty miles an hour.

The crash echoed through the night. The bar of the unlit rail crossing sliced across the top of the bonnet coming to rest an inch from the windscreen. A strange silence followed, broken by the rumble of an approaching train.

Now wide-awake with panic, everyone leapt out and started pushing the car. They managed to get it clear of the line before the express train thundered past, the driver oblivious to the drama. Shielding their faces from the dust, they pressed themselves against the sides of the Packard. As the barrier lifted, white-faced survivors stared at each other and then at the shattered aerial that dangled from the nearside of the car. The nose light was extinguished.

Lenny described what happened in his journal:

> We were quite mesmerised at the moment, chiefly annoyed at the
> damage so soon after an expensive repair, and when the gates,

60

manipulated from some distance away, were raised to clear the road, we set off again. But in a very few minutes the full extent of the danger we had escaped came over me with a shock, and I found that I could not go on driving in the dark. The girls were feeling rather shaky too, so we decided to stop where we were on the road and sleep in the car until daylight.

We raised up rather cold and stiff, about 5.30 am, having rested since about 2 o'clock. It was very dull and misty and the dew was so heavy that everything in the car was quite wet. We shivered and 'groused' a little, but as we wrapped ourselves up well and got on the move again, gradually we got warm and very hungry. We went for some 40 miles along a winding secondary road, most beautiful crossing the River Save several times, and catching glimpses of lovely views of the river as the road led us among the trees and hills around its valley.

With the aerial destroyed, they were unable to use the radio for the rest of the trip.

At the frontier, Yugoslavia was cleared without fuss, but the Italian border guards insisted upon a 1500-lire deposit for bringing the radio equipment into the country. The deposit would be returned as they left. Lenny was adamant that he was not going to pay, and five hours was lost in argument and negotiation. Finally, he announced he would cut Italy out of his itinerary and go through Austria instead, and that he would make sure the Italian authorities knew the reason. This did the trick; the deadlock was broken and they were allowed through free of charge. Actually, the threat was a bluff: Lenny knew they had to go to Trieste to pick up some of their baggage, which had been deposited there.

In Italy, they stayed at Lake Garda where they were severely bitten by mosquitoes. The remaining trip was uneventful and took them through Milan, Geneva, Paris and Boulogne.

Aether II arrived back in London at 2.30 in the morning of September 6th, 1926, having travelled 4,500 miles in five weeks. The car was in remarkable shape considering the rough treatment it sustained in the Balkans. Plugge boasted that the tyres were still filled with London air.

Dorothy, Florence, Mildred and Myfanwy returned to their jobs. Lenny went back to Grosvenor Place, the headquarters of the Underground Group, to tell Bill Wood all about his trip. As soon as he was able he phoned Mrs Oldacre who assured him that all his reports had been received and full advantage had been taken to ensure that the tour was well publicised in the national press. Most of the national dailies as well as the regional papers carried articles about his experimental tour of Europe.

A series of Selborne Society lectures was soon arranged. Captain Plugge travelled around the country and talked proudly about the trip, using lanternslides to illustrate the many places he had visited. One lecture particularly aroused press comment. In an address to the University of London, Plugge concluded that England was lagging behind the rest of the world in broadcasting. He pointed out that Germany had seven high-powered transmitters, providing sixteen hours of entertainment a day, whereas we had only one station giving eight hours a day. He also saw Italy and Hungary as being ahead. Plugge was severely criticised in the newspapers, which stated that although the German stations broadcast for more hours each day, many of their transmissions consisted of hour-long talks and early morning programmes of physical jerks. They were also prone to over modulation!

*

Aether III was soon on the drawing board. Having learned from previous experience, Plugge approached Standard Cars and proposed the installation of a permanent radio receiver and transmitter into one of its 14-horsepower Park Lane Saloons. It was agreed to mount all the car instruments to the right of the steering column, with all the radio controls on the left. Special lights were fitted to illuminate the dials, and the power was supplied to the radio by special multi-plugs fitting into sockets on the dashboard, below the receiver. Dummy sockets were also provided to take the plugs when the equipment was not in use. The loudspeaker, fitted centrally in the roof of the car, was a pleated paper type and incorporated an interior light. Volume controls were located on the steering wheel and in the back seat. A frame aerial, similar to those used before, was mounted on the offside wing. The receiver was a Standard Telephone nine-valve superhet. A small one-valve transmitter was also carried to cover the 45-metre band. Aether III was to become recognised as the first car to be fitted with a permanent radio.[1] The installation added one hundred pounds to the weight of the car.

The fawn and black Standard YR51 was to make its debut in December 1926. However, its first appearance caused Plugge some trouble with the law. He had parked outside the Café de Paris in Coventry Street to attend a dance at which the Prince of Wales was present. Upon leaving, two and

---

[1] See *Guinness Book of Firsts* and the subsequent *New Shell Book of Firsts*.

Capt. Leonard F. Plugge.

Bachelor of Science ; Fellow of the Royal Aeronautical Society ; Fellow of the Royal Meteorological Society'; Member of the General Committee of the Radio Society of Great Britain.

FROM LONDON TO THE SOUTH OF SPAIN IN A RADIO EQUIPPED CAR.

A Trip of 3,000 Miles through France and Spain in a Car Equipped with a Supersonic Heterodyne Wireless Receiving Set—Preparation, Difficulties and Complications in Entering Foreign Countries with a Wireless Set—Reception while Moving and Reception at Rest—Future of Radio Applied to Road Transport—General Review of Conditions in Countries Passed. (160 Slides.)

RECEPTION ON MOVING TRAINS THROUGH EUROPE.

18,000 Miles by Rail with Portable Sets covering Experiments on Wireless Reception on the following Railways:—

Southern Railway.	London, Midland & Scottish Railway.
London & North Eastern.	State Railways of Italy.
Austrian Railways.	Dutch Holandsche Spoor Maatscapy.
Danish State Railways.	German Reichbahn.
State Railways of Sweden.	Swiss Federal Railways.
Compagnie du Nord.	Compagnie de l'Est.
Chemin de fer de l'Etat.	Compagnie P.L.M.

Future Possibilities with regard to Reception on Moving Trains and provision of Entertainment for Passengers on long distance travelling.—A Review of what has been done in the various countries, including the Canadian National Railways and two-way communications on Moving Trains in Germany. (40 Slides.)

CONTINENTAL BROADCASTING STATIONS.

Description of Visits paid to Famous Broadcasting Stations—Their Situation—Their Gear—Their Methods of Transmission and the Characteristics of their Programmes—Foreign Radio Humour. (100 Special Slides.)

THE SUPERSONIC HETERODYNE METHOD OF RECEPTION.

A very comprehensive Lecture on this New Method of Receiving Long Distance Stations on a Frame Aerial.

The following points are fully described and explained by Slides : Selectivity—Long Range—Wide Wave Band—Simplicity of Principle—Case of Control—Constructional Details—General Practice in Various Countries. (100 Slides.)

At this Lecture a Demonstration may be provided with Reception on a Loud Speaker of music from five different European countries, and speech in five different languages. No Installation required, the Set being entirely self-contained.

THE INTERNATIONAL ASPECT OF BROADCASTING.

A Review of Broadcasting throughout the World—Its History—Its Influence on the Various Countries—The Various Legislations in Force—The Initial Difficulties encountered in each Country—Its Effect on International Relationship—The Question of Languages—The International Language for Broadcasting—To be English—The Future of International Broadcasting—Special Transmissions for other Countries—General Views. (With or without Slides.)

"*I have never heard anyone speak quite so fluently.*"—MR. E. BROWN, Headmaster of The College for the Higher Education of the Blind, Worcester.

"*I can say without hesitation both on behalf of myself and my fellow-members, that the lecture we have heard this evening is easily the most interesting we have been privileged to hear this year.*"—President of the Hounslow and District Wireless Society.

(London.)

Captain Leonard F. Plugge has travelled extensively through Europe where there is scarcely a country he has not visited and visited thoroughly. He is a fluent linguist, and is well known throughout the world for his writings on wireless subjects, the latter having been translated into some dozen or more languages, and published in every country in Europe, and also in America and other continents. He is admittedly one of the greatest authorities on International Broadcasting. It was he who first suggested the formation of the Geneva Conference in a lecture he gave on behalf of the Radio Society of Great Britain. He was the originator and Editor of the first British paper entirely devoted to Foreign Broadcasting. His lectures are illustrated by numerous slides which describe fully the various points to which he refers.

a half-hours later, he was confronted by a London 'bobby', who charged him with obstruction. Lenny's excuse was that the car was so unusual that it attracted a big crowd wherever it went. Nevertheless, he was fined 20 shillings at Bow Street.

The worthy Captain and Aether III appeared in many parts of the country over the next few months, including Edinburgh, Sheffield, and Broadway in the Cotswolds where he visited his sister Mina. Mina was married to Arthur Williams, a prominent local farmer, and lived at West End Farm a few miles outside the town. Lenny found that the farm was a handy place to store his cars. Incidentally, Arthur was later to divorce Mina and marry the mother of the first wife of Liberal MP Jeremy Thorpe who led the Party from 1967 to 1976.

A rare event was causing a lot of speculation in the press: a total eclipse of the sun was due on June 29th, 1927. Plugge planned to carry out transmission experiments during the eclipse before leaving again for Europe in July.

Several radio stations had agreed to take part and transmit special signals before and during the event. Radio Barcelona was to broadcast a half-hour talk in English; Berlin and Paris would transmit special signals. The BBC and the Radio Research Board together were also to send out signals. Aether III was to tour 'at high speed' the zone of totality that covered North Wales and the Midlands, monitoring transmissions. The Standard was equipped with a Marconiphone Super 8, which was to be operated by Lenny's friend, Horace Connell, who had designed this new 'one control' receiver. The car was positioned eight miles south of Darlington, and the two receivers were tuned to different stations. Plugge claimed that he registered the eclipse three minutes earlier than had been calculated. He noted that radio signals showed increased strength during the period of totality, and that once this had passed, the intensity of the signal declined. Their short-wave receiver also picked up the carrier wave of WGY Schenectady on 32.77 metres during totality, but they were unable to receive Schenectady distinctly. Lenny's experiments were not as successful as he had hoped and he was disappointed that cloud prevented him from seeing the eclipse.

Two weeks after the eclipse, Plugge left England with Aether III bound for Madrid. This time he was accompanied by Mrs Champness, Miss Mildred James and Miss Ivy Woodall. Five days later, Connell set out with the Packard. The two men hoped to keep in touch over a range of 500 miles. Both vehicles followed the same route to Paris at which point Plugge headed south via Clermont Ferrand and Toulouse while Aether II followed the western route to Bordeaux. Once in Spain, Plugge took the road through Barcelona and Madrid, and Connell took the west coast road through Portugal. They were to meet up near Gibraltar on August 1st to compare notes. Unfortunately, there are no records regarding the success of the inter-car communications.

Plugge's plan to take the car over to Tangier and run along the North Coast of Africa was dashed when he was unable to obtain the necessary permission. He and his companions had to cross by ferry.

The *SY Ceto*

"Ceto" Personnel

Officers:
Capt. Frank Rollo   A. Mathieson
J. Ritchie   R. Adie

Crew:
J. Maclean   J. Irvine
J. Leggatt   W. Dingwall
D. Hebington   Wm. McKee
J. Reid   C. Woods

"Daily Mail" Representatives:
W. Ridgeway and W. S. Scott

Announcer: Stephen H. C. Williams

Loud Speaker Engineers:
P. J. Linford   B. G. Anstruther
L. A. Wilson

Daily Mail Engineers:
George Thomas   A. Fraser

H.M.V. Records: G. M. Fenwick

General Supervisors:
Valentine Smith   W. J. Garnham

Ceto personnel

Stephen Williams at the
microphone as *Ceto* visits Bournemouth

Leonard Plugge

Frank Senior and Emmy

Lenny in St Marks Square, Venice

George Shanks

Richard Meyer

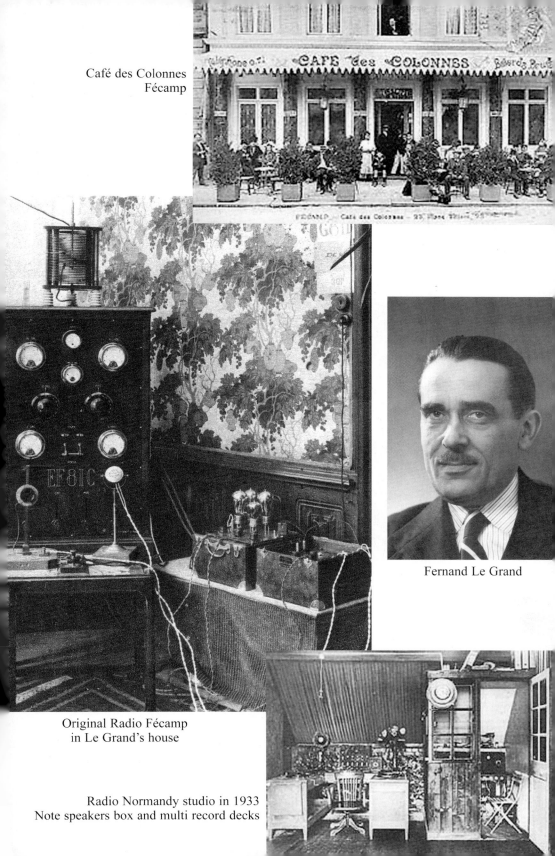

Café des Colonnes
Fécamp

Fernand Le Grand

Original Radio Fécamp
in Le Grand's house

Radio Normandy studio in 1933
Note speakers box and multi record decks

Fécamp – HOTEL DE LA POSTE - Avenue Gambetta - Journée Voyageur
Restaurant - Prix fixe et à la Carte

Garage pour 30 Voitures
Tél. 59

Salle de Fêtes
pour 200 couverts

Hotel de la Poste, Fécamp – home to the first English presenters

Max Stanniforth arrived on December 26th, 1931

Stephen Williams arrived a
Fécamp in February 1932

Max and Diana Stanniforth

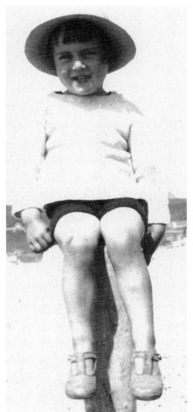

Rosamund Stanniforth
of "Happy 'turns" fame

Stephen Williams, Diana
Stanniforth and Rosamund

Roalnd Violette

Renee Malandaine

Bob Danvers Walker

Tom Ronald

Benjy McNab
arrived in
January 1933

orge Busby

Roy Plomley
arrived in Fécamp
in November 1936

David
Davies

Jack Hargreaves
joined as a
production
manager in 1936

Radio Pictorial July 20th 1934. No. 27

DAVY BURNABY ! **STAINLESS STEPHEN** "AT HOME"
TEARS BEHIND MY SMILES *EXCLUSIVE*

RADIO PICTORIAL

2ᴰ
EVERY FRIDAY

MARGARET RAWLINGS

B.B.C GOVERNORS — **WHAT THEY DO!**
A PERSONAL VISIT to **RADIO NORMANDY**

Radio Pictorial – July 20th, 1934 – No. 27

For the return journey from Spain, both cars followed the same route through Portugal. On August 10th, on the way to Lisbon, the party stopped at Elvas for a picnic. Lenny was exploring the airwaves when he picked up the following SOS broadcast from 2LO:

> Will Miss Ivy Woodall, travelling either in Spain or in Portugal in a motor-car, return to London at once as her father, Mr Thomas Woodall, of Cloncurry Street, Fulham Palace Road, S.W., is lying dangerously ill.

Ivy was preparing dinner on a camp stove some way from the car and did not hear the message. Unbeknown to her, Lenny rushed off a cable saying that she was on her way home. He did not tell her the news until two days later when they reached Lisbon. Here, a port strike stopped her from taking a boat, so they decided to proceed to France where she could take a flight back to London. Ivy arrived home a week later to find her father recovering from a stroke.

This personal story received enormous press coverage as it demonstrated dramatically the potential importance of the work that Plugge had put into the use of mobile radio, laying the basis for the future car phone.

During the tour, the group attended a bullfight. Lenny filmed the event with his 16mm movie camera and later showed it at several lectures that he gave for clubs around the country. He expressed his abhorrence of bull fighting, particularly the cruelty suffered by the horses. He added that the bulls probably preferred to fight for their lives rather than be slaughtered as in the UK, but even so, he backed moves to ban the 'sport'.

In contrast to the trouble-free Balkan trip in 1926, this trip clocked up twenty-one punctures. This was due to the terrible condition of the roads, particularly in Portugal. The passengers' heads were banged and their arms bruised from being thrown about in the car bumping its way over the rough roads.

During November 1927, Aether III, together with maps and diagrams of the route, was exhibited at the well-known department store, Whiteleys of Bayswater. The store was the brainchild of William Whiteley who was murdered by his illegitimate son in 1907. Five years later, the actual opening was quite an occasion as it was the first department store in Britain. In the same year, the then well-known music hall artist, Harry Fragson, wrote a song about it entitled *The Other Department If You Please*. Strangely, Fragson was shot dead by his father in Paris the following year. The store eventually closed in 1981 and reopened as a shopping complex and cinema in 1989.

5

1928-1930
Ships and Stunts

Voyage of the *SY Ceto* – Stephen Williams presenting
International Broadcasting Company (IBC) registered (1930)

As the year 1928 dawned, Plugge was working towards his goal to set up an alternative British broadcaster to the BBC. He was not the only man with ideas of commercialism and radio in mind.

Valentine Smith, the chief of publicity for the *Daily Mail* Group, was searching for a way to increase sales of his newspapers: the *Daily Mail*, the *Evening News* and the *Sunday Dispatch*. Smith hit on the idea of fitting out a ship with a transmitter and sailing it around the coasts of Britain, but outside territorial waters, and broadcasting music and advertisements to the happy holidaymakers on the beaches. A steam yacht, the *Ceto*, was chartered. Moored three miles off the coast and with the necessary equipment installed, Smith began test transmissions. Unfortunately, his ideas were more advanced than the equipment available in the late twenties. The experiment was brought to an inauspicious end when the transmitter was unable to produce a stable signal because of the swaying of the ship and the varying distance between the mast-rigged aerial and the sea (which comprised the 'earth'). Yet Smith did not give up that easily and he started work on new ways of achieving this unique publicity stunt.

The *Daily Mail* had a history of such stunts since its inception in 1896. The newspaper's chairman, Harold Harmsworth (Lord Rothermere), believed in exploiting publicity to the full in the competitive sphere of the press. Following deprecating remarks from Lord Salisbury referring to *Daily Mail* publicity stunts, Harmsworth replied:

> Don't use that stupid word; a stunt is merely what jealous newspapers call something their rival has done that they had not the brains to do for themselves.

Probably the *Mail*'s most notable stunt was to offer a prize for the first man to fly the English Channel, resulting in Blériot's famous flight. It had previously delved into radio by sponsoring Dame Nellie Melba to broadcast from Marconi's studio at Writtle in June 1920. In addition, the same newspaper had arranged broadcasts with an amateur station in the Hague, operated by Mynheer Van Dyck. Holland had many small amateur stations but the only one to survive was Hilversum, run by Nederlandsche Seintoestellan Fabriek, with a 100-watt output. It was taken over by Hilversumsche Draadlooze Omroep and, even in 1927, was still financed solely by voluntary contributions. The Chief Engineer was an Englishman, W.G. White.

Valentine Smith, the resourceful publicity officer, hit upon another idea: he decided to remove the transmitter from the *SY Ceto* and replace it with massive amplifiers plus four very powerful Siemens loudspeakers. This meant that the output would not be a radio transmission, and so there was no longer a need to broadcast from three miles out. Now the ship could sail within a mile or two of the coast.

A young Cambridge undergraduate, Stephen Williams, was engaged as a presenter to play records and read advertisements. Looking for something profitable to do during the long summer recess, he had written to Leslie Mainland of the *Daily Mail* asking if he could put him onto something. Mainland remembered being impressed with Williams's clear diction when he had heard him reading the lesson in his father's church, and had asked him to contact him when in London. Williams would be ideal for the *Ceto*, and Mainland put his name forward to Valentine Smith, who agreed. His Master's Voice was to provide the records, and Williams was told to co-ordinate with Gordon Fenwick of HMV to choose suitable recordings.

At last, all was ready and Stephen Williams took the train to Dundee to join the *SY Ceto*. The cruise took them down the east coast, visiting the major resorts. The rough North Sea tested the young announcer: one moment he was calling for young ladies to take part in a beauty contest, the next he was hanging over the rail, 'feeding the fishes'. The cruise continued around the south coast in July, and then travelled up the west coast to reach Blackpool on August Bank Holiday. Several times, they were invited to visit a resort to give a special concert, and quite often the local mayor would proudly welcome them and give a short speech through the *Ceto*'s microphone.

Stephen Williams's voice had extolled the virtues of reading the *Daily Mail*, *Sunday Dispatch* and *Evening News*, as well as suggesting that listeners should take advantage of the offers of free insurance to regular readers, which covered practically every eventuality, including having twins.

The *SY Ceto* returned via the Menai Straits, Plymouth and the south coast, eventually visiting the Thanet resorts and, finally, Southend where Jack Hylton's Band came aboard to 'broadcast' live. The journey of the 'Musical Yacht' ended at Greenwich. After a reception and a champagne supper, each person on board was given a turn at the microphone. To the strains of *Love's Old Sweet Song* and the National Anthem, the experiment came to a successful conclusion, the like of which was not repeated until the days of the 'pirate ships' in the late fifties. Valentine Smith would wait another three years, until 1931, for a further opportunity to become involved in commercial broadcasting.

In the meantime, Stephen Williams went back to Cambridge.

*

In 1929, Lenny entered Aether III in a Radio Rally in France. Organised by the Automobile Club de France, the Automobile Club de L'Ile de France and the Parole Libre TSF, the rally started in Paris on June 30th and ended in Fontainebleau a week later. Fifty cars took part, but none came up to the sophisticated standard of Aether III, which attained first prize for being the best wireless-equipped touring car.

It was also ideal as transport for Lenny and his friend Stella on a grand tour of Europe. Apart from the fact that she travelled with a large wardrobe of fashionable clothes that filled the back seat of the car as well as the luggage rack, Stella remains a mystery character. They filmed themselves cavorting through Germany to Venice and Rome, Stella wearing a different outfit in every sequence. It was a testament to the joys of travelling in the late twenties.

Lenny also tasted the delights of cruising: he was invited by Grant Morden, a Canadian financier and MP for Brentford and Chiswick, for a Mediterranean holiday on his yacht. Accompanied by friends, they left Barcelona to visit Majorca and Minorca. Time on board was spent happily playing deck quoits, and skipping and dancing with Pat and Peggy, Morden's lively daughters. Once again, Plugge's cine-camera was at hand to record the happy scenes. In Algiers, they took an extended trip down to the Atlas Mountains, visiting oases and, with great discomfort, riding camels. To Lenny, the social climber, this holiday was to remain in his mind as another step along the road to success.

He realised that he was going to have to concentrate his efforts if he was to attain his ambitions. His job with the Underground Group at a salary of £200 per annum would never make him rich, although it had allowed him, with the help of Lord Ashfield, the scope and the time to travel and make his name in the field of broadcasting.

Together with his old university friend, George Shanks, he began making plans to build on the foundations that had been laid over the last few years, and turn the investment into a worthwhile business. Radio International Publicity Services had prospered under the watchful eye of Shanks and Mrs Oldacre, and they now felt the time was ripe to try to introduce sponsored programmes, broadcasting to England via some of the Continental stations Plugge had visited during his trips.

George Shanks was a man of great charm. Tall and languid, he was a Catholic of Anglo-French descent and had spent much of his childhood in St Petersburg. He had inherited a sound financial backing from a celebrated champagne firm, was the recipient of several orders and decorations, and held the prestigious Privy Chamberlain of Sword and Cape. The latter is a Vatican appointment that involves waiting on the Pope. He and his rich Portuguese wife lived in a magnificent house in Park Square, Regents Park, in London, which he had filled with antique Russian furniture. Shanks was to play a very important part in Plugge's budding empire.

Plugge resigned from the Underground Group and founded the International Broadcasting Company, which he registered on March 12th, 1930. The nominal capital was £200 including £100 from Albert Leonard, the solicitor who handled property deals for Lord Waring of Waring & Gillow. The International Broadcasting Company directors were George Shanks and Aubyn Harold Raymond Wilson, who held 99 shares apiece. Plugge was the Chairman and figurehead. The company's first location was at 11 Hallam Street in central London, practically next door to where the BBC's new headquarters, Broadcasting House, was under construction.

Within a month of the formation, Richard 'Dickie' Meyer joined as manager. Born in South Africa and educated at St Paul's School in London, Meyer was to be the lynchpin of the organisation, the person who turned Plugge's ideas into reality and made them work.

The office set-up consisted of a back room and a junior typist. This was soon expanded to two back rooms and three typists. In the typists' room, there were two card tables, and many cardboard boxes for storing audience mail. The second room was for the manager, Richard Meyer, who was very short and extremely conscious of the fact. Anyone entering his office was immediately told to sit down.

Arrangements were made with Radio Toulouse to transmit a half-hour programme each Sunday, sponsored by a record producer. Surprisingly, they were heard by a large number of listeners in England.

Later that year, the IBC obtained an agreement with Radio Publicity Limited to handle a proportion of the sales of airtime for Radio Paris. Radio Publicity was an English company with offices in Aldwych, which held the concession from La Compagnie Francais de Radiophonie for the UK sales of airtime on the Radio Paris station. It was owned by a Mr Alfred who had a Paris associate called Monsieur Jacques Gonat. The following year Alfred withdrew and Gonat carried on with the company, re-registered as Radio Publicity (London) Limited and based in Chancery Lane. The IBC then lost its concession, probably because it was taking too high a margin on the sales. *The Sunday Referee* and its associates took over.

The International Broadcasting Company was set to go, but it was to rely on its Chairman to really get it moving.

6
1931-1933
Radio Normandy Early Days

Plugge visits Fécamp
First 'disc jockey' to broadcast in English from the Continent
The Sunday Referee
The BBC tries to ban Radio Normandy

The 1931 English summer had been miserable and wet; the August holiday period was spoilt by wind and rain. Hoping that the gales would subside, Lenny once again loaded his car onto the ferry to Dieppe. He was bound, on his own this time, for a short stay in Deauville. The boat docked early in the morning and, as he drove out of the town on the D925, the coast road was still shrouded in a morning mist but at least the rain had stopped. Passing through St Valery-en-Caux, he eventually arrived at the fishing town of Fécamp. Driving past the docks, he pulled into Place Thiers and parked in front of a small café, stretched and looked up at the sign over the door – 'Café des Collonnes'. He strolled into the warm interior and settled himself at a corner table, placing his hat on the seat next to him.

Monsieur Savoie appeared from the back room and walked over to where Lenny was sitting.

"Bonjour Monsieur, c'est froid, n'est pas?"

Lenny, fluent in French, agreed that it was cold for the time of year, and passed the time of day before ordering his lunch. The Frenchman shouted his order through to the kitchen and continued the conversation.

"What brings you to Fécamp, Monsieur?"

"I am on my way to Deauville for a few days. Tell me, Monsieur, is Fécamp famous for anything?"

Savoie thought for a few moments.

"Frozen cod, mainly. We are the largest supplier in the whole of France. Of course, we have the Distillery, the Benedictine Distillery. In fact, shortly we are to become better known. Our transmitting station, Radio Fécamp, is to become the main radio station for the whole of Normandy."

71

Lenny's relaxed pose changed to one of eager interest. "Transmitting station? What transmitting station?"

Monsieur Savoie explained. "A junior director of the Distillery has a small set in his salon and broadcasts during the evenings; he is very popular. A friend of mine, a shoemaker in Le Havre, was telling me just the other day that Monsieur Le Grand mentioned his shop on the radio a few weeks ago and his trade has picked up considerably."

"But this is wonderful!" Lenny exclaimed. "Can you tell me how I can meet Monsieur Le Grand?"

He explained his interest in wireless and was soon given directions to the Benedictine offices. He set off straight away to see Fernand Le Grand, who welcomed him into his house in rue Georges Cuvier. Le Grand was delighted to discuss his favourite subject with such a well-known personality, and said that he, too, had been bitten by the radio bug. He explained how he had first become interested in wireless when he was at school and had experimented for some years.

His family had not taken his venture into wireless seriously. His grandfather Alexander Le Grand, who had discovered the lost recipe for the Benedictine liqueur,[1] was particularly against the idea. Despite opposition, Fernand was not to be deflected from his dream. He set up a local Radio Club and became its President. The club obtained a transmitting licence in 1926, which enabled it to operate on an amateur basis. In 1929, Le Grand officially registered with the PTT (Posté, Télégraphés et Téléphonés) as a private station EF81C. He had the two fifty-metre aerial masts erected on cliffs about three hundred metres from the house, which meant that he could broadcast over a radius of 100 kilometres, taking in Rouen, Le Havre and Dieppe.

Lenny had been distracted by a very pretty girl hurrying about the house. Le Grand, noticing his interest, explained that she was his secretary, Francine Lemaître. Because of her pleasant manner and excellent speaking voice, he had high hopes of using her as a speakerine,[2] especially after she had taken over the announcements when he had been delayed one day, prompting a remarkably good response from the listeners.

The transmitter, EF81C, was standing on small tables behind the grand piano, a jumble of loose wires connecting the various units. Lenny

---

[1] Benedictine liqueur is produced from a mix of 27 herbs and the key to its success is the careful blending. The herbs were all grown on the cliffs overlooking the town.

[2] On the Continent, a woman announcer was referred to as a 'speakerine' whereas the men were called 'speakers'. The term 'speakerine' was used in both French and English.

described his plans for his newly formed International Broadcasting Company and went on to say how he felt that Fécamp could be expanded to provide an alternative station for British audiences. In doing so, the investment he would provide could also build Fécamp into a major transmitter to cover northern France.

Le Grand listened quietly as the Englishman babbled on; the Captain's ideas seemed to suit him admirably. Lenny suggested that if Le Grand agreed, he would like to make a start as soon as possible.

"What is your fee for broadcasting time, Monsieur?" he asked.

"Is 200 francs an hour alright, Capitaine Plugge?"

With a rate of exchange of about 120 francs to the pound, he immediately agreed and arranged for the first transmission to be at 10.30 pm on the September 6th. The only problem now was how organise to it. He decided to drive into Le Havre, draw some money and buy a selection of records.

In Le Havre, Plugge immediately went along to the English Bank, a consortium of Lloyds and National Provincial. The chief cashier, William Kingwell, served him and during the transaction, Plugge explained his plans for Fécamp. He asked Kingwell if he knew an Englishman in the area who might be interested in taking some records he was about to buy over to Monsieur Le Grand's house in Fécamp, and play them over the air for a couple of hours on Sunday evenings.

"I would rather like to take on the job myself, Captain Plugge, if that's okay with you. I have a motorcycle and it's not far. It sounds rather fun."

Lenny was delighted and accepted. He then scoured the shops in Le Havre, eventually managing to purchase twenty English recordings, which he delivered to Kingwell at the bank. After a few brief instructions on the presentation of the proposed broadcast, he phoned Le Grand to tell him of the arrangements. An evening spot was confirmed for the forthcoming Sunday from 10.30 pm to 1 am. Plugge hurried back to England to tell the IBC directors the good news and to worry about how they would raise the promised investment.

On September 6th, 1931, Radio Fécamp, the embryonic Radio Normandy, began with the faltering voice of William Evelyn Kingwell, the first 'disc jockey' to broadcast an English programme from the Continent. And with all the power the transmitter could muster: half a kilowatt.

Upon his return to London, Plugge was faced with three important tasks: one, to advertise his planned broadcasts; two, find a professional to take the place of Kingwell; three, obtain sponsors for his enterprise.

Tackling the first of these, he drew up a short letter entitled 'Special Foreign Broadcasts for British Listeners', giving details and times of the transmissions. He sent copies to all the Sunday papers but the only one interested was *The Sunday Referee*.[1] The letter had landed on the desk of Stephen Williams who had joined the paper as a special reporter on radio affairs. A meeting was arranged and the Editor, George Mussibini, agreed to give it a shot for two or three weeks. Contents Bills were printed with SPECIAL BROADCASTS FOR BRITISH LISTENERS and distributed throughout the south of England.

Miraculously, that October weekend, the paper sold out within a couple of hours; additional supplies were sent out with all the representatives they could assemble. People were definitely interested; at last, there was an alternative to Reith's traditional Sunday programmes.

Now to find a presenter. An advertisement in *The Daily Telegraph* drew a response from a 'professional' although his expertise was in the field of railways. Max Stanniforth was an Oxford graduate and classical scholar. He was also an ex-army Major, which appealed to Plugge, who liked titles. Stanniforth had spent several years in Europe, and later South America, selling coal to the railway companies. He had settled in South America and had held the post of assistant traffic manager with the Entre Rios Railway Company. After seven years, he had returned to England with his wife and young daughter.

The Depression still cast its gloom over the country and jobs were hard to come by. Having decisively ousted Labour in the October 1931 elections, people waited to see how they would fare under the new National Government, with Ramsay MacDonald remaining as Prime Minister. The tremendous increase in the crime rate, due to high unemployment, was causing great concern. The draconian measures necessary to protect the pound had failed and devaluation of 30 per cent was a reality (from US$4.86 to $3.40). International confidence in the pound was at an all-time low. Britain was forced off the gold standard.

Not the best of times to be on the dole. Plugge's advertisement was a thread of hope, and Stanniforth grasped it. At his meeting with Plugge, he mentioned having driven the Fishguard Express from Neath as a volunteer

---

[1] *The Sunday Referee* was established in 1877 and had a reputation for a go-head approach. Several of Dylan Thomas's early poems were first published in its 'Poet's Corner' in 1933.

during the General Strike whilst on leave in 1926. This appealed to the interviewer; here was a man after his own heart. He himself had driven a train for the strike-bound London Underground. The common experience, combined with Stanniforth's pleasing personality and affable voice, decided Plugge to offer him the job there and then at £4 per week, adding that he would be pleased if Stanniforth would use his title of 'Major'.

Following the success of their advertising campaign, another meeting was called at the *Referee* office. This time Isodore Ostrer, the co-owner and managing director of Gaumont-British, was present as well as Mussibini and Valentine Smith, who was now Publicity Director of *The Sunday Referee* after leaving The *Daily Mail*.

Gaumont-British was originally the UK subsidiary of the French Gaumont company, but in 1922 became a solely British company run by Isodore Ostrer and his brother. It had recently bought the controlling interest in Baird's failing television company.[1]

The Sunday Referee insisted that the station's power was increased ten fold to 5 kilowatts. Exactly how the necessary investment was found is not clear but it is understood that the IBC's solicitor, Albert Leonard, arranged it to the sum of 400,000 French Francs (approximately £3,500). This increased Radio Normandie's capital to 500,000 FF. Whether the sum was given directly to Fécamp or through the IBC is not recorded. The success of the station enabled it to increase its power yet again in 1932 to 10 kilowatts and ultimately to 20 kilowatts in 1933.

The station was renamed Radio Normandy for the British audience but retained the French spelling for France, although the staff continued to refer to it as Fécamp.

Regarding the 'man on the ground' in Fécamp, Plugge told his IBC colleagues about the ex-army Major, Max Stanniforth, a true professional albeit in the field of railways. His appointment was agreed, but *The Referee* also wanted a man with experience in broadcasting; they had one – Stephen Williams. The rough trip around the shores of England on the *SY Ceto* had qualified him as a broadcaster. Valentine Smith felt that Williams had potential. He was not wrong.

---

[1] Baird's recently agreed broadcasting permit in conjunction with WMCA in the USA was revoked upon his return to the UK, as the Radio Corporation of America appealed on the grounds that a foreign controlled company should not be allowed to broadcast in the USA. By 1933, most TV stations in the US had shut down, as electronic television was incapable of supplying a service and mechanical TV, although satisfactory, had programme limitations and a restricted number of receivers. A similar problem had occurred in the UK in 1930 and the Baird shares fell, eventually forcing Television Ltd into liquidation.

Kingwell had been struggling along by himself since September and was finding the work harder and harder. He had been gassed during the War, and the regular trips to Fécamp on his motorbike were becoming increasingly tiring. On one occasion, his voice gave out and he had to resort to asking his son to step in. The arrival of 'Major' Max Stanniforth on December 26th, 1931 was a great relief. As soon as it was possible, Kingwell gave up the job of 'disc jockey' and returned to Le Havre.

Radio Normandy in the early days could not be described as imposing. It had moved from behind the grand piano to a new location: the hayloft of the old Benedictine stables. Access was achieved by a ladder from below; for sound insulation, the walls were hung with old horse blankets and carpets. The 'speaker's cabinet', designed to cut out the noise of the traffic, was about the size of a telephone box. With no ventilation, the atmosphere in this booth left a lot to be desired. The English speakers dreaded using it immediately after one of their French colleagues, who tended to overdo the garlic. All announcements had to be made from within the 'box' and then the speaker had to squeeze out to put the records on the heavy turntable. The place was heated by an antiquated evil-tempered wood burning stove that was very difficult to get going and was nicknamed 'Le Buggre'. The signals were carried by overhead cable suspended on poles to the transmitter, now situated with its tall twin antennae in the herb garden at the top the cliffs.

Stanniforth's first job was to go down to the port and clear boxes of records through customs. These then had to be listed and arranged in playing order. About twenty-six records were required for a three-hour broadcast.

He had been given strict instructions by Plugge that at no time must he let their audiences know of the scant accommodation and actual size of the station. Exaggeration was the name of the game, and this had to be used at every opportunity. Mentions of "our other studio" and the "IBC Band" were often to be heard over the air. Of course, there was no such thing as another studio and the 'IBC Band' was a recording of a well-known English one, unaccredited of course.

Max Stanniforth, who was to take up Holy Orders in 1937, found more of interest in Fécamp than frozen cod. The local history fascinated him and he made mental notes for potential subjects for talks on air. The Benedictine Distillery produced a liqueur first made by the monks in the 11th century and based on plants grown on the Normandy cliffs. After William the Conqueror's invasion, some monks from this monastery were sent over to England to take up positions of authority. They were simple men and were chosen for their piety and learning. Two of them, Remy and de Losinga, were given the bishoprics of Norwich and Dorchester. Soon after being appointed, they sent back to France for skilled craftsmen and artisans and started a programme of cathedral and abbey building. It is to these people that we owe the cathedrals of Westminster, Canterbury, Gloucester, Chester, Bath, Winchester and many more. The Abbey Church in Fécamp is one of the finest examples of Norman architecture. Behind the high altar in the Seventh Chapel is a sixteenth century marble ciborium and, as it is reputed to contain some of the blood of Christ, it attracts many pilgrims.

Whenever possible, live acts were introduced by co-opting friends who had any musical ability. Stanniforth produced a serial talk based on the 'Story of Fort Vaux', which he found in a book he had bought at the local 'Tabac'. Fort Vaux was the site of a famous First World War battle in the Verdun region, between the French and German armies. His readings were popular.

It was agreed that the station should have a closing-down melody, and Plugge decided that it should be *The Goodnight Waltz* by Leo Wood, Irving Bibo and Con Conrad, played by Ted Lewis's Band. This was followed by *Ma Normandie*, the local anthem.

From early in 1932, the station closed with *The Grand Goodnight*, written by Richard Meyer and spoken over *The Goodnight Waltz*. In the later days of Radio Normandy, Roy Plomley read these same words:

The Grand Goodnight

To those of you who are keeping watch on board ships of the
Seven Seas, fair winds' fine weather and a good passage.

To those of you who man the lighthouses of our sea washed
shores, may your night proceed peacefully, immune from fog.

To those of you who are rising to resume the early morning shift,
especially our miners, police officers, postal officials, railwaymen
and other transport workers, may your day of toil be fruitful.

To young mothers who tend their little ones, may the sweet
ministry of sleep restore your strength and to aged mothers whose
thoughts are with their children far away, may the joys of
motherhood ever be with you.

To nurses and to all who ease the burden of the weak and the
suffering, good cheer and courage throughout your unselfish and
merciful vigil of the night.

To all of you, who by choice or necessity are seeing the darkness
out and the daylight through, good morning.

To the rest of you and especially to those who at this moment may be sick or wakeful or otherwise in grief, may this message on the aether waves convey our thoughts.

Good night and happy dreams.

Stephen Williams arrived at Fécamp in February 1932, with a crate of two hundred gramophone records. At that time, he spoke only schoolboy French, which made it difficult for him to find the studios. From his unpublished memoirs:

> I shall always remember my first arrival in Fécamp. I had crossed from England by night, reaching Dieppe in the very small hours. My train for Fécamp did not leave until a little after 5 a.m., but I found two Englishmen in the waiting room of the 'Gare Maritime' and we whiled away the time and kept out the cold night with black coffee laced with rum, at the same time blessing the more liberal Gallic attitude towards the consumption of alcoholic beverages at all hours.

> I arrived in Fécamp at about a quarter to eight. My French was of the usual standard then taught in English schools, quite good as far as it went, but it did not go very much further than somewhat useless enquires as to the whereabouts of the pen of my aunt. Nevertheless, I tried it on the Stationmaster: "Ou est la Radio Fécamp," I asked. After I had said 'pardon' several times in answer to his torrential reply, I decided to try elsewhere. Being ignorant of the French for cloakroom, I abandoned my luggage on the platform and made for a building labelled 'Hotel de la Poste'. Here I was morally strengthened by large white letters proclaiming 'English Spoken'. Unfortunately, the speaker of our native tongue was still in bed so I ordered and consumed several 'cafés' while waiting for him or her to appear. This occurred after my fourth cup. It was a 'her', and if only her English had been half as good as her looks … but alas it was a little less comprehensive than my French, so I gave up and decided to explore on my own.

> Almost at once, I was encouraged by the sight of two quite tall pylons, which I thought, correctly as it turned out, must be the aerial masts of Radio Fécamp.

> I would never have believed that such obvious landmarks as those two pylons would be so hard to find, but although I could see them from every point of the compass, I just could not find a road that led to them. By 9am I had learned to gesticulate like a native and armed with my new accomplishment, I enlisted the help of an official of some sort, a postman, I think, but he might have followed any calling, which provided a uniform and a peaked cap.

Together we reached those pylons and hopefully rang the bell of the wooden building between them. Imagine my disappointment when I discovered that this was the transmitter building, that there was nobody about but the caretaker and that the 'le studio' was elsewhere in the town. To make matters worse, it became obvious that my guide had business in another direction. He did his best to explain the road I should take and 'quelque francs' changed hands after which he left me to my own devices.

I went back to the hotel and tried the telephone. By luck, Fernand Le Grand was at the other end of the wire. He spoke excellent English and he would meet me at 10.30 and take me to 'le studio'. He met me as arranged and Le Grand conducted me, in some state, over the studio.

The tour did not take long but I was introduced to three French youngsters who helped him with his radio transmissions in their own language. Mlle Francine Lemaître, 'La Speakerine'; a vivacious girl in her early twenties; and the other two were the men 'Speakers' or announcers, Monsieur Violette and Monsieur Malandain. All three were very friendly and since none of them could speak English, my French improved no end.

All our contacts were either at work or at occasional social functions. We did not really fraternise and there was never any doubt that my charming lady colleague would certainly not have agreed with any Upper-Sixth-Form 'sophisticated' nonsense that the only way to learn a language was to sleep with the Dictionary – and I would certainly never have suggested such a thing!

Stephen Williams was appalled at the state of the studio and the lack of facilities. With Max Stanniforth's enthusiastic approval, the aid of a local carpenter and parts acquired in Le Havre, he set up a suite of turntables in the form of a horseshoe, which enabled a presenter to move from deck to deck.

The signals from the studio to the transmitter hut in the herb garden on top of the cliffs were carried by overhead cables suspended from poles set in the hillside, a matter of four or five hundred yards. As they were not very firmly fixed, the poles would occasionally move in the wind and had to be adjusted back into position.

Williams and Stanniforth hit it off straight away. Williams relates:

We only had about 250 English gramophone records (all 78s) and just the two of us, Max and I, to arrange them into some sort of programme and then to announce them.

Naturally, we pressed into service, for love, since we had no money to pay, anyone passing through or near Fécamp who could say a couple of words in English, or better still sing in it.

The presentation needed a bit of ingenuity. Generally speaking, listeners in Britain were accustomed to 'live' broadcasting from the BBC and we were a bit dubious as to how our programmes, though much lighter than the BBC's, would be accepted when it was realised that almost all of them came off gramophone records. We tried to overcome this with a little harmless camouflage.

By dividing our turntables into pairs and elevating them to 'Studio' status, we were able to refer to items played on pair 1, for example, as coming from Studio 1 and so on.

As another dodge, I introduced a new technique for those days by starting to speak just as a musical item was finishing and beginning to play the succeeding number just as the announcer's speech was ending. A fade-in/fade-out effect helped to hide the needle noise at the beginning and end of records. Incidentally, this had an unexpected side effect. It gained for us the reputation of presenting 'slicker' programmes, as the BBC in those days, invariably paused for several seconds between announcements and items. Listeners were quick to notice that we did not do this and were soon telling us that they liked our method.

There were also comments on the strange fact that each piece played lasted for about two minutes fifty-five seconds or about four minutes. These, of course, were the standard playing times of ten-inch and twelve-inch records, respectively. The station responded with the following statement:

Our programmes, which are reproduced from electrical transcriptions (records), are presented in such a manner as to give listeners the same impression they would get if actually present in a theatre or concert hall.

The IBC had demonstrated to its potential sponsors that Radio Normandy had a considerable audience. The next question was whether it could sell products to all these listeners. Further demonstration was needed. Plugge and IBC Director George Shanks discussed this problem and came up with an idea. Shanks had noticed a recipe for a beautifying cream in a housekeeping book belonging to his mother. The ingredients were readily obtainable and the preparation looked simple. So, the necessary constituents were assembled and, using a saucepan on the stove in Shanks's mother's kitchen, the unguent was prepared. They obtained some little pink glass pots decorated with two naked ladies in gold, filled them, and sent a couple of samples over to Fécamp with the instruction to sell it. It was to be called Renis Cream. The 'company' producing it was 'Classic Beauty Preparations'.

Williams and Stanniforth thought long and hard as to how to demonstrate selling a new product on air. When faced with a challenge, Max Stanniforth would cogitate, perhaps for a day or so, hardly speaking to anyone, until he gave birth to a remarkable idea. On this occasion, he suggested that they dream up a romantic story regarding a beautiful Persian princess and an old beggar – and this is how it went:

> Once long ago in the streets of Persepolis a beautiful Princess was being carried in her litter when she found her progress barred by a disturbance in the roadway. On summoning her attendants, she found that the disturbance was caused by some young students ill-treating a poor old Egyptian slave, which touched the soft heart of the beautiful Princess and she sent for the poor old man who had been ill-treated and rewarded him with gold and other precious objects. The poor old man went on his way rejoicing and years later when the beautiful Princess was being married, she found among her wedding gifts, a present from the old Egyptian she had rescued and succoured so long ago. The gift was in the form of a beautiful alabaster box containing some precious ointment or salve that according to the accompanying legend would beautify even the most beautiful of women. The preparation, of course, over the centuries was lost, but not very long ago, it was rediscovered by some scientists engaged in some form of excavation. The ingredients were identified; they had been purified and gathered together again and are now presented to the ladies of Britain in the form of Renis Face Cream, a beauty preparation, made by Classic Beauty Preparations of 10 Great Stanhope Street, London W.1. It may be obtained in pink glass pots at two and threepence a time from Classic Beauty Preparations, 10 Great Stanhope Street, London W1.

The address in Stanhope Street was in fact the home of George Shanks's mother. The response was immediate and Renis soon became popular. Demand for the product was soon too great for the Shanks's kitchen: a commercial chemist had to be found to take over the manufacture. However, the production of Renis was discontinued when it was found to compete with one of the chemist's own products. Nevertheless, Renis had served its purpose and made its point to the potential sponsors, much to the delight of Captain Plugge.

Gradually the number of sponsors increased, but not to the satisfaction of Plugge. He needed a way to demonstrate the size of the audience Radio Normandy was attracting and the potential market for the sponsors' products. Stephen Williams suggested the creation of a listeners' club, which was taken up, and announced over the air in June. Fifty thousand people enrolled on the first day and the membership eventually rose to nearly half a million. A newsletter was introduced in April of the following year giving details of all IBC programmes.

One of the first sponsors was Spink and Son Limited; their advertisement reflected the situation in England in early 1932:

> Here is a great opportunity. Most of our listeners have unwanted gold jewellery of some kind. Spink and Son Ltd. of 5, 6 & 7 King Street, St James' W.1, will buy old gold jewellery in any form. The prices now being given are a record, owing to the enormous increase in the price of gold. Sell your gold to Spink and Son, an all-British firm that have been established for 160 years. By so doing you will help yourselves and help your country, because your country needs all the gold it can get. Such things as watches, bracelets, rings even if quite out of date are valuable today. Send them all to Spink and Son, 5, 6 & 7 King Street, St James', London SW1 and send them by registered post if you are unable to call in person.

Other early sponsors were Ardath Tobacco and Filmophone, who manufactured flexible records that could be rolled up and delivered in a cardboard tube. HMV and Broadcast Records soon followed these.

Some of the early sponsors had somewhat unusual methods of paying: they developed a barter system. Philco, for instance, supplied twelve radio sets for a dozen mentions per week for six months. A gents' underwear manufacturer offered a selection of its products in return for a month's announcements.

Plugge's empire was growing. Apart from Radio Normandy, the IBC was still selling time and producing evening programmes on Radio Toulouse from 10.40 for thirty minutes. Radio Paris was broadcasting between 11 and 12 midnight, but would soon be replaced by Poste Parisien.

Arrangements had also been made with Juan-les-Pins (Radio Côte d'Azur) and several stations in Spain, including a short-wave transmission from EAQ Aranjuez. All the work he had put in with his car tours in the late twenties was eventually paying off. The IBC Club and the Renis projects had proved sufficient for the sponsors to be pouring in.

Monsieur Le Grand – or 'Biggs' as he had been nicknamed by the English team – was also a happy man. Stephen Williams described him as...

> a bit pompous and prone like a Frenchman often is to emphasise his craftiness by laying a forefinger alongside his nose and expressing himself inarticulately by what can only be called in the vernacular, a 'raspberry'.

Le Grand of course had his French operation, his studio being opposite that of the IBC studios in rue Georges Cuvier. The team included three speakers: Pierre Garnier, Roland Violette and René Malandain. In addition was the delightful speakerine, Francine Lemaître, who made Stephen Williams go weak at the knees with her flirtatious manner. Despite a language barrier, relations were very friendly between them all. Pierre Garnier had come to Radio Normandy from Poste Parisien where he had gained the nickname 'Radiovox', which stuck. At first, his English was limited, but after rubbing shoulders with the English speakers for a while, he became reasonably fluent. His main job was to give French translations of the music titles during the IBC concerts; this was a requirement of the station. He sometimes took part in *Nursery Corner*, as Uncle Pierre. Most evenings, Radio Normandy transmitted programmes from Rouen, Le Havre and other Normandy stations, which were relayed to it by landline.

The BBC's *Children's Hour* presenters were referred to as 'Uncles' and 'Aunts'. Uncle Mac (Derek McCulloch) – with his not-to-be-forgotten "Hullo Children" and "Hullo Twins" – read out birthday greetings. In April 1932, Radio Normandy started its own children's programme, *Nursery Corner*, with its own Aunts and Uncles.

Max Stanniforth's wife, Diana, and six-year-old daughter Rosamund Ann arrived from England to live in Fécamp. Diana Stanniforth took part in *Nursery Corner*. She read stories about Romulus, one of the studio's nine goldfish kept in a tank installed by Stephen Williams. During a visit to the studios, Rosamund Ann was warned that she must be very quiet and not make a sound. As with most small children, she was unable to comply for very long and her little voice was heard by the listeners, who wrote in asking if they had really heard a child's voice over the air. This gave rise to an idea and from thereon, Radio Normandy had a real live little girl to say "Happy returns" to those who wrote in. The fact that it came out as "Happy 'turns" only increased the appeal; even adults hoped to hear Rosamund Ann say "Happy 'turns" for them. The programme's popularity was boosted by this additional role and the number of people writing in grew rapidly.

Nursery Corner – with Rosamund at the mike and Uncle Stephen behind

On September 11th, 1932, sixty requests were received in the one day. From the thousands of letters received from the fans, one example remains. It was from the mother of Bonita Winter, a little girl of nine, who lived in Southsea. The profusely illustrated letter included a story:

MAGIC VOICES

Once upon a time, a mamma had her little baby girl christened an old Spanish name – Bonita – which means good and beautiful. She grew old enough to go to school. Now Bonita's Papa was a sailor man, who sailed the good ship Nelson, flagship of the British Navy.

BONITA

One exceptionally lonesome time, with Papa sailing the high seas, the mamma and little girl set off from Southsea, Portsmouth, to see Grandpa and Auntie Alice at Manchester. When they got there, Grandpa HAD A RADIO. Bonita had never heard the magic voices of Radio-land before. How THRILLED she was, to hear Uncle Eric Fogg, Uncle Harry and Auntie Muriel on North Regional.

They got back in time for the return of the Atlantic Fleet. They told Papa all about it. Very well, said he, you shall have your Radio-land for those times I must leave you lonely.

So it came to pass, the next time the dear sailor-man departed he left behind a Radio Fairyland for Mamma and Bonita. Mamma had to learn how to pick up the places where the magic voices and fairy music came from.

84

Oh dear... she was half afraid to touch things. Then one Sunday, by accident, she discovered Radio Normandie. She heard a little baby voice. Is it a fairy Mamma? asked Bonita. I do believe it is, replied Mamma. It was too, a baby Princess named Rosamund Ann, introducing an enchanted Bonita to a magic world. There was *Alice in Wonderland*, Romulus the Goldfish, three darling Uncles, who were Little Boys – Grown-up, and one Auntie with a voice like a silver bell... Diana.

Just imagine... one goddess, one princess and three little-boy-Uncles.

Stephen Williams recalls that things did not always go according to plan:

Now and again, we did transmit items we thought were interesting in their own right, like some rather nice music we relayed from Le Treport once a week. Halfway through one of these concerts a peculiar and loud rasping noise developed over the music. I tried to raise the local post office to complain about a noisy line but could not get any reply. Finally I went down to the Exchange in person to find that the only operator on duty in this rural set-up had plugged his headset across the programme lines and finding the music so soothing had fallen asleep. His snores were the origin of the extraneous rasping noise we had transmitted to the world.

In the summer of 1932 there was a large Anglo-French gathering at Fécamp. We broadcast the proceedings in which one of the Britons taking part obviously had his speech written out for him phonetically in French. He was having a bit of trouble with the pronunciation and I can hear now the hoot of delight from the mainly French audience when he announced dramatically that it was international gatherings like this which have done so much to strengthen the beds which have for so long united our two nations. He had meant to say 'bonds' (liens) but left out the last syllable which, of course turned the word into 'lits'.

Beds for some reason, remind me of baths which in 1932 were fairly few and far between in Fécamp. Max and I lodged in 'digs'. My Madame had a pretty daughter who used to put a can of hot water outside my bedroom door and then run like a hare.

Max's Madame had a son who performed a similar function and who worried his mother no end because he had no girl friend which, said Madame, was not natural at the age of sixteen. One day, in fact, she wished, looking first at Max and then at me, that some older man would take him to the brothel and show him what's what, a chore for which neither Max nor I volunteered.

She was naturally a motherly soul and she made lunch for Max
and me every day. She was always dressed in peasant style but we
noticed that even when her skirts were coloured her stockings
were always black. One day, though, she hurt her leg and we saw
with amazement that where she had bathed it her 'black stocking'
had turned flesh coloured!

Embarrassing moments were not confined to their digs. Williams
continues:

At the radio station one night we were told we had broken down,
'en panne' they called it and would we please play a record
continuously to give the engineer something to test on. An hour
went by and the phone rang again. This time it was London.

"Are you drunk out there?" demanded Captain Plugge. "You have
played the same record seventeen times with no announcement to
explain why."

"I excuse myself," came the reply. "The loudspeaker became
unplugged. I must have tripped over the leads."

On another occasion the engineer rang through from the
transmitter. "We are *en panne*," he said. "Each time I switch on,
my fuses blow themselves."

"Perhaps your aerial's fallen down," I suggested. There was a
longish pause and back he came on the phone. "You have reason,"
he said in his Gallic way. "It has."

Radio Normandy was developing better than Plugge could have hoped.
Early in 1932, *The Era* had provided him with an appropriate slogan, 'Plug
in for Plugge'. Unfortunately, the slogan did not work because until he
entered politics Lenny pronounced the 'e' at the end of his name, so it did
not rhyme with 'plug'. *The Era*'s article referred to his enterprise as
"entirely praiseworthy and deserving support". It went on to say:

The IBC contains the germ of an idea that may serve to bring
about the emancipation of English listeners from the B.B.C.'s
tyranny of dullness. Plug into Plugge next Sunday.

All his life, Plugge was fascinated by gadgets. One day, Stephen Williams
met him off the ferry only to see him proudly walking down the gangway
playing with a yo-yo. "Think you can sell them, Mr Williams? I've got a
whole box with me."

In September of 1932, Henley's began using Radio Normandy to advertise
the new SS1. This car was a product of Swallow Coachbuilding of
Coventry that specialised in the manufacture of sporting bodies on Austin,

Morris and Standard chassis. It was developed from the Swallow Saloon of the 16-horsepower Standard, using Standard mechanical components throughout, but with a special under-slung frame. The 2,054cc, 6-cylinder, side-valve engine was left untuned. With its long sleek looks, it had the lines of a car costing three times its actual price of £310.

As soon as Lenny saw the SS1, he wanted it. The first he bought was named Aether IV. As new models came out, he went on to buy two more: Aether V and Aether VI. The latter was a very special version in a white finish, and upholstered in green leather with silver piping. The fittings were in ivory with chrome trim, including the steering wheel, gearshift, handbrake lever and instrument board. Of course, each had a radio installed, and all three were entered for various Cours d'Elegance.

In November 1932, Max Stanniforth was transferred to Radio Toulouse, although his family remained in Fécamp. Tom Ronald moved from Toulouse to Normandy. It was not long before Stanniforth was complaining and asking Plugge to post him where he and his family could be together. This eventually happened, and Max and family were transferred to London. Bob Danvers-Walker, who had recently arrived in Radio Normandy, was then moved to Radio Toulouse. The announcers regularly moved between stations in the IBC group, usually at short notice.

Max Stanniforth had never been happy about being addressed as 'Major', but Plugge had insisted. However, by the beginning of 1933, Plugge relented and agreed that he could revert to 'Mr Stanniforth'. Lenny always liked the idea of a 'Band of Gentlemen' running his affairs: he felt that Williams having a Cambridge degree and Stanniforth with an Arts degree from Oxford put his organisation on a par with Reith's BBC.

The Sunday Referee had continued its support of commercial broadcasting since its inception, and sponsored Sunday broadcasts from Radio Paris and Radio Normandy. This eventually caused trouble and, in February 1933, *The Referee* was expelled from the Newspaper Proprietors' Association (NPA). This decision was based on a binding agreement that the NPA had with the BBC to the effect that no member shall use broadcasting for paid advertising or publicity purposes. The consequence of this was that *The Referee* was no longer allowed to use the NPA's special newspaper trains and transport services. In an article in the issue dated February 19th, the paper stated:

> Should any concerted action be taken against *The Sunday Referee*
> by the Association or its individual members, we shall lay the

whole of the facts before the public in our issue next Sunday and allow them to judge. We believe this is a matter of the gravest public importance.

The Referee's case was based on the argument that other newspapers were continually receiving subtle advertising from the BBC in the form of broadcasts of public functions organised by newspapers. A particular reference was made to a broadcast by Amy Johnson from the Cape of Good Hope when listeners were told that the *Sunday Express* had the exclusive on the full story of her flight.

The NPA in return argued that it had no power to stop the BBC from broadcasting public functions, and that in any case *The Referee* was paying for its advertising while other papers were not. The newspaper was not prepared to back down, and immediately made plans to ensure the distribution of its papers despite the efforts of the NPA to prevent it, thus making newspaper history.

Valentine Smith set up a special office in the Strand and, assisted by a team of clerks and typists, worked up to twenty hours a day to make the arrangements. They succeeded in doing what no other newspaper had ever dared attempt: to organise their own private distribution service. On the Saturday night, as the papers rolled off the presses, they were packed in such a way as to prevent them being sabotaged. Staff, in specially arranged private cars, rushed them to the railway terminals. Because of the complexity of the operation, the publisher had to utilise one hundred and fourteen trains instead of the usual fifty-two. To foil any attempts by other newspapers to interfere, the packs of newspapers were sent in bulk to certain stations outside London where staff were waiting to tear off the original labels and replace them with others bearing the actual destination of the parcels. At each destination point, a fleet of fast cars and motorcycles was waiting to convey them to their final location. Blizzards frustrated deliveries in the more remote areas such as Scotland, but a great many readers did receive their copies.

The following weekend, with the addition of aeroplanes and even motorboats, full coverage was achieved and *The Sunday Referee* arrived in several places hours before the competition. The paper was prepared to continue with its own distribution network for as long as necessary. The Gaumont-British transport (being part of the group) was available to it as an emergency backup, but was not needed.

The Referee was appalled that the other newspapers followed the NPA instruction not to cover the story. Nevertheless, *The Referee* had strong support from its readership, and public opinion was generally that it should not be put out of business by an NPA ban on its distribution.

The battle against commercial broadcasting in English from Europe to the UK was just beginning. The BBC, being of the view that these transmissions were in direct contravention of its charter, approached the French Government with the idea of having them severely curtailed, if not abolished. Despite its motto, "Nation shall speak unto Nation", Reith obviously did not consider that they should be heard outside their own country, particularly dance music interspersed with commercials, which was strictly against his aims. He clearly stated his views in his book, *Broadcast Over Britain*:

> I think it will be admitted by all, that to have exploited so great a scientific invention for the purpose and pursuit of 'entertainment' alone would have been a prostitution of its powers and an insult to the character and intelligence of the people. ... few know what they want and very few what they need. ... In any case it is better to overestimate the mentality of the public than to underestimate.

In his diary, he referred to himself as "a sort of broadcasting doyen of Europe" – some would say a title more relevant to Plugge than to Reith.

It is interesting to note that for many years the small print on the back of a wireless receiving licence dictated restrictions on the use of a receiver. In 1930, clause 5 read as follows:

> The Licensee shall not use or allow the station or the portable set to be used for the receipt of messages other than messages intended for receipt thereby or sent for general reception. If any other message is unintentionally received the Licensee shall not make known or allow to be made known its contents its origin or destination its existence or the fact of its receipt to any person (other than a duly authorised officer of His Majesty's Government or a competent legal tribunal) and shall not reproduce in writing copy or make any use of such message or allow the same to be reproduced in writing copy or made use of.

By 1933, the first sentence of this clause had been rewritten:

> The only messages received by means of this station or the portable set shall be those intended for receipt thereby or sent by a duly authorised broadcasting station for general reception.

This, in essence, made it illegal for people to listen to Radio Normandy, Radio Luxembourg or any other station that the Post Office or the BBC considered 'unauthorised'. This clause was not referred to in any of the arguments for or against commercial broadcasting and yet the issue must have had a bearing on the change of wording quoted above. The press had a field day, claiming that listeners would destroy their wireless sets if such legislation were successful. In the House of Commons, E. Doran, Conservative MP for Tottenham North, championed the case for broadcasts from the Continent and aimed his criticism at the Postmaster-General, General Sir Kingsley Wood, who had responsibility for the BBC.

He asked if the PMG had been consulted by the BBC before it made representations to the French Government, who assumed that the Corporation was speaking with the full authority of the British Government. Kingsley Wood advised him that the BBC denied making any approaches to the French. However, it seems that the BBC's representatives discussed the matter in 1933 at a conference of the International Broadcasting Union in Lucerne where it was decided that the use of one country's stations for another's propaganda was contrary to the interests of broadcasting generally. This decision had allowed the French Government to take steps to absorb privately owned Radio Paris into the State network, which would bar any commercial broadcasts. This also meant that *The Sunday Referee*'s agreement with Radio Publicity was now null and void. The IBC had already been informed that its broadcasts from the rebuilt Toulouse station could not now go ahead due to these decisions. Radio Paris closed its doors to the UK advertisers by the end of 1933 – around the time of the opening of the new station, Radio Luxembourg.

The Newspaper Proprietors' Association was totally against any form of sponsored radio advertising and had a strong influence within the BBC, encouraging the Corporation to strengthen its monopoly of the airwaves. The NPA had already told *The Referee* it could not publish details of the BBC's programmes because it would infringe *The Radio Times* copyright. This provoked the comment from the supporters of commercial radio: "Not only does the BBC decree *what* we shall listen to, and *where* we shall tune in to, but apparently also *how* we may find out what is on."

It looked as though all the effort that Plugge and the IBC had put in to developing commercial broadcasting was to be of no avail, although they had tremendous support from the listeners who, having become accustomed to their late night radio, were appalled by the obstructive attitude of the BBC and its backing from the Government.

During the debate in the House of Commons, it was suggested by one MP that, since a lot of money was going to these foreign stations to advertise British goods, we should set up a second station in England to advertise these goods. The idea did not gain any support. By 1934, there were 340 British companies using commercial stations abroad, spending £200,000 on fees and programmes.

Plugge had already made plans in case his broadcasts from Fécamp were banned. He intended to continue broadcasting by fitting out a yacht as a transmitting station and sailing up and down the channel. It would have had to be a very big yacht and, if the experiences of the *Ceto* were anything to go by, they would need some robust broadcasters.

However, action did not proceed any further due to the considerable pressure from the radio advertisers, whose interpretation was that advertising did not constitute propaganda, and anyway the Lucerne Agreement had never become official. Little more was heard of the 'radio wars' for some considerable time. Radio Normandy carried on together with the other privately owned French stations at Poste Parisien and Juan-les-Pins.

Radio Normandy was still the IBC's flagship and, surviving the battle, it was going from strength to strength. Australian-born Bob Danvers-Walker had joined the IBC in 1932, and replaced Max Stanniforth in December of that year. He had served his apprenticeship with the Herald Broadcasting Station (3DB) in Melbourne as a junior announcer before joining the Australian Broadcasting Company's national stations, 3LO and 3AR. Danvers-Walker's voice was to become one of the best-known in both radio and newsreel.

The departure of Max Stanniforth and family meant the loss of Rosamund Ann, the 'naughty little girl' in *Nursery Corner*. This was resolved when Benjy McNab arrived as a new announcer in January with his little sister, Flossie. Tom Ronald also joined at this time in a management role.

Bob Danvers-Walker recalls[1] that Plugge frequently visited the studio during transmission times and enjoyed introducing the occasional record himself. He was primed by the presenter as to what to say but regularly got it wrong. Sometimes he would send other people to have a go on air. On one occasion, Bob Danvers-Walker was warned that Bill Crofton, the son of an old friend of Lenny, was coming over. He was told that Bill suffered from a stammer and that it was thought that exposure to a microphone might assist in curing him of the affliction. Bill duly arrived at the studio and Danvers-Walker showed him how things worked. The rehearsal they attempted turned out to be dreadful: Bill was barely able to manage a coherent sentence, and Danvers-Walker decided to pass him over. Plugge

---

[1] Bob Danvers-Walker in an interview with the author – 30th January 1983.

phoned the following day, saying that he had been listening out for Bill and wanted to know why he had not been on, and instructed that he be put on the following evening. This turned out to be a half-an-hour of pure hell: Bill would start a sentence and Danvers-Walker would eventually have to step in to get it completed.

The following day, letters poured into the IBC headquarters at 35 Portland Place. Listeners, thinking that the presenter was drunk at the microphone, expressed their disgust at the 'disgraceful performance'.

The group of young Englishmen away from home did at times behave in higher spirits than their French colleagues could accept. Stephen Williams, in his unpublished memoirs, recalled one occasion when he received a phone call to his office in Radio Paris from Captain Plugge asking him to make a flying visit to Fécamp:

> Le Grand, who flatteringly described me as 'sympathique' to him had asked to meet me privately to try to sort out a 'catastrophe', which had occurred in the town.

> I travelled north to Breaute Busseville where 'Biggs' himself met me. On our drive to Fécamp he exposed the lurid details. The town was almost in an uproar. His 'anglais' were suspected. Some nights ago there had been some trouble at the local brothel. According to the 'bouncer' the culprits were English. The red shade bearing the brothel's official number had been stolen and had turned up a little later deliberately placed over the all-night white light of the local convent. The Holy Sisters had been woken up all night by drunken sailors demanding women. He was deadly serious. This was no laughing matter – although I must confess to a stifled giggle or two.

> Le Grand took me to meet the Commissaire de Police. They had no proof of the identity of the miscreants but there were now several broadcasting 'anglais' living in Fécamp and, well, they would be Protestants whereas in a Catholic Country like Normandy .....and so on.

> I saw the Reverend Mother and as tactfully and sincerely as I could I apologised profusely if any unspecified countrymen of mine should have been concerned in such an outrage.

> Apparently my efforts appeased both sides, civil and spiritual. I do not say suspicions lingered but all agreed that the case was not proven against Messieurs des Grand Britaniques.

> Back at Breaute Busseville, 'Biggs' fingered his nose, blew a 'raspberry' and said goodbye.

Plugge visited Radio Normandy regularly during the early months together with either Shanks or IBC Manager Richard Meyer. If the staff wanted to please the captain, they would suggest that it would be a good idea if he broadcast a personal message to the listeners. In 1933, he was to give an Easter Message. It was duly recorded and sent, with other material, to Fécamp. Benjy McNab, who had recently joined the team, remembers the instructions arriving, but the recording of the message was nowhere to be seen. The specified time for the broadcasting was fast approaching, but still the record could not be found. At the appointed time, McNab stood at the microphone and announced:

> I am sure that our listeners will appreciate this is a particularly
> serious moment in the Christian calendar, so to mark this we will
> now have... three minutes silence.[1]

Plugge was furious. No culprit was ever discovered, but several listeners wrote in saying they had appreciated the sensitive treatment of a solemn occasion. Nevertheless, the Captain continued to give talks over the air at appropriate occasions.

Religion did not play a prominent part in the Radio Normandy transmissions, although it did broadcast *Thought for Today* by the Bishop of Durham on Sunday afternoons. Plugge also negotiated a religious broadcast through his connections with American Jehovah's Witnesses. This was the first time such an 'alternative' approach to religion was heard over the air in England, and it was not popular. Benjy McNab's father approached Plugge to have it taken off, which he did.

In April 1933, Stephen Williams left Radio Normandy and took up the post of Directeur Artistique at Radio Paris. His employer was now Radio Publicity (London), which managed all English programmes including those from Gaumont-British Picture Corporation and *The Sunday Referee*.

Increasing numbers of listeners trawled the wavebands and explored the aether. Major stations such as Radio Paris, Munich, Leipzig, Brussels and Bisamberg in Austria were well known. IBC programme information had been published in *The Sunday Referee* since October 1931 and, from April 1933, the *IBC Programme Sheet* was sent weekly to its Club members.

Radio Normandy started a late news bulletin on the June 18th, 1933, but this was discontinued by the following February. It was decided that it allowed scope, even if unintended, for possible claims of political bias. The idea was not repeated until the start of Radio International at the beginning of the war. For the same reason, none of the commercial stations

---

[1] Benjy McNab in an interview with the author – February 1983.

broadcast English-language news, although Radio Luxembourg issued a daily news bulletin in French and German.

In October 1933, Bob Danvers-Walker received an instruction from Plugge to meet him in Madrid to discuss the taking over of Union Radio. He arrived at the hotel late in the evening, extremely tired after a long journey. Lenny was buoyant and his usual chirpy self; always the night bird, he generally went to bed at about five or six-o-clock in the morning and got up around midday. They settled themselves in the dining room and Lenny suggested a drink. Calling the waiter, he ordered a dozen grapefruit and a dozen oranges together with a fruit press. The night was spent pressing fruit and discussing how the station was to be run.

The IBC liked its broadcasts to be slick and fast moving, but Danvers-Walker found that the Union Radio Spanish engineers had a rather *manana* attitude. Unlike in Normandy, the system did not allow the presenter to start the record himself; this had to be done by an engineer in a separate room. The problem was that the engineer would delay for several seconds before putting the needle down. Danvers-Walker came up with the bright idea of giving a signal to start the record. Using a small mallet, he would hit the water pipe next to his chair, thereby transmitting a 'ding' to the engineer's room. This worked very well except that the listener also heard the ding before each record.

In addition to working at Union Radio, Bob Danvers-Walker spent some time on the short wave station EAQ Aranjuez before returning to Normandy in 1935.

One approach introduced by Radio Normandy to attract listeners was to nominate each week a particular town or county in the UK, from which a special concert was broadcast. Included were references to local events, although the music played did not reflect the particular location. According to letters from listeners, reception was very good, despite the mere 20-kilowatt output. Reports came in that the programmes had been received in Sweden, Iceland and even New Zealand.

7

1933-1934
And The World Listened...

Radio Luxembourg
Listeners love the voices
Radio Pictorial

Radio Luxembourg was to be a far greater worry to the BBC than all the other commercial stations put together. It was not party to the Lucerne Agreement and, at 200 kilowatts, it was the second most powerful in Europe, exceeded only by Radio Moscow with 250-300 kilowatts.

Since mid 1933, Plugge had been hinting in his Club Programme Sheet that the IBC would get the sole concession for the new Luxembourg station English broadcasts. However, it was not to be, and he was annoyed at losing out to Radio Publicity (London), which had held the Radio Paris concession. Radio Paris had already complained about the excessive profit the IBC was making on its sales of broadcasting time, so its reputation was under a cloud, which may have influenced the decision.

The plans had been on the board for a couple of years and eventually, on Sunday December 3rd, 1933, Radio Luxembourg began transmitting on 1191 long wave.[1]

Stephen Williams, who had been operating from Radio Paris since he left Fécamp, told his listeners that in future, to hear Radio Publicity English programmes, they should listen to the new station in Luxembourg. They were both on the long wave but at opposite ends of the dial. To make it easy to find the new station that evening, Radio Paris and Radio Luxembourg broadcast the same programme. Williams told his listeners to tune from Paris along the dial until they heard his voice again – on Radio Luxembourg.

This ended commercial broadcasting from Radio Paris, but it was not long before a new Paris station had taken over. Poste Parisien started sending out IBC sponsored programmes on December 17th, 1933. A variety concert was broadcast from 10.30 pm until 11 pm and *The Goodnight Melody* was played. Tom Ronald was appointed to take care of the new

---

[1] The change to 208 metres medium wave – with the familiar station slogan, '208: Your station of the Stars' – was not introduced until the 1950s.

Paris station in early 1934, when the Sunday-only broadcasts were extended from 5.30 pm until 11.30 pm. He carried on his work at Radio Normandy until Benjy McNab took over the responsibility.

Those families who could afford to buy a wireless set in 1933 were introduced to a new world of increasingly familiar voices. Some listeners fantasised that the announcers, or speakers as they were called on the Continent, were friends or even lovers. This was reflected in the popular Flotsam and Jetsam[1] song, *Little Miss Bouncer*:

> Little Miss Bouncer
> Loves an announcer down at the BBC
> She doesn't know his name, but how she rejoices
> When she hears that voice of voices
> Absolutely tireless sitting at the wireless
> Poor little Miss B
> It's the man who announces with such a lot of passion in it
> The Daventry shipping forecast will follow in a minute
> Little Miss Bouncer loves an announcer
> Down at the BBC

The song goes on to say how Miss Bouncer eventually writes to her hero and receives a letter back from his wife enclosing a photograph of her with the children.

In the early days of broadcasting, it was BBC policy to keep its radio announcers anonymous. Listeners knew and loved the voices but were left to wonder what these announcers looked like. However, by the early 1930s this was beginning to change. In 1933, W.D. & H.O. Wills published a series of *Radio Celebrities* cigarette card series, which included popular stars like Derek McCulloch, Gracie Fields, Gillie Potter and Jack Payne – with the BBC's Chief Announcer Stuart Hibberd as Number One and Frederick Grisewood, the Assistant Chief Announcer, as Number Three.

Radio announcers were recognisable by their distinctive voices and repeated phrases. For example, Stuart Hibberd's "Goodnight, everybody, good night" was "loved by young and old", and Eric Dunstan became known as "the man with the golden voice".

The trend of popularising announcers continued with the publication in January 1934 of *Radio Pictorial*, a new weekly magazine that included photographs and brief biographies of broadcasters. There were articles describing visits to various foreign radio stations, with pictures of the presenters. Plugge had started this idea back in the twenties, but his articles

---

[1] A popular comedy double act. Flotsam was pianist B.C. Hilliam, known for his high voice. Jetsam was low-voiced Australian Malcolm McEachern.

were published in magazines aimed at the wireless enthusiast and amateur constructor rather than the mass audience. *Radio Pictorial* offered sets of twelve "beautiful photographs" of radio stars, with an album available free to those who have purchased twelve sets.

Part of page 16 from *Radio Pictorial* – August 24, 1934 – No.32

BBC programme listings were copyright of *The Radio Times* and therefore *Radio Pictorial* could publish only commercial radio listings, which it did under the heading of 'Your Foreign Programme Guide'. Listings included IBC stations Radio Normandy, Poste Parisien, Juan-les-Pins (Radio Côte d'Azur) and EAQ Aranjuez as well as Radio Luxembourg programmes provided by the IBC. Also on the page was a limited selection of listings from other foreign stations – German, Russian and American.

BIGGER AND BETTER THAN EVER

40 pages 3D

RADIO PICTORIAL

EVERY FRIDAY

INCLUDES FULL
ENGLISH PROGRAMMES
FROM THE CONTINENT

ANNA MAY WONG

Radio Pictorial
August 31, 1934
No.33

In this issue: J. Murray Smith, John Trent, Godfrey Winn and Whitaker-Wilson

Radio Pictorial, Number 33, was the first *Radio Pictorial* to include "full English programmes from the Continent". The IBC Programme Sheets provided by Plugge were now published in full, with complete programme details of the IBC's entire output, and covered several pages.

In November of that year, *Radio Pictorial* started publishing details of all the Radio Luxembourg programmes provided by Radio Publicity (London) and, in the same month, started its own *Celebrity Concert* on Radio Normandy on Sundays and Fridays together with another on Poste Parisien on Wednesdays.

By the end of 1936, the BBC had given up trying to keep their announcers anonymous and the Christmas number of *The Radio Times* published an 8-page supplement called 'Here are your Announcers' with photographs and short notes on Stuart Hibberd, Freddy Grisewood, Alvar Liddell and Lionel Gamlin as well as the regional announcers.

Radio Pictorial – No.33

More and more stations across the globe were taking to the air, broadcasting every hour of the day, entertainment for all – and the world listened.

8

1934-1936
Marriage and Parliament

Lenny and Ann
98 Park Lane
IBC new division: Universal Programmes Corporation
Plugge becomes an MP

Lenny Plugge had become wealthy and successful. The year 1934 promised excitement of a more personal nature. He had met the beautiful young Ann Muckleston at a party in the home of the owner of Meltonian Shoe Creams at Pinkneys Green. The family originated in Muckleston in the county of Shropshire, a few miles from Shrewsbury. Ann's parents, Frederick and Mildred, lived in Onslow Gardens, Muswell Hill, not far from the Alexandra Palace in north London.

An actress and model, she was twenty years younger than Lenny – but he always liked a challenge. Her name was Gertrude Ann but she preferred to be called Ann. Her mother had wanted to call her Nancy but her father thought it was not a proper Christian name. As a child, she had always been known as Nancy and, in her theatrical career, she appeared in several West End revues under the stage name of Nancy Rigg. Her good looks enabled her to take up modelling, which entailed trips to Canada and the United States.

Ann was not impressed by the short, tubby gentleman in his mid forties, particularly when compared to the handsome young men who were already courting her. She was about to become engaged to the head of a dairy company, and there was Greville Stevens, the well-known cricketer. But Mildred was an ambitious mother and a strong influence: she wanted a 'good' marriage for her daughter and encouraged Ann to consider Lenny as a potential husband; he was very rich and could provide her with security and comfort. Little did she know of the life into which she was urging her daughter.

Lenny was very keen to take part in the various *Concours d'Elegance* held in England and Europe, and entered Aether VI into shows in the South of England as well as in Dieppe. Ann, together with Marie Louis Bloch

(Lenny's niece), dressed in matching white raincoats and hats to complement the white car and walked away with a prize. *The Autocar* featured them on the front cover of its November 1934 issue.

Lenny had proposed to Ann more than once. While in the States, he had another try, this time over the phone. Ann accepted. They decided to marry in New York, and to take the SS1 and spend their honeymoon touring America.

Ann arrived in New York aboard the *Aquitania* on October 16th. She was met by Mrs Shelby Bracey, who put her up until the wedding. Lenny stayed at the Waldorf Astoria.

The New York press had been well informed and the forthcoming marriage was the subject of numerous reports. Even though Lenny had visited the States only a couple of times before, his reputation was well established and he was entertained by New York society, who were enchanted by his glamorous young fiancée. The couple held a dinner for friends at the Rainbow Room of the RCA building in the Rockefeller Centre, during which Lenny officially presented his future bride.

Ann and Lenny were married at St Thomas's, Fifth Avenue on October 25th, 1934. The church was decorated with palms and white lilies. Ann wore a gown of ivory satin with a high neckline and long train. She was given away by George Townsend of Greenwich whose daughter acted as bridesmaid. Patrick Egan, a well-known yachtsman of the day, was best man. Neither of Ann's parents nor Lenny's father was present. The reception was held at the Waldorf Astoria.

Plugge, a romantic at heart, had received a prize in January 1932 for his entry in the *Daily Express* Golden Rules of Marriage Contest:

Love Bond

1   Love one another, but make not a bond of love and give each other your hearts although not into each other's keeping.

2   You will give little when you give of your possessions: it is when you give yourself that you will truly give.

3   Stand together, but not too near together, so that the winds of heaven may blow between you, for you shall be together even when these winds scatter away your days.

4   You may give your children your love but not your thoughts for they have their own thoughts and you may strive to be like them, but seek not to make them like you, for life does not look backwards nor does it tarry with yesterday.

The honeymoon lasted six months during which the happy couple toured in their white SS1 all over America. They stayed in New York until early December before travelling to Los Angeles where they stayed as the guests of Mrs Alan Keith, Baroness Fern Andra.

From Los Angeles, they took a trip to the Grand Canyon and rode mules down the Bright Angel trail to the banks of the Colorado river where they stayed overnight in a Ranch Hotel. They also visited a Dude ranch and entered into the spirit of things by donning ten-gallon hats and leather chaps, and sporting six-shooters.

The newly-weds caused a sensation whenever they stopped for gas in out-of-the-way filling stations. The locals would stand and stare at the couple in the beautiful little foreign sports car.

In Hollywood, they rented a comfortable but not pretentious house in Mariposa Avenue. Whilst there they visited the film studios where they met May Robson who was filming *Strangers All*, and Charles Vidor, the director. He offered Ann a character part, which she declined.

They also spent a few days with William Randolph Hearst, the infamous press baron, and his film star wife, Marion Davis, at their fabulous house at San Simeon. Hearst, whose life was the basis of the Orson Welles film, *Citizen Kane*, liked to surround himself with well-known people. Ann and Lenny were allocated one of the four self-contained guesthouses, which were named in Spanish after the sea, mountain, field and river. Theirs was the Casa Mare. The guesthouses were decorated and furnished with fifteenth, sixteenth and seventeenth century oak. The walls were hung with beautiful paintings and the shelves and tables were laden with fabulous *objets d'art*. For the guests' enjoyment, there were two luxury swimming pools, one in the open air with a Roman theme and the other indoors, heavily decorated with Italian-style mosaics on the walls and the bottom of the pool. There was also a private menagerie with exotic animals, as well as tennis courts and stables. On hot days, guests could ride through a two-mile long shady pergola.

Before the meal, guests would assemble in the Reception Room where Hearst and his wife would make a regal entrance. In the Refectory, four very long oak tables, bought from an Italian monastery, would be laid out for the guests. At the time, no alcohol was served at San Simeon because Marion, an alcoholic, was 'on the wagon' – but Ann noticed that the Hearst sons were provided for, on a special ledge under the oak table. The food was not exotic: hamburgers were often served, with bottles of ketchup on the table.

For the many millions of unemployed, the economic situation in America was as bad, if not worse, than in England. Envious eyes must have greeted the sleek white sports car as it sped across the countryside, carrying the obviously rich couple without a care in the world. *Brother, can you spare a dime?* was just a popular song to them. The black clouds of depression were as real as the black clouds of dust destroying the Mid West, wiping away the livelihoods of thousands of the farming communities, and it showed little sign of coming to an end.

The 1929 Stock Market crash, where many people had lost everything, was followed by the worst period of history that the United States had faced. Many well-known figures were now broke, including Jerome Kern, Flo Ziegfeld, Eddie Cantor, Groucho and Harpo Marx; the Rockefellers lost four fifths of their fortune. Buying 'on margin' (putting up ten per cent to buy stock and borrowing the rest) had wrought disaster for the middle classes. Lenny never had confidence in the Stock Market and liked to be in control of his money. Years later his son Frank, who was born in 1937, came to suspect that this distrust originated from Lenny's experience of seeing his own father lose a goodly part of his savings in some financial collapse, the fortunate consequence being that Lenny had avoided financial disaster and was able to enjoy his honeymoon with his beautiful young bride.

Whilst in Los Angeles, the couple attended a bike marathon with Baroness Fern Andra and Prince Sagfragi of Persia. Mrs Claude Beddington (Lenny's old friend, the hostess who had introduced him to Lord Ashfield all those years ago) turned up. There were several members of 'refugee' royal families amid the social whirl of New York and London in the thirties. Prince and Princess Obelensky of Russia attended Lenny's party in New York. Their son was at Oxford and made his name by playing rugby for England against New Zealand, scoring two tries and enabling England to beat the All Blacks for the first time.

Aether VI created a lot of interest in the press. During an interview for the *New York World Telegram*, the reporter commented on the car, and Lenny's response was, "Not bad is it? She's taken all the prizes. I designed her myself!"

Lenny filmed the honeymoon on his 16mm camera, as a permanent record of this most happy time. In addition, he kept up his study of radio stations, and broadcast from several during the trip. Ann kept notes.

Whilst in the States, Lenny sent a telegram to Bill Wood asking him to find them a house – furnished and staffed, in a good neighbourhood, where they could entertain – to be ready for when they returned. For the few years prior to marrying, Lenny had lived at Rex Lodge, in Rex Place, a spacious mews house in Mayfair, just off Park Lane. This would not be large enough to accommodate the guests he was planning to entertain, now that he had a beautiful hostess to impress them.

Bill found 98 Park Lane, sumptuously furnished with antiques – a far cry from Lenny's little fifth-floor flat in Pall Mall Place just twelve years before. The house, which still exists, is one of a terrace of ten with a private access road. Each house is designed in a different style, some with bow fronts and others with square bays. Comprising basement, ground floor and four stories, it came complete with elegant Georgian furniture and oil paintings on the walls. The drawing room took up the whole of the first floor; the dining room was situated on the ground floor, together with a study/library. The kitchen and staff quarters were in the basement.

Having left the Underground Group in 1931, Plugge was now making all his money from the IBC, which had built up a network of stations in addition to Radio Normandy. Its programmes were broadcast from Poste Parisien, Union Radio Madrid, Radio Valencia, Radio Barcelona, Radio San Sebastian, Radio Côte d'Azur, Radio Athlone, Radio Dublin and Radio Cork. Short-wave transmissions were being made from EAQ Madrid on 30 metres, which were received in the States, but these and other Spanish station transmissions were to end in February 1936 due to the civil war. Trouble had been brewing in Spain for some time and, even in 1934, revolutionary activities had made it uncertain whether the IBC broadcasts would actually go on air. The announcer there was S.H. Gordon-Box, and many were the times when he had to risk rebels' bullets to get to the studio and present the programmes. He was handling the IBC programmes from Union Radio Madrid, Radio Valencia, Radio San Sebastian and Radio Barcelona, but eventually all were commandeered by the Government, which ended IBC's broadcasts from Spain.[1]

The IBC was expanding and had set up a new division, Universal Programmes Corporation, to provide a service for manufacturers not having their own advertising agents or to agents who did not have a radio division of their own. It could supply a complete design of programme to the customer's requirement, or offer a programme that was already on air that the customer could sponsor. Programmes could be made up of records chosen from the massive library and presented by an IBC announcer. A half-hour variety show recorded in a theatre with an audience of over two thousand people was another option.

---

[1] See Appendix A.

In its first three years, the Universal Programmes Corporation produced 94 different series, 2100 programmes, and was the biggest and most experienced company in its field. It had also become the exclusive European agents for the Canadian Broadcasting Corporation.

Plugge had become involved with politics and, in October 1935, he was nominated as Conservative candidate for Chatham in the forthcoming election. The Rochester and Chatham Joint Conservative Association had been trying to find a candidate as the National Government member for Chatham since Sir Park Goff resigned due to ill health. Former Conservative MP for Lincoln Sir Alfred Davies had been approached, but he had recently suffered a serious illness and was unable to stand. Plugge was selected out of five candidates for the Chatham seat.

The Captain chose to fight the campaign on the grounds of the weakness of Britain's defences. The country had been setting a good example to the rest of Europe by disarming; unfortunately, this had not been followed by others. Some other countries, rather than disarming, had increased their armaments in excess of international agreements. Britain now had only half the number of ships as in 1914; the territorial forces had been reduced by a similar amount and the regular army was only 80 per cent of its 1914 strength. The RAF was in an even worse situation, being only a quarter of its 1918 strength. Plugge advocated that Britain should have a defence force of comparable size to the largest in the world, and promised to press for this should he be elected.

He recommended the continuation and expansion of the policies of the National Government over the previous four years, in the reduction of unemployment, building of new houses to replace slums, increased exports and lower taxes. He stated, "Every man has a right to work. It is his heritage." He attacked the Socialist programme of nationalisation and supported private enterprise and individualism. Commenting on the League of Nations, he said:

> We are faced today with a test case of collective security. It is for us to partake of this test and see to what degree we can rely on collective security.
>
> We shall be able to see by this test whether collective security is a practical proposition.
>
> If it is not, my policy would be in favour of withdrawing and breaking the bridge which links us with the European continent and turning to a more real and practical League of Nations – that of the Commonwealth of the British Empire.

> My policy may be summarised in a few words: I favour power without arrogance. I demand a powerful Navy, a powerful Army and a powerful Air Force, used as a power for defence and a force for peace – peace at home, peace in the Empire and peace in the world.

Ann, often referred to as the Captain's 'first lieutenant', gave her opinion of the candidate:

> My husband is the most dependable man I have ever met and you could not have a better person to represent you than him. Nothing is too much for him and I want to assist him in every way to make him the best Member of Parliament you have ever had. He is my husband and he will never let you down.

Plugge's opponent was Hugh Gaitskell, representing Labour, who became a good friend of the Plugges.

The Conservatives suggested that, out of respect, there should be no campaigning on Armistice Day, then held on November 11th. Labour disagreed, arguing that the Conservatives' attitude to defence and rearmament was warmongering and would create an arms race; not to electioneer on Armistice Day would be betraying the Glorious Dead. However, as the day came nearer, Gaitskell and Plugge agreed not to actively canvas on that day.

When making a campaign speech, Plugge would become so excited about his subject that he would gradually speak faster and faster. Noticing this, Ann thought of a handy solution. When he began accelerating, she would pass him a piece of paper with 'SLOW DOWN' written on it.

Heckling was something to which the new candidate had to become accustomed. Among the dockers, there were some hardened Labour supporters who took every opportunity to embarrass the speaker – but Plugge had his supporters. The well-known voice of radio, Christopher Stone,[1] spoke at meetings on Plugge's behalf and wrote a piece in *Radio Pictorial* confirming his support following the election.

The white SS1 – Aether VI – was part of the small convoy of cars used for Plugge's campaign. The leading car, with its large placard declaring

---

[1] Until he was poached by Radio Luxembourg at the then fabulous salary of £5000 per annum, Christopher Stone was a well-known voice on British radio (often referred to as the BBC's first disc jockey). Such was his popularity as a presenter that he appeared on stage at the London Palladium sitting in an armchair next to a radiogram upon which he played a selection of gramophone records. The BBC never forgave Luxembourg for stealing its star, and did not use him again until the war, when he broadcast his popular record programmes once again. Stone was also the inspiration for the BBC's popular long-running programme, *In Town Tonight*. In 1923 he was cofounder (with Sir Compton Mackenzie) of *The Gramophone* magazine, which he edited for many years.

'PLUGGE FOR PLUGGE', was becoming a well-known sight around the streets of Rochester and Chatham. Ann would escort her husband everywhere, and they stood in the sleek white SS1 with their heads through the sunshine roof, waving at the prospective voters. Shouts of encouragement from the Conservatives and shouts of derision from the Labour supporters greeted them. Campaign songs were a feature of Plugge's meetings. For instance, when he addressed a group of ladies the following song was enthusiastically chorused to the tune of *Daisy Bell*:

> Ladies, ladies give him your answer, do
> Good old Pluggie has fallen in love with you
> Don't list' to the Free-trade fogey
> With his worn-out dear-loaf bogey
> Just be sweet, put PLUGGE IN THE SEAT
> Let him see you are Red, White and Blue

Polling day was November 14th, 1935, and with a 71 per cent turnout, the National Government was re-elected with a Conservative majority, although considerably reduced by the large gains made by Labour. Both Ramsay MacDonald and his son, Malcolm, lost their seats. Captain Leonard Plugge had a comfortable majority of 5,897 votes in a straight fight with Labour. To show his gratitude, Plugge gave his agent, R. Harris Brand, a motorcar as a Christmas present.

There were shadows cast over the election, including the challenge to the authority of the League of Nations by Italy's invasion of Ethiopia, and the ill health of King George V, which made it impossible for him to attend the opening of the new Parliament.

Parliament met in early December and addressed the defence problem by placing orders for seven new destroyers. Much to the disappointment of the newly elected Member, Chatham did not have the facilities needed to win any of the contracts. The Christmas adjournment was agreed for December 20th to February 4th, but a Labour member, Mr Batey, moved that they should meet earlier, on January 21st. His motion was defeated, but turned out to be prophetic: due to the death of the King, they were recalled on the 21st.

Ann and Lenny started their holiday in Saint Moritz, where, much to Ann's amusement, Lenny had a go at skiing. They also visited Vienna and Prague. Now that Lenny was a Member of Parliament, his status and reception in these countries was even greater than during his previous visits. He revelled in the feeling of increased importance and the chance to mix in the social circles he had always desired. Upon receiving the news of the King's death, the couple returned to the UK to take part in the mourning ceremonies that are expected of an MP on behalf of his constituents. To suit the mood of the nation, the IBC changed the content of the majority of its programmes broadcast from Radio Normandy and associated stations.

One of the many charts from 'Facts About Radio Advertising' published by the IBC for potential customers in 1937

The matter of commercial broadcasting raised its head once more in the House of Commons in February 1936. The Postmaster-General, Major Tryon, was again bombarded with questions from both sides of the fence, those in favour and those not. Plugge, of course, was heavily biased and stated that "61% of British listeners heard these programmes and liked them". Another Member asked if a better way to compete against the commercial broadcasters "was for the BBC to produce better programmes". Following questions as to whether he had taken any official action, Tryon advised that the Government had from time to time addressed the foreign governments concerned, calling attention to the resolution of the

International Broadcasting Union, and asking whether they proposed to take any action in regard to the practice adopted by certain stations in their territories of broadcasting advertisements in English. As the Government's policy would be decided by the report of the Ullswater Committee, he suggested that they await the outcome of their findings.

This committee had been set up the previous year to consider the future of broadcasting in the light of the imminent expiry of the BBC's first charter. Although the report reiterated the view that the Post Office and Foreign Office should take steps to prevent broadcasts of foreign programmes in English that include advertisements, its main concentration was on future policy for the BBC. As expected, the BBC was not allowed to advertise on radio, but it was given the option of using sponsors for its television broadcasts, a concession that was hotly contested in Parliament. It was argued that, like radio, it should be publicly funded. The objections rumbled on, but nothing serious was done to stop the commercial radio stations.

Oswald Mosley was watching Plugge's operations with interest. His Fascist organisation was subjected to a complete media boycott in Britain, and, in April of 1936, the Public Order Act banned political uniforms. Mosley needed a way to keep his Party in the public eye. Former MP W.E.D. Allen suggested that a radio station be set up on the lines of Radio Normandy, broadcasting non-political programmes, but with Allen receiving a share of the advertising revenue, and Mosley a percentage. The two men set about trying to find a suitable site for this station. They considered Ireland and Sark but finally entered into negotiations with Germany. Complete secrecy was necessary so that potential advertisers would not be put off by knowing that Fascists were behind the operation. The main problem had been one of wavelength: the Germans did not have any to spare. This would be solved by the takeover of Austria in 1938 (*Anschluss*) when the Austrian wavelengths became available. Eventually, with Hitler's approval, a station was set up on the island of Borkum, in the North Sea, with the transmitter aimed at Britain. Peter Eckersley and German engineers designed the station. It did not achieve its original commercial purpose but would instead be used for broadcasting propaganda during the War.

Plugge gave his maiden speech in the House of Commons on April 29th, 1936 and, not surprisingly, it concentrated on broadcasting. The report of the Ullswater Committee regarding the transmission of English programmes from the Continent formed the initial subject of his speech. He informed the House that, according to a survey carried out over 10,000 households, radio sets were owned by 7,700, of whom 61% listened to and

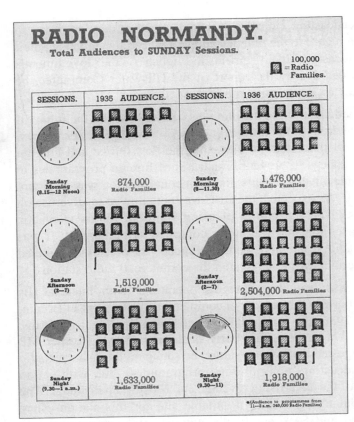

RADIO NORMANDY.

Total Audiences to SUNDAY Sessions.

100,000 = Radio Families.

SESSIONS.	1935 AUDIENCE.	SESSIONS.	1936 AUDIENCE.
Sunday Morning (8.15—12 Noon)	874,000 Radio Families	Sunday Morning (8—11.30)	1,476,000 Radio Families
Sunday Afternoon (2—7)	1,519,000 Radio Families	Sunday Afternoon (2—7)	2,504,000 Radio Families
Sunday Night (9.30—1 a.m.)	1,633,000 Radio Families	Sunday Night (9.30—11)	1,918,000 Radio Families

*(Audience to programmes from 11—1 a.m. 340,000 Radio Families)

Charts comparing audiences from 1935 and 1936

enjoyed the commercial broadcasts from Europe. He pointed out that although the BBC may have the monopoly in this country for the building and operation of wireless stations for the twelve channels under its control, it did not hold the monopoly for the use of the English language over the aether. Radio advertising was advantageous to British manufacturers in the export market. He quoted from a speech given at a meeting of the Incorporated Society of British Advertisers:

> If foreign Governments decided of their own accord to prohibit British advertising whilst allowing that of other countries, we (the British advertisers) should all protest in the most energetic manner and demand that the National Government take immediate steps to remove such an injustice. That our own Government should initiate such action against its own nationals is as inexplicable to foreign Governments as it is to ourselves.

Plugge went on to compare the transmissions available in other countries. While London, with a population of ten million, had the National and

RADIO NORMANDY.
Total Audiences to WEEKDAY Sessions.

🔲 = 100,000 Radio Families.

SESSIONS.	1935 AUDIENCE.	SESSIONS.	1936 AUDIENCE.
Weekday Morning (8.15—8.45)	422,000 Radio Families	Weekday Morning (8—10)	841,000 Radio Families
Weekday Afternoon (4.30—6)	211,000 Radio Families	Weekday Afternoon (3.30—6)	510,000 Radio Families
Weekday Night (11—1 a.m.)	760,000 Radio Families	Weekday Night (12—1 a.m.)	166,000 Radio Families

It will be noticed that the audience to the weeknight session has considerably decreased, due, of course, to the fact that this session now starts at midnight instead of 11 o'clock.

Regional stations (plus the English overseas service), Paris, with half the inhabitants, had eight stations from which to chose, and Brussels four. New York had twenty-two, transmitting at all times of the day and night. He also argued that the press should not be concerned about radio advertising being a threat – 60 million pounds was being spent on newspaper and magazine advertising compared to a mere two hundred thousand on radio. The advantage of advertising on the radio, he pointed out, is that it reaches the whole world and not just our own country.

During his many visits to Europe, Plugge had noted that his counterparts received the total co-operation from their Governments in assisting them in their endeavours, whereas our own diplomatic service did little to back him and even denigrated his efforts. He summarised as follows:

> I do not know what Honourable Members may think of that position, yet such is the position in broadcasting today. I submit that the Government and their representatives abroad should give every facility and every assistance to any British subject in his

endeavour to utilise facilities available to advertisers in this manner in any part of the world. Broadcasting covers every field of life. Indeed broadcasting is life itself. It comes under the jurisdiction of every Government Department, including the Ministry of Agriculture, the Board of Education and the Air Ministry, and therefore it is most proper, as suggested in the report, that there should be a Minister of Broadcasting, responsible to the House at all times. I am glad that that subject has been dealt with in the report and I would ask Honourable Members that when they consider the report they may give support to this important measure, so that we may ourselves be at all times responsible for the policy of so important a field, a field which concerns the lives and happiness of 30,000,000 of our constituents. I thank the House for their indulgence during this my maiden speech.

The following day a heated discussion took place in the House, and the BBC was strongly criticised. Stafford Cripps claimed that the Director General with "unlimited dictatorial autocracy" had, by frowning upon employee associations and unions, created an unhappy and insecure staff. Commercial radio stations were again criticised, but Plugge (now becoming known as the 'Shirley Temple' of the House because of his round juvenile face and bland youthful voice) defended them. The Reverend Campbell Steven, the Independent Labour Party MP for Camlachie, attacked the BBC's religious services, describing them as "mawkish sentimental Holy Willie stuff" and their tone as "most disgusting". He added that the BBC had been the most anti-religious influence in this country in recent years because of the way in which it tried to "shove it down the throats of the people". There were loud cries of "Nonsense!" Strong stuff, indeed.

The Postmaster General remarked that an alternative, brighter Sunday programme would remove many difficulties. There were significant cheers, none louder than Plugge's.

The 1936 Ullswater Committee Report, issued prior to the renewal of the BBC charter, outlined its recommendations for the future of the Corporation. It concentrated mainly on programme content, commending the BBC for its news coverage but chiding it for its lack-lustre Sunday entertainment. Political issues had to be addressed so that the views of both Government and opposition were given equal airtime. It was also suggested that time be given to minority and unpopular points of view and that the political parties should be consulted on major issues. These recommendations were to be totally ignored by the Government as the power of radio as a propaganda tool became apparent.

Plugge settled comfortably into the routine of the House of Commons and became a voluble member. He held the record for the number of questions asked: one hundred in his first year. Some of the issues sound rather odd today, but at the time were considered important, for example, the case of the guardsman who was court-martialled after refusing to shave off his moustache, which caused a great deal of ribaldry in the House and in the press.

Most of his questions related to the dockyards; the Chatham constituency included one of the largest naval dockyards in the UK. He also regularly addressed matters connected to broadcasting. Regarding transport, he suggested that traffic lights were set to amber at night, when traffic was light; and that car parking was restricted to one side of the road only, on alternative days, as he'd seen done on the Continent.

The Member for Chatham certainly attracted his full share of press attention. When the House had an all-night sitting, lasting twenty-two and a half hours altogether, a picture of Plugge leaving the House in full evening dress appeared on the front of nearly every newspaper. Always well turned out, he was often to be seen with an orchid in his buttonhole. A reporter for the *Belfast Telegraph* wrote:

> ... when Captain Plugge took his seat other MPs were apt to be eclipsed by his smartness. None of the men has a black coat, which is so deep a black nor striped trousers so emphatically creased and the jacket is worn in a way that accentuates the military carriage that is habitual to him. As he walks he is every inch a soldier, but it must be confessed that like lesser men he relaxes after he has been in the House some time and he has a habit of clasping his hands over his diaphragm.

In 1936, a new battle was waged, but this time between the radio advertisers themselves. From before the start of transmissions from Radio Luxembourg, Plugge had regularly publicised in his newssheets that he would get the concession for its English broadcasts. Plugge had gone so far as to announce in *Radio Pictorial* that, as with other IBC stations, *The Goodnight Melody* would be played at close down.

Plugge had made himself unpopular with the station owner, Compagnie Luxembourgoise de Radio Diffusion, over previous negotiations and was *persona non grata*. Radio Publicity (London), the appointed concessionaire, was well aware of this, as was Richard Meyer, the IBC's General Manager. Meyer spent part of his honeymoon in the Grand Duchy but kept well away from both companies and did not see the Radio Luxembourg studios and transmitter.

Unfortunately, Radio Publicity (Universal) Limited – Radio Publicity (London)'s associate company – was not aware of Plugge being unpopular with Compagnie Luxembourgoise and, as it was short of advertisers for the early part of Sunday and some weekdays, it arranged with the IBC to fill up this airtime. The IBC was delighted to oblige, and publicised the fact with its programme listings in *Radio Pictorial* and in its own newssheet. *Radio Pictorial*, which later published full weekly Radio Luxembourg programme listings as supplied by Radio Publicity (London), not apparently realising that it was duplicating some of those listings under the IBC schedules. This double billing was eventually picked up in Luxembourg and suspicions were aroused that Radio Publicity (London) had sublet airtime to the IBC. This decided Compagnie Luxembourgoise to revoke Radio Publicity's concession and operate through a new company.

Radio Luxembourg sent out the letter announcing that the exclusive rights for the sale of 'air time' in the UK had been taken over by Wireless Publicity Limited (a Canadian company with five directors based in Montreal). As a result, Compagnie Luxembourgoise was issued with a writ from the IBC – and two more from Radio Publicity (Universal) and Radio Publicity (London). Wireless Publicity Limited was also issued with writs: one from the IBC and one from Radio Publicity (London).

Stephen Williams, the Director-General employed by Radio Publicity (London), was approached by Compagnie Luxembourgoise to join Radio Luxembourg. He refused the offer and defended Radio Publicity's right to a hearing – hence the court case to defend Radio Publicity (Universal) and the IBC's claims to loss of rights. However, although supplying programmes to Radio Luxembourg, the IBC in fact had no contract with Compagnie Luxembourgoise. Consequently, its claims to loss of rights (the subject of the writs) did not stand up and Mr Justice Luxmore dismissed the case.

Radio Publicity lost its concession, Wireless Publicity took over and Radio Luxembourg continued to close with *It's Time to Say Goodnight* by Al Bowlly and Ray Noble. Stephen Williams remained in Luxembourg until the outbreak of the war, when the Germans invaded the Grand Duchy and his office was taken over by William Joyce ('Lord Haw Haw').

9

1936-1939
The High Life

Lenny buys a yacht
Birth of first child, Frank
Hamilton Place
War

Lenny and Ann again spent the summer recess in Monte Carlo. They attended the 'Night of Jewels' at the Summer Sporting Club, a fabulous occasion attended by princes, princesses and many other aristocratic figures. Lenny revelled in it and later shared the experience with his old friends, Sir Frank Sanderson MP, Sir Henry Lyons and Captain Arthur Evans MP. He talked about the prettiest Monte Carlo girls stepping from a huge jewel box onto the glass dance floor, and how the gems they wore, glittering in the terrace lighting, were valued at more than two hundred thousand pounds. The show was staged by Van Cleef and Arpels, the jewellers, but was almost overshadowed by the extravagant jewellery worn by many of the guests.

Back in England, the staff of the IBC, now numbering eighty-one, were having their first annual outing. The *SS Royal Thames* took the happy crowd to Hampton Court. George Shanks accompanied them in the absence of Plugge who sent a goodwill message that was read out on air at lunchtime. Radio Normandy also broadcast its best wishes.

Sometimes, what came over the air was unintended. One such occasion was in the late Summer of 1936 when Peter Taylor was spending a few days holiday in Fécamp with his parents. His mother was a friend of announcer John Selby who had joined Radio Normandy earlier in the year. Selby showed them around the studio, and Peter was intrigued by the towering piles of gramophone records. Also visiting the studio that day was a senior representative of Currys, a sponsor of long standing ("Britain's Biggest Radio Retailers"). He had decided to make an unexpected call on the radio station that handled his advertising and seemed pleased with what he saw. It being a beautiful day, he invited some of the staff, including Peter and his parents, to a picnic. John Selby left a couple of people in charge of the station and joined them. The picnic was set up in the adjacent field. Everything was perfect and the radio was switched on so that Selby could monitor what was happening at the station. Suddenly, an enormous crash burst from the loudspeaker followed by a stream of unrepeatable oaths. They raced back to find the floor strewn with records, some shattered, and the two red-faced presenters staring in disbelief. One of the towering stacks had toppled.

Meanwhile, at Orchard Cottage[1] in Kent, Lenny was holding a small garden party for a group of influential friends. It was a particularly quiet spot and the wireless was tuned to Radio Normandy. The friends were admiring the garden as Ann pointed out her favourite flowers when the background of pleasant music was shattered by the almighty crash at the studio and the stream of expletives. In stunned silence, everyone turned to stare at Lenny who was rooted to the lush lawn. He never swore and to hear these profanities come over the wireless from his pride and joy, Radio Normandy, was shocking. History does not record exactly what took place next, but John Selby left Fécamp within a couple of weeks to join the BBC. He went on to achieve a distinguished war record with the RAF.

In 1936, the National Broadcasting Company (NBC) of America issued a bronze medallion to mark its Tenth Anniversary 1926-1936. It was inscribed, "To those who have shared with us in the advancement of broadcasting". Lenny received his from the NBC President, Merlin Aylesworth, duly engraved to "Captain Leonard F. Plugge MP, Chairman and Founder of the International Broadcasting Company, London".

Whilst in the South of France, Lenny achieved his ambition to join the yachting set. In 1936, he purchased a 115-ton twin-funnelled motor yacht, an American ex-World War One submarine chaser. It was 110 feet long and fitted with two General Electric 500-horsepower petrol engines direct-coupled to each propeller and fired by compressed air in both directions. Renamed the *Lennyann*, she was converted into a luxury yacht with dark oak panelling on the walls and comfortable furnishings. At one end of the saloon was a highly polished dining table with seating for eight. The three-piece suite was generously sized and the windows were fitted with floral patterned curtains. Lenny and Ann's sleeping quarters boasted a large four-poster bed.

The *Lennyann* was moored in Cannes and, with the crew of nine, the couple decided to sail to London via the canals of France. They left in early October and reached Paris on the 28th, having passed through 170 locks

---

[1] Plugge rented this country retreat near Chatham so that he had an address in his constituency.

along the way. The superstructure had to be dismantled several times to enable them to pass under low bridges. They sailed on to Le Havre where they moored before returning to London. Lenny later arranged for the yacht to be brought to England and moored on the Surrey side of the Thames, opposite the Houses of Parliament. This gave rise to rumours in the press that he intended to use her for visiting his constituents. This was not what he had in mind but the publicity did him no harm and impressed his fellow MPs. He also purchased a twin yacht, and when asked why, he replied that it would be "useful for spares".

Captain Plugge had taken his seat in the House in time for the debates on the plans for the forthcoming Coronation, which was soon to be abandoned because of the abdication of King Edward VIII on December 10th, 1936. The Duke of York inherited the throne, and the Plugges attended the first court of the new Sovereign, as well as the Coronation. Lenny was in the full dress uniform of an RAF flight lieutenant, busby-like headdress and all, and Ann, expecting their first child, looked more radiant than ever.

Leonard Frank was born on January 13th, 1937 in the bathroom of 98 Park Lane, which had been fitted out as a temporary delivery room; the birth was attended by qualified nurses. As soon as 'Frank' was born, a nurse and nursemaid were added to the staff. Lenny chose a home delivery because he was afraid that if the birth took place in a hospital, he might go home with the wrong baby.

The christening ceremony was held in the crypt of the Palace of Westminster, attended by 150 guests. Oswald and Vi Short, Lord Sempill and Olive Newton were godparents. The *Daily Mirror*, announcing the birth, described Ann as "one of the most beautiful Westminster wives". At a meeting of the Rochester and Chatham Conservative Association, on January 20th, 1937, Lenny talked about his newborn son. The *Chatham Observer* reported:

> "He was 21 inches long, weighed eight and a quarter pounds and has got a lot of hair and by brushing his hair we have decided he is fair. He has a round face like a ball and everyone thinks he is exactly like me. I can't say that I agree; I am glad to say he is just like his mother. He has got large eyes – blue – and they are far apart like mine. He is exceptionally quiet and doesn't cry at all. He sleeps as much as he can. I have heard other parents say theirs is the most beautiful baby they have ever seen and now I think *he* is the most beautiful *I* have ever seen."

> When this remark was greeted with laughter, he exclaimed, "I believe it! He has not been able to express any wish about the

constituency, but I am sure he will want to come down here as soon as possible. The nurse told me he will be able to go out in two or three weeks time. Good photographs of him will be taken and distributed in the constituency by way of the Press. I have already taken some photographs of him, but I am not sure that they will come out. He has already been made a Friend of St Bart's and I see no reason why he should not be made a member of the Conservative Association."

Years later, Frank's maternal grandmother, Mildred, told him that as a baby, with a mass of dark hair, he was not very attractive.

In all, 1937 was a good year. Apart from being granted a son, Leonard Plugge was also awarded the *Croix de Chevalier de la Legion d'Honneur* by the French Government for his work in broadcasting. In addition, the IBC was now housed in the palatial 37 Portland Place. (The old offices in Hallam Street and Duchess Street were purchased by the BBC to create an extension to Broadcasting House.) Prior to the move, IBC programmes had been recorded in a studio in Kilburn High Road. Roy Plomley, in *Days Seemed Longer*, remembered it as:

> ...having originally been an Irish Dance Hall and then it was a studio of the record company which issued the Sterno label. ... It was shabby and ramshackle, with a frayed grey carpet and hanging drapes round the walls which attracted every particle of dust. The control cubicle, which had no visual contact with the studio, was in an exterior lean-to.

The IBC was expanding rapidly and, not long after moving to Portland Place, it extended yet again, this time into the properties on either side. The premises, 35-39, covered a total area of more than a hundred thousand square feet, each of the five floors of offices and studios being nearly twenty-three thousand square feet. In the imposing reception hall hung a large portrait by Cowan Dobson of its Founder and Chairman, Captain Plugge, in full dress uniform.

Moving into the bright modern complex was something to celebrate and it was decided by the IBC that a staff dance be arranged for Friday April 22nd at the Suffolk Galleries in Suffolk Street, London. Lenny and Ann hosted the evening with two hundred people attending, including the staff of the IBC's subsidiary company, Universal Programmes Corporation. Producer Tom Ronald of Universal was the Master of Ceremonies for the evening and music was provided by Marius B. Winter's Orchestra. There were cabaret turns by some of Universal's artists, including Brown and Starr who entertained on the Alka Selzer programmes.

Originally an announcer on Radio Normandy, Tom Ronald had by the mid thirties become Universal Programmes' first producer. Jack Hargreaves joined as a production manager in 1936, becoming Director of Programmes in 1938. He was to become well known for his BBC broadcasts after the war. Other producers were Philip Slessor and Roy Plomley. The object of the division was to co-operate in an advisory capacity with their clients and other production units, as well as producing programmes from scratch

Don't forget that your liver requires two pints of digestive juices every day

Tom Ronald at the Normandy mike in 1936
Cartoon by Burgess

for advertisers who did not have their own agents experienced in radio advertising. The IBC was able to call on most of the major stars of the day to take part in its programmes, and the man in charge of this side of things was Harry Fletcher who boasted forty years in the entertainment business. Although some programmes were still broadcast live, many were recorded on disc at 33⅓ rpm and sent to Normandy. The IBC was thriving.

Radio Normandy Calling – a series of outside broadcasts – was in essence a touring revue that proved to be popular. A typical preview of one of these shows appeared in the *Kent Messenger* in April 1938:

> Commencing on Monday next you can see and hear some of your favourite radio stars at the Royal Hippodrome, Chatham in the IBC's touring revue, *Radio Normandy Calling*.

> What's more, if you can sing, whistle, impersonate, or think you can entertain a radio audience, this may be your chance to broadcast, because an amateur talent spotting contest will be held at every performance and the finalists will be included in a broadcast from the stage on the Radio Normandy wavelength.

> Heading the cast is Alfredo and his famous Gipsy Band and that inimitable comedian Joe Young in new and screamingly funny sketches. Maisie Weldon does some delightful impersonations and Ward and Draper sing cheery songs at the piano.

The dancing side of the show is particularly strong. Wolkowsky and Grand are seen in beautifully produced ballet scenes and Joan and O'Shea do lightning acrobatic dances. The eight Belles of Normandy form a captivating chorus.

One of the high spots of the show is a reconstruction of an actual broadcast from Radio Normandy studios, in which you get an authentic and exciting glimpse behind the scenes of radio.

'Radio Normandy Calling' is a show not to be missed.

10.0 p.m.
RADIO NORMANDY CALLING
Strelsky and His Russian Band
Ward and Draper
Maisie Weldon
Final of Weekly Talent Spotting Competition
Compère
Joe Young
Presented by Macleans, Ltd., *makers of* Macleans Peroxide Toothpaste and Maclean Brand Stomach Powder, Great West Road, Brentford, Middlesex.

From *Radio Pictorial*
April 15, 1938

Roy Plomley was often the compère and all the station's outside broadcasting efforts met with the same success. Some of the so-called live shows broadcast from Fécamp were actually pre-recorded. On one occasion, a 'live' performance was from a theatre that had been burnt down a few days before.

*

Occasionally, Lenny and Ann made trips from Cannes to Monte Carlo in their yacht. In January 1938, Lenny threw a special birthday party there for Ann. The dinner was held in the prestigious Empire Room of the Hotel de Paris. The guest list included most of the Plugges' closest friends: Lady Hulton, Lady Orr-Lewis, Mr and Mrs George Repton, Lord Annersley, Sir Frank and Lady Sanderson, Mrs Gerald Donner (a well-known beauty), Major and Mrs Frank Goldsmith (parents of James), Mr N. Zographes, Mrs O'Moilley-Keys, Mrs Forester Agar, Mr Gilbert Beal, Mrs Molly Edgar, Mr Herbert Guschiner, Mr Ashley Dodd, Mrs Connie F. Shaw, Mr Reginald Purbrick MP, Mr Golding, Mrs B. Docker, Mrs Clarence Newton, Mr Henry Clews, Mr Dudley Tocan, Mrs Wooley Hart, Mr Bromley and Captain D'Arcy Rutherford.

Lenny gave Ann a splendid diamond necklace and presented each of the guests with a silver Cartier watch in the style of a roulette wheel.

Back in London, Lenny wanted to move to bigger premises. While strolling down Park Lane with Bill Wood, he noticed that a large house in Hamilton Place was vacant. A residence of palatial proportions, it was built at the beginning of the nineteenth century and first occupied in 1812 by the 4th Earl of Buckingham, Robert Hobart, the Colonial Administrator who gave his name to Hobart in Tasmania. He was followed in 1817 by the first Marquis Cunningham, whose family stayed for three generations, ending with the third Marquis, who sold the house in 1878 to Leopold de Rothschild. The architect, William Rogers, was employed to carry out several modifications and extensions. One of these was to add the stone cladding to the exterior. Upon the death of Mrs Leopold de Rothschild, the lease was put up for sale by the trustees, the Crown Estate Commissioners. Bill Wood negotiated the purchase and, later in 1938, Lenny and family moved from the top of Park Lane to Hamilton Place.

Number 5 was and remains one of the most spectacular of the few mansions left in London. In the late thirties, Londonderry House (almost opposite number 5) still stood, as did Number 45 Park Lane, home of the Sassoon family, but most of the great mansions had been pulled down in the twenties and thirties to make way for hotels, office blocks and apartments. Grosvenor House (formerly the site of the home of the Dukes of Westminster) Dorchester House, Devonshire House, and Brook House (the home of Lady Louis Mountbatten) were now a block of top-of-the-range apartments.

In those days, Hamilton Place branched off the southern end of Park Lane, and consisted of six houses built in the French style. Number 4 held the offices of the Royal Aeronautical Society. Number 5 was on the north corner with a garden of about two acres, three or four times larger than the others, and backing onto Hamilton Garden, which stretched up as far as Marble Arch in the north and East Carriage Drive on the east side of Hyde Park. Hamilton Garden was private to the residents of Park Lane, Hamilton Place and the large houses in Piccadilly adjoining Apsley House (the home of the Duke of Wellington, still known as Number One London). The Duke and Duchess of York and their children, Princess Elizabeth and Princess Margaret, lived adjacent and were often to be seen there. Today, except for a little strip of green, it has all but disappeared, lost when Park Lane was widened in the 1950s. All that remains of Number 5's two acres is the Italian patio hiding behind the high white wall alongside the exit from the Park, the rest having been demolished to make way for the one-way system around Hyde Park Corner. Only two of the original six houses in Hamilton Place are left, Numbers 4 and 5. Hotels have replaced the others. Frank Plugge remembers:

> Number 5 has an extended basement with numerous staff bedrooms, staff hall, butler's pantry, strong room, wine cellar and huge white tiled kitchen. This extension was not only under the house, but spread out under parts of the garden and even the pavement.

On the ground floor was an enormous marble dining room where the extending table could accommodate fifty people. The walls were lined with white Carrara marble from Italy; two fountains with mythological figures played constantly between the long French windows. On the ceiling was a French style painting of angels and cherubs. A large fireplace with a mirrored overmantle was placed centrally in one long wall opposite the fountains; this was also fashioned from Carrara marble and was beautifully carved with the Rothschild crest over the fire opening. The crest contained five arrows, one for each of the five sons. The heavy curtains were of deep red velvet. When the house was built, Lionel Rothschild had the best craftsmen in wood and marble brought over from Italy to carry out the interior decoration. Most of the original furniture was purchased with the house.

Through connecting doors to the front of the house was the library, Lenny's favourite room. The walls were panelled in heavily carved dark walnut that also framed the many bookcases; a large fireplace with corner alcove seats and comfortable red velvet sofas on which to relax and browse some of the many books that filled the room.

From the library, the doors opened onto the magnificent main stair that swept up to the first and second floors. The sidewalls boasted tapestries in carved wooden frames of floral arrangements or hunting scenes. On the first floor, in the centre of the elaborately carved balustrade, were the entwined initials of Lionel Rothschild 'LR'. With the help of a skilled carpenter, the 'LR' was changed to 'LP' to reflect the change of ownership. All other motifs were similarly dealt with.

On the first floor was the large drawing room, extending the length of the house and furnished with Louis XVI furniture. Lenny had the large portrait of Ann in her wedding gown hung to the left of one of the two fireplaces; a Canaletto of the Doge's Palace in Venice took pride of place over the fireplace itself.

From the southeastern and southwestern corners of the drawing room, doors led into two smaller rooms, the Empire Room, totally furnished in 1st Empire furniture, with contemporary paintings; the other being the Lady's Boudoir, a gem of a room with satin wood panelling incorporating painted allegorical scenes. All the furniture was also in satin wood, some of which is still in the hands of the Plugge family.

The second floor contained the two principal bedrooms. The master bedroom facing west with a huge balcony and a bathroom/dressing room; the principal guest room, known as the

Franz Josef room, named after one of its famous occupants, also had en-suite bathroom.

The third floor could only be reached by crossing to the back staircase, which ran from the basement the full height of the house. This floor consisted of the nursery suite (day nursery, night nursery and daughter room), a further guest room and the Chinese Room entirely furnished with black lacquered furniture made in Europe in the Chinese style.

The fourth floor contained the cinema, projection room and photographic studio as well as a nurse's bedroom.

The property also came with a mews house immediately opposite the front door, but with its entrance in Hamilton Place. The mews could accommodate our seven cars: a Rolls Royce, a Daimler, a Ford V8 shooting brake, the SS1 ('Aether VI'), a Buick and two small run-a-bouts for my mother to use. Upstairs was a flat for one of the two chauffeurs.

To look after such a large establishment required a staff of fifteen – butler, two footmen, chef, two kitchen maids, two housemaids, lady's maid, two chauffeurs (one each), a nanny, nursemaid and two gardeners. Even with this staff, when large banquets were held, extra staff would be called in.

The Plugges held many grand parties in the marble dining room. A hidden photographer would take pictures of the guests seated at table. These would be processed in the small photographic laboratory on the top floor, next to the cinema, and prints presented to the guests at the end of the evening, much to their astonishment.

Sometimes, before dinner, friends would be invited up to the top floor to the specially built cinema, which had seating for fifty people. Two professional 16mm projectors were housed in the projection room at the back. A projectionist would be employed for the evening to show films taken by Lenny of his many trips abroad. Drinks were available from the bar in the corner of the auditorium; its fittings were of solid silver.

Ann was never comfortable as hostess at these large parties, many of which were official functions to welcome various foreign dignitaries. It was not in her nature to pander to all the notables that Lenny invited to Hamilton Place. Sometimes, during a party, she would disappear for long periods.

Bill Wood, his wife and their daughter, Joan, were sometimes invited. On one occasion, the Arch Duke Franz Josef of Austria was staying in the house and, taking a liking to Joan, said he would visit her the following day at Harrods where she worked. The morning duly arrived, as did the Grand Duke. As Joan remembered, he swept towards her with his entourage, wearing one of the longest overcoats she had ever seen. He chatted to her quietly and, much to her embarrassment, suggested an intimate dinner that evening. She politely declined.

With the war looming, the Plugges' luxurious lifestyle with fifteen servants and seven cars could not last. As a Member of Parliament, Plugge was well aware of the situation and he must have foreseen the end of the 'good life'. It was an end, too, of the journeys through France to Cannes, Ann and Lenny in the Rolls Royce followed by the nanny and baby Frank in the Buick, and Bill Deane, the butler, bringing up the rear on his motorcycle. The *Lennyann*, now back in the Mediterranean, was used mainly for entertaining or day trips, and the family stayed at the Carlton Hotel in Cannes the rest of the time.

Germany was broadcasting a great deal of propaganda in English, but the appeasers in Britain – led by the Prime Minister, Neville Chamberlain, and supported by US interests – were not succeeding in getting their message across. In an attempt to inform the German people of the British Government's willingness to avoid a conflict, the BBC Overseas Service was instructed to broadcast translations of Chamberlain's speeches in German and Italian. However, the translations were of poor quality and, in September of 1938, Captain Plugge wrote to Sir Robert Vansittart, offering the services of the IBC to set up stations in Romania to transmit these broadcasts.

Consideration was given to this offer on the grounds that other powers would be stopped from using these stations. Nevertheless, the idea was gratefully turned down because it was thought that commercial broadcasts in English might accompany the transmissions and this was against agreed policy. Plugge was assured that he would be contacted if need be. Eventually the German and Italian studios of Radio Luxembourg were used for these sensitive broadcasts, but these transmissions were kept secret from the public. When the Duke of Windsor made a speech on appeasement from Verdun in May 1939, the whole world was able to listen, except Britain.

Just prior to Christmas 1937, the foundation stone was laid for Radio Normandy's new transmitter at Louvetot, 35 kilometres from Fécamp, on the main road between Yvetot and Caudebec-en-Caux. It would be linked by underground cables to the new studios being set up in the converted

Plugge and Le Grand, centre; Max Brussett, left, wearing glasses;
George Shanks, right, with a cigarette holder
Dated 1938 – possibly connected with the opening of the Caudebec Studios

Chateau of Caudebec-en-Caux, beautifully situated on the banks of the River Seine, five kilometres away. Fernand Le Grand performed the ceremony; Georges Mandel, Minister for the PTT, and Monsieur Pellenc, Inspector General of La Rediffusion attended, as did Captain Plugge and his cohort, George Shanks. The transmitter building was designed in the local style and, considering its purpose, was to be a very elaborate structure. Local stone was used for the walls, and the end gables were decorated with contrasting materials. The small gables over the entrance and side extensions were half-timbered; the slate roofs were high pitched, and a tall spire decorated the entrance lobby, giving the building a church-like appearance.[1] The transmitter would not come into operation until December 1938 when, yet again, the wavelength was changed, this time from 212 to 274 metres.[2]

The transmitter buildings included a powerhouse with twin diesel engines working alternately to supply the energy to drive the generators in the main transmitter building. Standby was provided by a link to the local power supply. In front of the transmitter was a large fountain, which acted as part of the cooling system for the huge transmitting valves. The 565-foot aerial mast was situated in front of the building and mounted on porcelain cups containing crystal balls that allowed it the necessary movement in storm conditions.

---

[1] After the war, the Louvetot transmitter building was converted to a church.

[2] There had been a change from 269.5 to 212 metres in the previous April.

125

The Broadcasting Studios in the Caudebec Chateau were to become a tourist attraction, with regular tours of the facilities, and aperitifs served at tables dotted about under colourful sunshades. Unfortunately, this idyll was not to last: within nine months of its opening, the station would be commandeered by the French government.

In January 1939, the Plugges went on a high profile holiday to Egypt. During an interview for *The Egyptian Gazette*, Lenny gave his views on the European situation:

> Well I can say that we are now better prepared than any other country in the world. I think the state of our unpreparedness at the time of the crisis was greatly exaggerated but anyway great steps have been taken since then. The present head of A.R.P. Sir John Anderson is a very strong and able man. Given a free hand, I think we have nothing to fear in that respect. Regarding our military preparations, I think that it is a good thing that our air force is fully prepared. Aircraft become obsolete so rapidly that to get ready an air force much in advance of its use would merely mean that your aircraft would be out of date. The only thing that is necessary to create in advance is a fleet that takes years to build and cannot be caught up to during a war. That is why I feel secure about our position. Our fleet is so much in advance of others that they cannot catch up. Air forces can be created quite rapidly once the framework exists. Airplanes can be built in so many places at the same time and pilots can be trained in great numbers over short periods, in much the same time that it takes to train an army. In time of emergency, we could rapidly put a large army into the field, as we did at the beginning of the last war and also a formidable air force. I heartily agree with the plan of purchasing a token supply of American aircraft because it lays down a potential source of supply. American factories will know what we want and will be able to accelerate production, as will our own factories if the necessity arises.

> You must take into consideration that the next western war, if it were to come, for I most certainly think it will not, would be, like the last war, an economic struggle. Our troops and those of the enemy dug themselves in and stayed in roughly the same positions for nearly four years. Then Germany's civil population cracked under the economic strain and the army had to withdraw. I think that is what will happen again. Our resources are immensely greater than those of any other country, and we have our unrivalled fleet to keep the seas open for us. I do not hold the opinion that the airplane will prove so decisive a factor in modern warfare as some are led to believe.

> Germany is actually, economically speaking, at war today. Her economy is on a wartime basis and has been for the past four years and the country is gradually growing weaker and weaker in that respect. I do not think Germany will, or could go to war unless colonies were surrendered to her. Once owning colonies, she would have bases and supply possibilities indispensable for waging war. England will not and cannot surrender colonial territory to anyone and so I do not fear any western war.

A brave speech indeed, and one that he would regret a few months later.

The Plugges arrived back in England with a souvenir of their trip, a huge embroidered desert tent to set up as a marquee in the garden. It was never used and eventually rotted away in the basement.

The last few months before the war seemed to be one mad round of social occasions. The 'season' in Cannes was more hectic than ever, the parties more flamboyant, the yachts packed with people apparently making the most of what was left of the old style. Lenny and Ann were in the midst of this, and were to be seen at every event. Their yacht, berthed alongside the Jetée Albert Edouard, was the venue for several cocktail parties, usually followed by dinner at the Ambassadeurs. Cannes was the meeting place for several exiled kings and queens, who took advantage of their titles in being welcome guests at many of the lavish parties.

In May of 1939, King George VI and Queen Elizabeth were making an official Royal Tour of Canada. Lenny and Ann, also visiting North America, were in Ottawa to film the Royal arrival. Plugge took the opportunity to broadcast over the Canadian network.

In Connecticut one evening, driving over the Merritt Parkway, a four-lane fast highway, Lenny noticed glass curb reflectors that marked the outline of the road at night. He pulled over and studied them in detail with the aid of a torch. He later contacted the Connecticut Highways Department and asked for samples and manufacturing details, saying that he intended to suggest the use of them on English roads. Somewhat embarrassed, the officials informed him that they were copies of those in use on the road from Evesham to Worcester in England.[1]

The BBC tried to steer its unbiased course through the political pressures of the Foreign Office, but staying on track was difficult when its programme producer, Guy Burgess, was following his own agenda of spreading the communist doctrine. As mentioned earlier, the Ullswater Committee recommendations regarding the use of the medium for

---

[1] Percy Shaw in the UK invented 'Catseyes' in 1934.

propaganda purposes were all but torn up. The Nazis had used radio successfully in steering the result of the plebiscite on the Saarland in their favour, and the Italians used the airwaves in an endeavour to encourage Britain, their ally in the previous conflict, to support their invasion of Abyssinia. The use of radio, however, as a means of broadcasting to the enemy was limited, mainly because transmissions could be jammed.

A system similar to one devised in Germany to overcome the problem of jamming was developed by Peter Eckersley who, having left the BBC in 1929, was employed by one of Oswald Mosley's companies, Airtime. The system involved signals being transmitted through the mains electricity supply. It employed a special receiver without a tuning facility: a switch was used to select any one of its four channels. Even when the unit was switched off, an incoming signal would set off an alarm to indicate an impending transmission, thus ensuring that important messages were not missed.[1] Eckersley and Oliver Hoare, the brother of the Foreign Secretary Samuel Hoare, presented the idea to the Government. It was initially given a good reception but was dropped, possibly due to the Mosley connection. The idea was used after the war for simple intercoms, such as baby alarms, in private houses.

Another system being discussed in Parliament was the provision of wireless programmes over the telephone. It was proposed that the National and Regional Services would be used, and initially would be available only to existing telephone subscribers. Plugge asked whether other stations, namely Radio Normandy, would be allowed to make use of the service. This was unlikely, as the control of the system would have been in the hands of the Post Office who had no love for the commercial stations. Although it was felt that there would be certain advantages during war, the idea went no further than the discussion stage.

Peter Eckersley's ex-wife, Frances, stayed on in Berlin after the outbreak of war and began working for an English speaking propaganda station. Her big achievement was to recruit William Joyce (Lord Haw Haw) and his wife to the station. It was made very clear in the House of Commons that any British broadcaster involved in foreign propaganda would be treated as a traitor.

German propaganda broadcasts, termed 'black radio', were becoming a matter of great concern to the British Government, as they purported to be coming from a station based in England. One of the major worries was the New British Broadcasting Station (NBBS, sometimes referred to as the

---

1 *Truth Betrayed* by W.J. West (Duckworth 1987)

Ann Muckleston

Ann, the model

Ann in pantomime at the Lyceum in 1925

Cover of *The Autocar* for November 1934
showing Plugge's SS1

98 Park Lane,
Ann and Lenny's
first home together

Portrait of Ann
in her wedding dress
1934

The drawing room

Captain Plugge MP leaves t
House in full evening dress a
an all night sitting

The *Lennyann* with luxury interior – bought in 1936

Skipper Lenny

Plugge in full dress RAF uniform.
The portrait by Cowan Dobson that hung
in reception at the IBC building

IBC Headquarters, Portland Place

Party on board the *Lennyann*

Captain Plugge, having received t
Legion d'Honneur – 1937

The Plugge's moved to their new home
in Hamilton Place in 1938

The staircase with Plugge's initials

The library

The drawing room

A dinner party at Hamilton Place

Bill Wood
was a regular guest

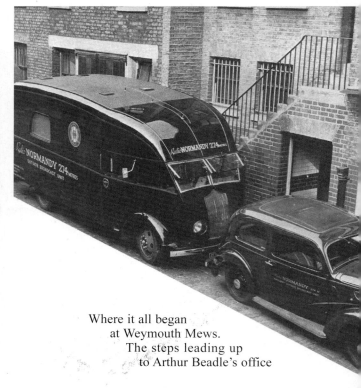

Where it all began
at Weymouth Mews.
The steps leading up
to Arthur Beadle's office

IBC staff party – 1937

Louvetot Foundation Stone laid
December 1938

The aerial pylon
at Louvetot

Radio Normandy daytime coverage – 1939

New BBC) whose printed leaflets advertising its broadcasts were fly-posted in London and the suburbs. The convincing, cultured English accents of the announcers preaching a message of conciliation and co-operation with the Germans posed a danger to morale. Another such station was the Workers' Challenge, which, using a rough cockney voice, appealed to the workers to throw off the yoke of the bosses and strike against the war and for a negotiated peace. Equally dangerous was the Christian Peace Movement, with a pacifist theme. The existence of these stations was a closely guarded secret: the BBC and other communications media were not allowed to mention them. Eventually their broadcasts were jammed, but unfortunately not before the NBBS had broadcast a claim that it had previously worked for the International Broadcasting Company. Plugge vehemently denied this, and the only possible reason for this claim would have been to add an air of authenticity to the NBBS's broadcast, and to support the impression of its being an English station.

The British were not averse to carrying out similar activities. We broadcast propaganda under the cover of popular music programmes allegedly emanating from a radio station in Frankfurt, but actually coming from our own 'black radio' base at Crowborough, which was under the control of Harold K. Robins. Initially, the responsibility for British radio propaganda was in the hands of the Joint Broadcasting Committee (under the directorship of Hilda Matheson) which was later absorbed into the BBC.

In July of 1939, during a meeting at the Home Office, the possibility of using other commercial stations was discussed, particularly Juan-les-Pins and Radio Ljubljana (Yugoslavia). Plugge had strong connections with these stations as their English broadcasts had been organised by the IBC for several years. He offered the use of them to the Government for whatever purpose it desired – possibly as 'goodwill' stations broadcasting light music and entertainment as a cover for propaganda to Germany.

War was declared before these plans could be put into action. At this point, all broadcasts from Radio Luxembourg were suspended in order to preserve the Duchy's total neutrality. When Luxembourg was overrun in May 1940, the radio station was taken over and used for German news bulletins. With some foresight Stephen Williams had had all the recordings transferred to safe storage, in the hope that one day he would be back to carry on.

Radio Normandy closes down (September 1939)
Ann and Frank evacuated to New York – Jack Bouvier
Lenny persuades Ann to come home
The twins are born

One of the last good deeds that Radio Normandy was able to perform was for a good friend of Plugge, Lady Mountbatten. She had lost her dog, of which she was very fond, and all efforts to find it had failed. Lenny broadcast a message over the air and the dog was found within hours.

Radio Normandy broadcast its final programme on September 7th, 1939, after which the station was closed down and the employees at the IBC in London put on half pay. The directors held discussions with the War Office about taking over the recording facilities and studios for the production of Forces entertainment, but their offer was not taken up. The technical staff, over several pints in the Dover Castle public house in Weymouth Mews, discussed how to spend their time while they were waiting for decisions to be made. They agreed to set up a laboratory in the basement of Portland Place where they experimented with time fuses and other lethal devices. One idea they came up with was a propaganda shell; this consisted of an unbreakable loudspeaker with a trailing cable attached and a spring-loaded spike on the end. The idea was to fire it from a mortar towards the enemy lines so that it landed on its spike, whereupon it could be used to bombard the unsuspecting Germans with propaganda. A prototype was produced and demonstrated to representatives of the War Office; it worked, after a fashion, but was not developed further.

Much to the annoyance of the Le Grand family, the French Government requisitioned Radio Normandy's new Louvetot transmitter, which had been in use for barely more than a year. However, the Le Grands retained the ownership of the Fécamp transmitter.

Through his advisory role on the British Expeditionary Force Wireless Entertainment Committee,[1] Plugge continued to press the idea of

---

[1] Presided over by Field Marshall Lord Birdwood.

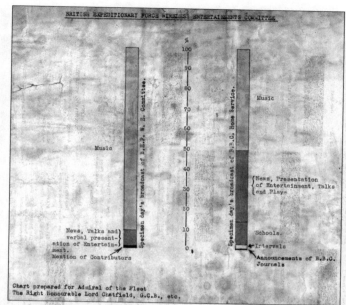

One of the four charts prepared by Plugge to convince the Government of the advantages of using Radio International compared to the BBC for entertaining the BEF

providing radio for the troops. He supplied the Committee with comparison charts of programme content, showing how the IBC intended to use the Fécamp transmitter for Radio International. Radio International's output was compared to the BBC and *Blighty* magazine, which was very popular with the soldiers. He also produced charts comparing content of eight of the major daily papers, ten of the Sundays and eight of the most popular magazines. The intention was that Radio International's programmes should comprise 90.63 per cent music, 8.38 per cent news and verbal presentation, and just 0.99 per cent allowance for credit to the sponsors. This last part was contentious, as the BBC had already stated its concern about any commercialism being allowed. Plugge agreed that no advertising would be used apart from a credit to those companies who had given their backing to the project. The title 'sponsor' would not be used under any circumstances.

Plugge kept up incessant pressure to ensure that the troops would get the sort of programmes that he believed they deserved. Fécamp was to be staffed by the regular IBC announcers: Bob Danvers-Walker, Philip Slessor and Charles Maxwell. George Busby was manager. It was intended that the Free Czechs and Austrians would also use the station, and their announcers were recruited in Paris. The regular sponsors were approached in the UK to gain their approval for their old pre-war programmes to be rebroadcast. Programmes started at 7.00 every morning and continued until 8 pm; the Austrians and Czechs then took over with two hours each.

rebroadcast. Programmes started at 7.00 every morning and continued
until 8 pm; the Austrians and Czechs then took over with two hours each.

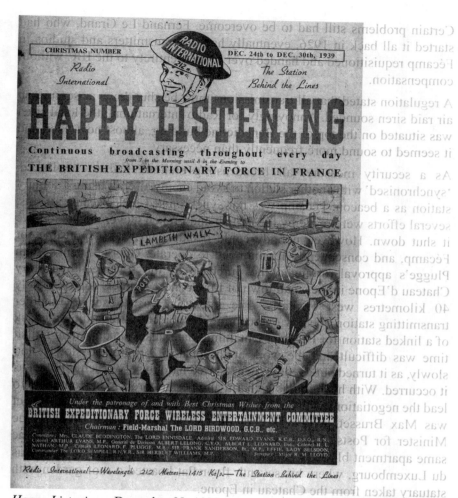

Happy Listening – December 22, 1939

Left:
Centre spread of Boxing Day programmes

A magazine called *Happy Listening* was produced in the IBC offices in Portland Place and issued free to the troops in France, listing the programme details and encouraging comment.

Certain problems still had to be overcome. Fernand Le Grand, who had started it all back in 1926, eventually had his transmitters and studios in Fécamp requisitioned and handed over in their entirety to the IBC without compensation.

A regulation stated that all transmissions must be shut down as soon as an air raid siren sounded. Annoyingly for Radio International, the local siren was situated on the top of the Benedictine building, almost next door, and it seemed to sound more frequently than necessary.

As a security measure, all broadcasting stations had to be linked, 'synchronised' with another station to avoid enemy aircraft using a solitary station as a beacon. Fécamp was not synchronised and, because of this, several efforts were made by the British and French Governments to have it shut down. However, nobody could decide who was responsible for Fécamp, and consequently it continued to operate. George Shanks, with Plugge's approval, arranged the purchase of the seventeenth century Chateau d'Epone in the small town of Epone, near Mantes, approximately 40 kilometres west of Paris. The intention was to set up another transmitting station, thereby overcoming the objections regarding the lack of a linked station for Fécamp. Obtaining materials and equipment at that time was difficult and the work at the chateau progressed slowly; too slowly, as it turned out. George Shanks tried hard to solve each problem as it occurred. With his inimitable charm and perfect French, he continued to lead the negotiations with the French authorities. His main political contact was Max Brusset, who was chef du cabinet to Georges Mandel, the Minister for Posts, Telephones and Telegraphs. Shanks moved into the same apartment block as Brusset at 28 Boulevard Raspail near the Palais du Luxembourg, where his seventh floor flat boasted a roof garden with statuary taken from the Chateau in Epone.

Lenny had known Brusset for some time and valued his position in the French Government. He arranged for him to take over the IBC's interests in France during the occupation, with the idea that a 'French' station would not be requisitioned by the Germans. With this in mind, the ownership of the new station at Epone was put in Brusset's name.

Brusset already held interests in broadcasting: he owned the Juan-les Pins station for a while, sold it and then repurchased it in 1937 when, due to new French laws, the name changed to Radio Mediterranean. It was later destroyed by the Nazis.

In November 1939, Roy Plomley arrived in Fécamp to replace Philip Slessor who had demanded to go home because he was finding the stress too much. David Davies, Ralph Hurcombe, Maurice Griffith and Godfrey Holloway had also been sent over.

George Busby had to attend weekly meetings in Paris with George Shanks and the Ministry of Foreign Affairs to discuss plans for the new service. Soon after he arrived, Roy Plomley was invited to join them. One idea was for a weekly programme to educate the troops in the ways of the French and even to teach them a few useful words and phrases. The job of producing the programme, to be called *Tommy's Half Hour*, was given to Roy with a committee of titled and cultured advisors. Many suggestions for programme items were put forward; Roy recalled such subjects as 'Stamp Collecting', 'A Tiger Hunt in Indo-China', 'Bird Song' and 'The Invention of the Turbine Engine'. *Tommy's Half Hour* was recorded each week in the Poste Parisien studios for transmission from Fécamp, but it was soon reduced to *Tommy's Quarter Hour*.

Although Radio Normandy had officially closed down, the station began its transmissions under the name of 'Radio International' soon afterwards. This caused a string of correspondence, classified as secret, between various authorities in England. While the Air Ministry wanted it shut down because it was not within the group of synchronised stations and could be used as a beacon for enemy aircraft, the GPO and BBC had its own reasons for wanting the Fécamp station closed. The Corporation denied jealousy, and some thought the BBC would provide a better service, while others believed that Fécamp was doing a good job. However, Lord Gort considered its entertainment value to be negligible in comparison with the prejudice to security, and concurred with the shut down appeal. The arguments went on until Fécamp was finally closed down in January 1940.

All members of staff were recalled to Fécamp for a meeting with Richard Meyer. He told them he could hold out no hope for future employment with the IBC, and they would have to make other arrangements themselves. Bob Danvers-Walker returned to London and took a job with Pathé Newsreels. Others, such as Charles Maxwell and Tom Ronald, obtained jobs with the BBC and were soon heard through loudspeakers in England. A 'wake' was held in the Café des Collones in Place Thiers, where Lenny Plugge had first asked the question back in 1931, "Tell me Monsieur, is Fécamp famous for anything?" The closing-down melody of Radio International – Ivor Novello's *Keep the Home Fires Burning* – was heard for the last time.

Shanks had decided to close the office at the Paris studio and move everything, including the records, to the apartment in Boulevard Raspail. He went to Epone with Dick Baines, presumably to see how the war would progress. They had not long to wait.

In June 1940, with the Germans approaching Paris, Shanks and Baines had to flee. This left Epone in the hands of Brusset. Despite the French ownership, the Nazis requisitioned the studio and used it to transmit propaganda to the UK.

Roy Plomley had gone back to Paris in the vain hope that Poste Parisien might have started broadcasting again. He found it hard to believe that Paris would fall, but it did, and he and his wife Diana just managed to get out of France at the last possible moment, narrowly escaping internment. Plomley, in *Days Seemed Longer,* described his meeting with Captain Plugge on his return:

> It was strange to be in the Portland Place building with so few people about: all my friends had left, and there was only a small administrative staff to keep things ticking over. When Captain Leonard Plugge heard of my arrival, he sent for me. It was the first time I had been in the supremo's office. I assumed that he wanted to congratulate me on my good fortune in getting back to England, or to ask for specific information about the situation in the Paris office when I had left, but his first question, in his usual high-pitched voice, was, 'Plomley, where's the French fleet?'
> This rocked me back on my heels a little because I was having difficulty in remembering exactly where I was myself. 'The French fleet is vital to us,' continued the honourable and gallant Member for Chatham, and he continued to look at me enquiringly.
> I could only reply that, although I had covered quite a lot of French territory during the past week or so, I did not remember having coming across the fleet, whereupon he lost interest and the interview came to an end.

Dickie Meyer was the next to leave the IBC; he was given the rank of Lieutenant Colonel in the Army and from 1943 was Director of Middle East Forces Broadcasting. After the war, he returned to South Africa, his country of birth, where he was involved with several radio and television companies. He came back to the UK and the IBC before becoming a Director of Associated Television (ATV) and Independent Television News (ITN) when these companies were formed in 1955. He founded Richard Meyer Associates Limited in 1960, and was Chairman of Isle of Man Broadcasting until his death on a golf course in Cannes in 1972.

Over in France, as the German forces approached Louvetot, the French army cut the cables from the transmitters to the Normandy aerials. One of the aerial pylons was destroyed in a violent thunderstorm on November 7th, 1940. The other was blown-up by the Germans in November 1943 in order to remove a landmark that might be used by Allied forces. The Germans took over the old studios in Fécamp. This marked the end of Radio Normandy. Fernand Le Grand, the founder of the original Radio Fécamp, died in 1953.

As for the Chateau d'Epone, in 1944 the Germans were in retreat as the American troops advanced. The studio and transmitters were destroyed and the citizens of the town were locked up in the civic centre; fortunately, the Allied troops arrived a day later. Max Brusset and his wife Marie, active members of the Resistance, had been arrested and sentenced to death. Thankfully, they were released by the American troops in time, and Brusset went on to become Mayor of Royan and to serve in the Government until 1958. He retained ownership of the Chateau d'Epone, although Plugge always claimed it was rightfully his.

Ann and Lenny continued to host large receptions at Hamilton Place, including one they called the 'pink party', which they gave for the Turkish Military Mission on its visit to London in October 1939, barely a month after the outbreak of war. General Kiazim Orbay, whose wife was at the forefront of emancipation for Turkish women, led the deputation. Field Marshal Lord Birdwood, who led the Anzacs[1] at Gallipoli, had greeted them on their arrival in England and was present at the party. There were pink roses and pink candles decorating the tables, and pink champagne served throughout. The object of the evening was for the Mission to meet MPs from all parties, but many notables such as the French Military attaché, Lord and Lady Sackville, and Lady Marchwood also attended.

In 1940, Plugge became a member of the Worshipful Company of Glaziers, one of the long established Livery Companies. The Guild of Glaziers became formally organised during the reign of Edward III, and its distinctive livery was defined at that time. When Plugge became a Steward, he was able to wear a special livery of a fur-trimmed cloak and carry a silver-topped staff, which he loved showing off to young Frank. The Guild was originally formed for the craftsmen in glass, particularly stained glass, to protect their industry from foreign competition. In recent times, the Glaziers have became more of a social club, accepting members

---

[1] Australian and New Zealand Army Corps.

not associated with the craft but still supporting and forwarding its interests.

In the early days of the war, Plugge entertained King George II of Greece, and his brother HRH Prince Paul who became King of Greece in 1947. Official receptions such as this could be charged to expenses, but Plugge suffered a severe drop in income. He donated the £600 a year he received as an MP to the constituency Conservative party. His annual income of £50,000 from the IBC was substantially reduced and his property and interests in France had to be signed over to George Shanks's associate, Max Brusset, who acted as his nominee. The many happy and carefree days of sailing in the blue waters of the Mediterranean also ended: the Germans sank the *Lennyann*, as well as its twin, which had been bought for spares. Fortunately, the yacht's tender, a Kriscraft, was hidden from the Germans by Plugge's faithful mechanic, Joseph, who returned it to Lenny after the war, when it was used for water skiing at Cannes during family holidays.

Plugge was not optimistic about the outcome of the war and, following Dunkirk, he felt very strongly that England would lose. He laid plans to evacuate Ann and Frank to America, where he would accompany them and settle them in with friends. They left from Liverpool on the RMS Duchess of Atholl in late June 1940, bound for Canada. Frank, unfortunately, contracted measles when they were only a few days out, and had to spend most of the journey in a darkened cabin. His favourite plaything was 'Minibrix', a construction toy that required special pins to connect the bricks together: Ann had brought the bricks but left the pins behind. Young Frank was not a happy boy.

After a long, slow crossing, they landed at Montreal and headed south where they stayed in New York with the Townsends whom Ann already knew from her previous stay during her honeymoon. Frank remembers them as very rich, having a beautiful house, but being very strict. His mother was expected to play bridge every evening, and if Frank dared to creep downstairs to take a peek, he was chased back upstairs by the lady of the house wielding a hairbrush. After a short visit, the family travelled on down to South Carolina where they stayed on the Belle Hall estate, owned by financier Bernard Baruch, near Georgetown. Baruch had been a friend and confidant of Winston Churchill since their dealings during the First World War, when he was the Commissioner responsible for raw materials on the American War Industries Board. He remained in a position of considerable influence all his life and was a special adviser to President Roosevelt. Both Churchill and Roosevelt visited the Estate for meetings with Baruch. He was nicknamed 'the old goat' by a mistress, Inga Marie Arvad,[1] who was also intimate with Jack Kennedy.

Meanwhile, in London, questions were being asked in the House about three absentee Conservative Members of Parliament as to why they had been granted exit visas. When Mrs Tate MP pressed the Home Secretary for an answer, she was informed that two MPs, Captain A.S. Cunningham-Reid and Roland Robinson (husband of the Woolworth heiress) had both gone to the USA to arrange for the evacuation of children in their constituencies. Captain Plugge left without informing the Chief Whip, his agent or his housekeeper. Upon his return in August, he satisfied critics at a meeting of his supporters, but no details were reported about his actual reasons for visiting America and Canada.

Soon afterwards, Plugge made a speech to the House regarding the use of radio for propaganda purposes. He also talked about his discussions with 'important' Canadians while he was away, but gave no other justification for his absence. If the truth were known, he did not want to return at all.

Ann, being of an independent nature, did not enjoy having to live in someone else's pocket. She and Frank moved to New York and stayed at the Grammercy Park Hotel until she found a two-bedroom apartment on 72nd Street. It was a couple of blocks from Central Park and had separate accommodation for a maid. As taking money out of England was next to impossible under the wartime restrictions, Ann had brought all her jewellery with her. By selling pieces, she was able to live comfortably, employing a black maid named Rose and a governess for Frank called Mademoiselle Chenelaut. In addition, she found herself an unpaid job as a receptionist for British War Relief, a charity that arranged gifts and food parcels for Britain. Ann quickly settled into the New York social life, renewing many of the friendships she had made from her previous visit. She was seen regularly at El Morocco, the 21 Room, and the Russian Tea Rooms. After a while, they moved again, to 125 East 74th Street, and Frank was enrolled at Buckley School.

It was on one of these social occasions that Ann made the acquaintance of Jack Bouvier, who asked about her arrangements for the summer season. He suggested that a cottage at East Hampton would be ideal: plenty of sea and sand for Frank and a pleasant social life for herself. Ann liked the idea and arranged to rent a modest cottage near the dunes. The war was a long way away – and so was Lenny.

---

[1] *The Dark Side of Camelot* by Seymour Hersh – for details of Arvad's meetings with Hitler and the concern of the FBI.

East Hampton was, and is, the summer playground of the rich New Yorkers and others from as far a field as Hollywood. Situated on Long Island, it was originally founded in 1648 by farmers and fishermen from Connecticut and has a distinct New England feel as well as having some of the best beaches to be found on that coast. Some of the families living there can trace their ancestry back ten or twelve generations.

One such family was the Bouviers who in 1940 lived at Lasata, situated on Further Lane. The house was owned by 'Major' John Vernou Bouvier, a successful lawyer and stockbroker with a penchant for embroidering his family history. He claimed to be descended from a French aristocrat, when his true ancestor was an ironmonger from Grenoble. He was looked upon as the family patriarch because of his position and wealth, which was displayed for all to see at Lasata, with its fourteen acres, paddock, riding arena, tennis court and formal gardens.

The Major's son, Jack Bouvier, did not have the same pretensions as his father but had followed in similar footsteps. He was also a stockbroker, but with vices: gambling, women and drink, not necessarily in that order. He was known as 'Black Jack', a nickname given to him by his business associates because of his dark complexion and success with the ladies. Unfortunately, his income, although considerable, could not support his excesses, as his income had been considerably reduced since the Depression.

In 1928, he married Janet Lee. He was attracted by her wealth and she by his social standing. They had two daughters, Jacqueline and Caroline Lee, who were the apples of their father's eye. The marriage did not last. Jack had numerous affairs, and they were eventually divorced in 1940. The daughters would spend the summer season at East Hampton with their doting father. Jacqueline loved horses and took part in the local riding events, but Lee lost her enthusiasm for riding following a nasty accident when her horse fell and rolled over her.

Into this environment came Ann and Frank, and it was not long before they were spending a great deal of time in the company of Jack and his two daughters. Ann was taken with Jack's good looks and charming manners; dinner at Lasata became a regular event. Although only two years younger than Lenny, Jack's persona made him appear much younger. In some ways, the two men were very similar: the interest in gambling and women was common to both, as was their tendency to spend their income as soon as it was received. A major difference was Bouvier's drinking, something that Lenny found abhorrent.

Ann soon found herself swept up in a passionate love affair with Black Jack, which did not go unnoticed by the gaggle of friends at the sports club. Five-year-old Frank knew only that he had a father figure in his life, and the memory of his own father was fading fast. Ann was happier than she had been for many months. A social person at heart, she enjoyed the company of the young people around her, in contrast to the formal hostess role expected of her in London. Jacqueline and Lee became close to her, finding her a very different woman from their own mother who had now found a new life and family with Hugh Auchincloss, the Standard Oil heir.

At the end of the season both families moved back to New York, each to their own apartments, but the affair continued. Frank still played with Lee and Jackie whenever they were staying with their father.

Lenny was not having a good war. Hamilton Place suffered considerable damage when a bomb landed in the garden and blew out nearly all the glass in the lower windows, and another direct hit that destroyed all seven cars in the mews. Most of the furniture had to be moved into the first floor drawing room, and the windows were boarded up. Due to his lack of income and the damage the house had sustained, Lenny was finding it difficult to manage Hamilton Place. He asked Bill Wood to approach the landlords in an endeavour to get the rent reduced or waived altogether until the end of the war. Bill, yet again, came up trumps; he was a brilliant negotiator.

In September 1940, Lenny moved into a rather luxurious bunker created in a room in the basement. It was all decorated in white, complete with a white fur bedspread. He retrieved the heavy curtains from the upstairs rooms and hung these around the walls. To keep warm he had a siren suit (à la Churchill), but made of furry material. And to ensure a supply of eggs, he kept chickens.

The Captain was terrified of being buried in the rubble if the house took a direct hit. Picks and shovels were placed conveniently in the room, and a tunnel of sandbags was built from the bunker to the area steps as an escape route. So that he could call for assistance, a microphone was fitted by his bed, and a loudspeaker mounted on an outside wall.

The bunker was equipped with radios, telephones, projectors and every possible comfort he could squeeze in. Piled up were canisters of 16mm film, home movies of happier times, which he watched as reminders of how much he missed Ann and his son Frank.

Lenny enjoyed having visitors, one of them being Randolph Churchill, who would join him on some evenings. According to Mrs Martin, the housekeeper of the Royal Aeronautical Society next door, he did not lack female company either, and often invited ladies from the Society to dinner. When it came to the opposite sex, Lenny could 'charm the birds off the trees'. On meeting an attractive girl at a party, he would ask for her phone number. When she showed surprise that he was not writing it down, he would say, "It is engraved upon my heart." He would then quietly slip away to jot it down in his little black book.

Just across the road was Shepherds Market where there were plenty of 'ladies' from which to choose – but Lenny vowed to his son, Frank, that he never paid for sex.

All the servants had long departed except for Adam and his wife who had been in his employ for several years, as valet and housekeeper. Adam had also stood in as bartender at the various parties that were held in happier times. When Lenny needed a break, he would either visit his sister, Mina, in Broadway, or cruise down the river in his motor canoe.

In the House of Commons, Plugge had been appointed Chairman of the Parliamentary and Scientific Committee. He led a deputation to see the Minister of Education, Rab Butler, to put forward recommendations regarding the setting up of scientific and technical staff to work closely with the Departments of Defence and Construction. They pressed for the staff to be men with scientific training. In case of invasion, with the enemy bound to requisition the major radio stations, Plugge suggested that as a matter of priority a number of small transmitters be built across the country. Whether or not because of Plugge's suggestion, the BBC did make plans to evacuate its studios to other parts of the country.

During his ten years in the House, Plugge spoke to Winston Churchill only once. He was called into the Cabinet Room where the Prime Minister told him that, as he was the only member of the House that spoke perfect French, he would like him to prepare a speech of welcome and congratulation to General Charles de Gaulle when he arrived in England in June 1940 after France had been occupied by Germany. Plugge delivered the speech in the House of Commons, finishing with the words "La France Eternelle", which delighted de Gaulle.

Ann was beginning to think about her future. What did she want? She wanted Jack Bouvier, warts and all. So, in the Spring of 1943, she wrote to Lenny, asking for a divorce. It hit him like a bombshell. Only a few years earlier they had been on honeymoon touring the very country where she now wanted to live. Hadn't he shown the film to their friends many times, and weren't they obviously blissfully happy? Apart from the hurt, the ignominy of a divorce would not look good at home. As a prominent MP, he would lose face considerably. He telephoned Ann and told her that he still loved her and was not prepared to give her a divorce. However, if she pursued the matter, he would obtain custody of Frank.

Lenny needed to make plans to fly to America to sort out the problem and, if possible, arrange for their return to England. After the trouble in the House over taking Ann and Frank to the States, he did not want to attract any more criticism; this time he would arrange it officially. There was a proposed Parliamentary Delegation going to Washington and he was determined to go with it. With the backing of a few fellow MPs, he managed to gain a place.

Frank arrived home from school one day and ran into the lounge, looking for his mother. Instead of his mother, he found an elderly man sitting on the sofa. Smiling, the man stood up and came towards him, saying, "Hello Frank. I'm your Daddy."

The boy was surprised and confused. The only father figure in his life was Jack Bouvier. He knew he had a father somewhere, but could not remember him; he did not recognise this old man. Short, bald and wearing glasses, Lenny was nothing like the suave sophisticated man Frank had come to know over the past two years. Ann had to assure him that this really was his father.

Lenny took his son out to places like the zoo and the movies. In an attempt to resolve the marital situation, he and Ann had many long discussions. Eventually, he persuaded her to come back to England and make a new start. The pressure and stress on both of them must have been enormous, and Lenny suffered a mild heart attack. On being discharged from hospital, he arranged for Ann and Frank to travel back to England on a Portuguese ship, the *Serpa Pinto*. Being of a neutral country, it was considered the safest way to travel. A huge Portuguese flag adorned the ship, floodlit at night with fairy lights outlining the masts, to ensure that the German U-boats would not sink her in error. Lenny had arranged for them to have first class treatment on the voyage. Frank remembers the crossing in April 1943 very well:

> The journey across the Atlantic on the *Serpa Pinto* was wonderful and was greatly enjoyed by my mother and myself. There was a little girl called Petra who was travelling with her mother and

baby brother; the two mothers became friends and Petra and I became inseparable. Lenny had arranged an introduction to the Captain and he made sure we had one of the best cabins and sat at his table. There was always so much to do on the boat and I had a thoroughly good time.

When we reached the Azores, passengers were allowed ashore for just two hours in alphabetical order. For some reason, my mother and I spent the whole two days ashore being driven around by contacts of Lenny. The same occurred when we reached Madeira.

They had the use of a chauffeur-driven car and took the opportunity to visit George Shanks's Portuguese wife who lived on the island. As they drove through the streets, young boys threw flowers into the open car, hoping for coins to be thrown back. The visit was all too short for Frank; the freedom of being on dry land and going back to the ship for fancy dress parties, was a joy. Soon they were on their way to Lisbon, where they intended to catch a plane to England.

On arrival in the capital, a very pleasant young man, arranged for by Plugge, took them to a hotel in Estoril and gave them money. They spent most of their three weeks in Portugal on the beach, where Frank played with his little girlfriend Petra and her family. One day, Ann told him they had managed to get a flight to southern Ireland on June 1st. There appeared to be an unwritten agreement that civil aircraft flying from Lisbon would not be attacked by the Germans. The night before they were due to fly, Frank suffered a serious attack of tonsillitis and was unable to travel. This sudden illness turned the hand of fate. The KLM Dakota upon which they were to fly was inexplicably shot down by the Germans over the Channel; it was the only civil aircraft on the route to be attacked during the war. Thirteen passengers were killed, including Frank's little friend Petra and her family. Film actor Leslie Howard was also among the fatalities. He and his business manager, Alfred Chenhalls, had visited Spain as members of an ENSA[1] group. Chenhalls bore a striking resemblance to Winston Churchill and Leslie Howard a resemblance to Walter Thompson, his bodyguard. There was speculation that one of the many Nazi spies in Lisbon at the time noticed them boarding the plane and, believing he saw British Prime Minister and his bodyguard, and informed Berlin.[2] Another theory was that Leslie Howard had been suspected of spying against the Germans. At the time, Lisbon was a centre for spies from all sides, rivalling Switzerland.

---

[1] Entertainments National Service Association.

[2] *Churchill's Bodyguard*. Documentary BBC2, 2005

Whatever the reason for the attack, it remains a mystery. It was the only civil aircraft on that route to be shot down by the Germans during the war.

Eventually, Ann got herself and her son onto a Short Sunderland flying boat back to Ireland. From there they sailed to England, landing safely on June 15th, 1943, to be met by Lenny. Oswald and Vi Short were godparents to Frank, and their christening present to him had been a model silver Sunderland flying boat on an onyx base – perhaps a portent of the time when his life would be saved.

Ann had regretfully said goodbye to Jack Bouvier and would not to see him again although she remained good friends with his daughters. Jackie was destined to marry Jack Kennedy in 1953 and to become First Lady. This role suited her even though JFK had similar vices to her father. A notorious womaniser, his reputation was protected in part by his father and his brother, Bobby. Needless to say, as President, nothing protected him from the assassin's bullet in Dallas in 1963. Jackie, having lost Jack, later became Jacqueline Onassis.

Lee's second marriage, in 1959, was to a friend of Jack Kennedy, Prince Stanislaw Radziwill of Lithuanian/Polish descent, who had left Poland during World War Two to set up a prosperous business in England. The Radziwills were an important aristocratic family with a long history, but under communist rule had been stripped of their money and property. Lee was his third wife and enjoyed her new title of Princess Radziwill.[1]

Ann now had to put her American lifestyle behind her and face up to the strictures of wartime London. Her heart must have sunk when she saw the terrible state of Hamilton Place, battered and scarred by the German bomb that had dropped in the garden. There was a huge crater where the bomb had landed, and the gardens were overgrown and desolate. The devastation of the mews and the wreckage of the cars were still there, and many of the house windows were boarded. Inside, the drawing room was stacked high with furniture, and the dining room was stripped bare. The only room that seemed to be intact and fully furnished was the library.

The worst of the air raids was over, but Ann occasionally had to wake Frank, whose bedroom was on the third floor, to bring him down to the bunker in the basement. Fortunately, the lift was still working. Young Frank, blissfully unaware of the danger, recalls the air raids as quite exciting.

Lenny was totally occupied with affairs of Parliament. Number 37 Portland Place, the new IBC headquarters, had been flattened by a bomb

---

[1] *Short History of the Radziwill Family* by Peter Paul Bajer.

and he had lost his large imposing office. It was not a total loss: Number 35 survived. He must have thought that the Germans had it in for him, first bombing Hamilton Place, then Rex Lodge, and now Portland Place. They even dropped a bomb on the House of Commons, forcing MPs to share the House of Lords.

Despite the war, Lenny decided that he and Ann would celebrate their tenth wedding anniversary in as luxurious a style as possible. More than 400 guests were invited to Hamilton Place. Not everyone was able to attend in evening dress, and many of the ladies were in afternoon frocks. Live bands provided the music: one upstairs for dancing and another in the marble dining room, beside the drinks and the oyster bar. Lenny boasted that he ate three dozen oysters that evening.

A buffet supper, including lobsters and turkey, was served. The whisky gave out at about 2 am, but the gin, like the party, lasted nearly all night. This was 1944; austerity was still the norm, and such a party attracted a lot of press publicity, most of it bad. It was looked upon as being thoughtless, considering the deprivation that most people had to suffer. Nevertheless, the Plugges were to give a number of extravagant parties while at Hamilton Place. The parties were held in the library and dining room, which were the only large rooms fit to use. The bomb damage to the house and garden was not repaired until the building was sold.

Aside from the luxurious parties, life at Number 5 was pretty uncomfortable. Lenny preferred to rent, but Ann had pressed him to purchase a house for her mother on Montpelier Street. Pregnant again and with Lenny spending little time at home, she and Frank sometimes stayed with her mother.

They also spent weeks at a time with Emlyn Williams, the playwright and actor, and his wife Molly at their house in South Moreton. Frank remembers the fun he had with his best friend, Brook Williams, at the neighbouring Potter's Farm. They would spend a whole day there helping with the haymaking and other farming pursuits. A much-polluted stream ran close by, which they enjoyed jumping over until one day Ann tried to do the same and fell in – a nasty accident for a woman who was eight months pregnant.

Mother and son also made extended visits to Lenny's sister, Mina. As all the able-bodied Englishmen were fighting the enemy, the farm was tended by Italian prisoners of war, and patients from the local psychiatric hospital. Frank recalls being befriended by Clum, one of these patients, who took him for rides on a tractor.

Following the death of his wife, Lenny's father had remarried and moved back to Belgium, where he lived throughout the German occupation. Mina received the occasional letter from him, which was routed through Switzerland.

In the Middlesex Hospital in Cavendish Street, on the afternoon of November 4th, 1944, Ann gave birth to twins – Gale Ann Mildred and Greville Roland Chase. Ann had always liked the name Greville. As a schoolchild, she had written a very successful essay about a tramp of that name. And the well-known cricketer, Greville Stevens, might have become her husband had he not had an affair with another cricketer's wife (who eventually divorced her husband and married Stevens).

Lenny and Ann were now renting a country house from the brother-in-law of Molly Williams. This lovely five-bedroomed residence on the river at Sutton Courtney, near Abingdon, was previously owned by liberal politician Lord Asquith. The lawn ran down to a backwater of the Thames. Along this stretch of water was a series of weirs, one being almost opposite the house, so the sound of falling water was always present.

There was a staff cottage in the grounds. Bill Deane, butler to the Plugges in pre-war days, moved in together with his wife. He had a job in London, and she attended to the Plugge family. Deane had just been demobbed from the RAF. He had been a navigator and had flown with Neville Heath, who was hanged in 1946 for the savage murder of two young women.

Lenny was away a lot, and visited Ann and Frank some weekends. From time to time, they would cruise the water in the motor canoe that he had purchased several years earlier. On occasion, they picnicked on the canoe, using a methylated-spirit stove to boil the kettle for tea. Frank recalls one such picnic: his father had lit the stove and was waiting for the kettle to boil when a passing motor launch created a bow wave that rocked the canoe, making the stove tip over. It landed in Lenny's lap. He stood up, shouting, "I'm on fire! My trousers are on fire! *What shall I do?*" A chorus of voices shouted, "Jump in the water. Jump! Jump!" And jump he did. The resounding splash immediately extinguished the fire, but not before he had received some nasty burns. Lenny never really enjoyed the country; he was a town person and most happy when at the heart of things – particularly when he was the centre of attention.

Ann, busy looking after the twins, was suffering from breast ulcers. Frank's nanny, May Gibbard, had retired because the new additions to the family were too much for her to cope with. Nanny Sutton took her place, relieving some of the pressure on Ann.

147

While the Plugges were living at Sutton Courtney, Frank attended a school in Abingdon. It was a girls' school, and Frank was one of only three boys there. Ann arrived to collect him one day and, seeing him playing with all the girls, decided it was time for him to go to boarding school. It was agreed that he should go to the school attended by Brook's brother, Alan. So, at the beginning of the Easter term, Frank and Brook went to Barmouth, in West Wales, where the Cottesmore School, normally based in Brighton, had been evacuated. They were there for two terms, and were joined during the latter by Tarquin Olivier, Sir Laurence's son. Frank recalls:

> It was an idyllic school, up a mountain, only 40 boys, few masters
> and those mostly past it, consequently very little discipline. We
> rode Welsh ponies bareback and formed ourselves into gangs; the
> black gang, the jungle gang and so forth. After games we could do
> what we wanted, so we would roam through the dense woods,
> fighting our own wars. If we had to play cricket, we would all try
> to get out as quickly as possible, so we could go off to the woods.

11

1945-1962
Diana's Hunting Lodge

The cost of peace
Ann and Lenny living apart
Tories trounced – Labour in power
Radio Normandy does not reopen
Radio Luxembourg is back, with a new image
Lenny rents an apartment in Dolphin Square
From Hamilton Place to Lowndes Square

The war in Europe was over and the masses started to hear about the horrifying cruelty suffered by prisoners in the German concentration camps. Six million Jews had been killed by the Nazis. Still to come were the USA atom bombs that ended the war in the Far East and the atrocities in the Japanese prisoner of war camps. With the obliteration of Hiroshima and Nagasaki, the world faced the fact that advances in science had given humankind the power to destroy all life on the planet.

On the UK political front, it seemed clear that a win for the Labour Party in the coming General Election was on the cards, and Ann knew that if her husband lost his parliamentary seat, it would be a major blow to him. In 1945, the Plugges prepared to meet the people of Chatham and

GENERAL ELECTION 1945.   CHATHAM DIVISION
PARLIAMENTARY BOROUGH OF ROCHESTER

THE PROGRAMME OF **CAPT. L. F. PLUGGE**

THE NATIONAL CONSERVATIVE CANDIDATE

CAPTAIN LEONARD F. PLUGGE, B.Sc., F.R.Ae.S.

Ladies and Gentlemen—

For the last ten years I have had the honour of representing you in Parliament, and I regard it as a great privilege to have been again unanimously adopted as the Conservative and National Candidate for the Chatham Division of Rochester.

The War in Europe has been won by an overwhelming victory, but the task is not yet finished. I wish that the Labour Ministers had been willing to stay in the Coalition Government until a similar victory had been gained over Japan. This, however, they declined to do, despite Mr. Winston Churchill's invitation, and a General Election therefore became inevitable.

SUPPORT FOR MR. CHURCHILL

I have given and still give my whole-hearted and unreserved support to Mr. Winston Churchill and his National Government, which is composed of men of goodwill of all parties and even of no parties. I believe that the most urgent task that lies ahead of us is the total and absolute defeat of Japan in the shortest possible time, and with the least loss of life. What you, as the Electors, have to decide is, who is the best qualified man to be our leader in attaining this objective. Mr. Winston Churchill, whose incomparable powers of leadership have brought us from the brink of disaster in 1940 to the European Victory we have so recently celebrated with our Allies, or Mr. Attlee and his friends? What personality have the latter to match up to men like Marshal Stalin and co-operate with the United States, China and France?

Rochester once more, but their mood was very different from a decade earlier. Lenny's opponent this time was Arthur Bottomley, a respected TUC man, who had been awarded an OBE for his services to Civil Defence. Plugge's majority of nearly 6,000 in 1935 was at risk of being turned around. Canvassing was difficult. Ann and Lenny were heckled; on one occasion, they were chased by dockers wielding staves as they ran for the safety of the party offices.

During the campaign, Plugge was able to review his career as an MP in his manifesto:

> During six years of the war, my main work has been in Parliament, where I have always been one of the hard working members. I served on many Parliamentary Committees, including the Dockyard Committee, the Aeronautical Committee, the Anglo-French, Foreign Affairs, Agricultural, Imperial Affairs, Kent Members Committee etc. For six years, I was the Hon. Secretary of the Inter-Parliamentary Union, a link between all Members of Parliaments of all Democratic Countries of the world.
>
> I was instrumental in creating the Parliamentary and Scientific Committee of which I was Chairman, for the first four years. This Committee was the means of securing relief from taxation for Scientific Research in Industry and large additional grants to Universities.
>
> During the war, a Committee was formed in London of all the Members of Parliaments of invaded countries who were accepting our hospitality. I was elected to be Member of their Executive Council as their Liaison Officer to the British Parliament. This Committee proved to be a valuable link with our numerous European Allies.
>
> Among outside contributions to the war effort, may I mention that during the first six months of the war I organised and provided, mostly at my own expense, the first broadcasts specially radiated for the troops. This service was operated continuously during 13 hours a day, every day of the week, including Sunday, from Radio Normandy and was provided free to the troops, who also received free a copy of a magazine, which I produced and published, entitled *Happy Listening*, containing one week of Radio Normandy's programmes.
>
> This method of large-scale entertainment for the troops by radio, has since been copied by the BBC, with their Forces programme and later by the United States of America and by many of the United Nations.

In 1940 I crossed the Atlantic by sea, being in America and Canada for five weeks, when I carried out an important and secret mission for the Minister of Aircraft production, Lord Beaverbrook.

As Chairman of the Appeals Committee of the Stage Door Canteen, I was greatly instrumental in creating, opening and operating the Stage Door Canteen in London and am still engaged on this work. The Stage Door Canteen has proved a great success and a boon to all enlisted men and women of the three services of all the United Nations. As many as 3,000 Service men and women have visited the Canteen daily and a different floor show has been given free every night, including Sundays, since its inception.

The election resulted in the Conservatives being thoroughly trounced. The number of Tory seats slumped from 358 to 189 while Labour's soared from 164 to 393. Winston Churchill, who had led the country so successfully for the previous four years, was now out in the cold and labelled a warmonger. Many things were to change, although it was to be another nine years before rationing was completely ended. Stafford Cripps, the Labour Chancellor of the Exchequer, cast an air of austerity over the country; Britain was broke.

Plugge had more work for his old friend, Bill Wood. He needed him to draw up claims for war damage to Portland Place. He also required compensation for the loss of the *Lennyann*. Bill was to receive 10 per cent of whatever sum he managed to secure. The exact sum received for the IBC offices is not recorded, but £30,000 was obtained for the *Lennyann* and, after some negotiating, Bill managed to get another £20,000 for the other yacht that had been purchased for spares.

Radio Normandy was never to reopen after the war. The Louvetot Transmitter building, which had sustained heavy damage from hits by Allied incendiaries in 1944, was to be rebuilt but without its spired tower. The Germans had blown up the 170-metre aerial pylon, so a new 120-metre pylon was erected, and the station used as a relay transmitter for Radiodiffusion-Télévision Française (ORTF). Eventually it became what it is today, an Evangelical Church and a local FM station Radio Fraternité.

Between April and November 1945 – as a 'United Nations Station' – Radio Luxembourg broadcast some of its own programmes and was used to transmit the *Voice of America*, initiated by the US Army. The Germans had done a great deal of damage before leaving, and only temporary repairs were carried out by the Allied Command. The Central Control Room had been entirely destroyed and a fair amount of equipment had been stolen or made unusable. The transmitter and the transmitting aerials at Junglinster (11 miles from the Luxembourg capital) needed a complete overhaul, and many pieces of apparatus had to be replaced. Much of the initial work was carried out by the US Army, which under General Patton had liberated the Duchy in 1945.

The station was handed back to its owners as an independent station on November 12th, 1945. Broadcasting a few minutes before midnight on the 11th, Colonel Clifford Powell, Acting Chief of the American Information Control Division, said:

> Radio Luxembourg has contributed largely towards the breaking
> of the morale of German soldiers and civilians and it has helped to
> organise the repatriation of millions of slave workers. It has
> fulfilled its military mission and can now be returned to its
> original owners.

The future of Radio Luxembourg had been discussed by the UK Government during the war, and Churchill and the exiled Prime Minister of Luxembourg agreed that it would be a good idea if the station relayed certain BBC programmes on its international service to South East Europe and occupied Germany.

Stephen Williams, who had been working with ENSA during his wartime employment with the BBC, was instructed to return to Luxembourg to put these plans into operation. He was told to contact the British Embassy in Brussels for further instructions, and to liaise with the recently opened BBC office in Paris and the new British Minister for the Grand Duchy, Colonel Watson.

Williams was pleasantly surprised that he was immediately able to recover the gramophone records that he had put in storage at the beginning of the war and began broadcasting in January 1946 from the studio previously used by Lord Haw Haw. An important discovery was made at this time in the shape of 27 tape recorders or 'Magnetophones' that the Germans had invented and which were completely new to the Americans and ourselves. Most of them were taken to America but two were given to the BBC and were developed by EMI.

Representing the newly elected Labour government, a belligerent Herbert Morrison visited Luxembourg and decided that the negotiations started under Churchill should be continued with the French government and the owners of the Luxembourg station infrastructure. Morrison returned to the UK to inform the House of Commons that negotiations started by the previous administration had run into an impasse due to objections from the

French and Russian governments, and therefore Radio Luxembourg was to revert to its pre-war status of a commercial radio station.

Stephen Williams returned to England in 1948, leaving the operation in the hands of his former assistant, Geoffrey Everett. His final job was to set up a London office for the station called Radio Luxembourg (Advertising) Limited. He returned to the BBC as a very successful producer.

Radio Luxembourg was up and running once more, but with a different image: its programmes were to appeal to the young. Disc jockeys became the norm, something that Stephen Williams would never have accepted. But the change of format was very successful and over the next three decades the new voices on air were to become some of the most familiar in popular music.

The war was over, but relations between Ann and Lenny were strained. They now lived apart and saw each other only when a special occasion arose. Lenny was still throwing parties at Hamilton Place and Ann disliked them more than ever, although she put on a brave face for the sake of appearances.

Lenny rented an apartment in Dolphin Square, near the Thames in Chelsea, which he equipped and furnished as a miniature Hamilton Place. He named it 'Diana's Hunting Lodge' after the painting of Diana, the Greek Goddess, which he had mounted on the ceiling over his bed. The visitors' book provided people with the opportunity to express their admiration.

Ann spent her time between Hamilton Place and Montpelier Street. Jimmy Newton, the son of her godmother, Olive, recalls his mother commenting that Ann was always in tears.

Ann's mother, Mildred, often visited her at Hamilton Place. One evening, they were standing at the window looking out over the garden, which had not been refurbished since the bombing, when they noticed a young woman disappearing into the chicken house with a man. After some time, the couple reappeared. Ann and her mother looked at each other in surprise. Upon investigation, they found that a carpet and mattress had been installed, and decided that the fence around the garden must be repaired to stop the park prostitutes making use of the chicken house.

Intent on trying to resurrect Radio Normandy, Plugge made enquiries with RCA in America regarding the purchase of 10- and 50-kilowatt transmitters, but the French authorities were not agreeable to the reinstating of a commercial radio station. Plugge then concentrated his efforts on making use of the recording expertise of the IBC in the remaining section of its headquarters at 35 Portland Place. The bomb-stricken Number 37 had been sold off to developers planning an apartment block on the site.

In 1946, Lenny embarked on a combined business and holiday trip to the States. There are no recorded details of the purpose of his business, but from the photographs of the trip it appears that he had an enjoyable time with some young friends at Palm Beach. Impressed by the colourful shirts on sale there, he bought several and wore them when he got home. He also purchased a large bright red drop-head Buick, into which he fitted the car phone recently introduced into the USA by the Southwestern Bell Telephone Company.

Having shipped the Buick back to the UK, Lenny decided to take it down to the *Concours d'Elegance* in Cannes, the first of these car exhibitions to be held after the war. He spent a couple of weeks in Paris on the way down. While there, he met with the Police Department to discuss the possibilities of car phones being used in police vehicles. There was immediate interest, and a trial of the system was agreed. The police appointed an officer to man a base station day and night in the headquarters building, while Lenny made calls from various parts of the city. There was considerable interest amongst the Parisians whenever he used his phone, which he did with great panache. The car was equipped with an enormous ten-foot long 'whip' aerial – something that proved irresistible to French anglers. It disappeared a few times before Lenny decided to remove it each night.

Once at Cannes, Lenny prepared for the *Concours d'Elegance*. Being the showman that he was, he put an attractive young lady at the wheel of his luxurious limousine. As she brought the car to a halt in front of the judges, she picked up the telephone receiver and said, "Hello Lenny, c'est moi. Comment ca va?" This *coup de grace* won them the *Grand Prix d'Honneur*.

Plugge was never given the recognition in Britain that he believed he deserved for all his work and achievements in the field of broadcasting and politics. He felt bitter that he was not even granted an OBE, and secretly harboured the hope of a knighthood. Ideally, he would have liked a hereditary peerage that he could pass down to Frank – but it was not to be.

At the end of the forties, Lenny decided he must sell the lease on Hamilton Place and find somewhere less expensive. One of the last things Ann and Lenny did at this grand residence was to throw a well-publicised party for the twins' fifth birthday. Attended by their nannies, thirty little girls and thirty little boys, all dressed in their best bib and tucker, crowded into the marble dining room and sat down to a tea of jellies and cakes. This was followed by games and a film show in the cinema and then a firework display in the garden. Among those present were comedian Leslie Henson's son, Nicky (who was later to become a star in his own right), Bonita Wilson, Tony Monson, Tommy Arnold, Miranda Moon, Nina Campbell and John Radziwill – all children of well-known personalities of the day.

Plugge found a buyer for the lease: one John Mills, a Polish man who had changed his name from Jean-Jean Millstein. He was allegedly the sole survivor of the Holocaust in the Polish town of Lodz, and had endeavoured to reach England as a Polish soldier via Lisbon. He had been interned in Spain for some time before arriving penniless. In 1941, he had managed to set up a club, Les Ambassadeurs, with bandleader Harry Roy, in Stratton Street, just off Piccadilly. It was rumoured that Mills had made an agreement with the intelligence services to use the club to assist in counter-espionage. This is unsubstantiated but, if true, could explain where the financing came from. What is certain is that Mills was able to offer £40,000 for the lease of Hamilton Place. He planned to convert the house for the relocation of Les Ambassadeurs, which, due to its extraordinary popularity with the 'in set', had outgrown the current location. Hamilton Place was later also to house a nightclub called the Milroy.[1]

Ann wanted Lenny to buy a freehold property with some spare rooms that they could let out to supplement the huge salary of £20,000 per year from the IBC. However, while she and Frank were on a skiing holiday in Austria with Emlyn Williams and his family, Lenny found a property with a 'good address' and bought the leasehold. On her return, Ann was surprised to find that she was moving into 15 Lowndes Square.

On moving out, Lenny stripped Hamilton Place of many fixtures and fittings, including some door handles, panelling and a small pair of inset chests of drawers from the boudoir. This act enraged John Mills who, on walking through the front door, pointed to the empty fireplace and said, "He even took the grate." As much furniture as possible was moved to Lowndes Square, the rest being stored in the coal cellars of 35 Portland Place where it subsequently rotted. Several of the door fittings and other small wooden panels went to Lenny's 'pad' in Dolphin Square.

John Mills's modifications to the house were less than desirable. Jimmy Newton's mother, Olive, who popped into the house while it was being converted, was appalled to see the white Carrara marble being painted pink.

---

[1] The name Milroy combined the name John Mills with Harry Roy whose band appeared there. Les Ambassadeurs was the home of several ventures other than the Milroy nightclub, including the Garrison Club and the Cercle, one of London's first gaming clubs.

Lenny's lease on 15 Lowndes Square was for twenty years – but the top floor was separately leased. The sitting tenants, much to Lenny's embarrassment, had to use the main entrance. Frank was annoyed, too, because without the top floor the family had only two bedrooms, which meant that he had to sleep in the nursery in the basement. Despite Lenny exploiting every opportunity to make life difficult for the tenants, they managed to see out their seven-year lease, after which time they moved out and Frank acquired a proper bedroom on the third floor.

The Plugges' manservant was Edward, an ageing Irishman who smelt of stale urine and imbibed heavily on the whisky that Lenny kept for visitors. He was paid three pounds a week and had his own little room off the kitchen. Lenny did not keep any clothes at Lowndes Square and only visited on Sundays for family lunch, which Edward cooked. He expected the family to speak French throughout the meal. It was at such times that he would tell the children that he proposed to leave them a million pounds each when he died.

By this time, Frank was at Eton and glad to be away for nine months of the year rather than suffering the miseries of Lowndes Square along with his mother and the twins. There was no central heating, so log fires had to be lit during the winter.

Frank recalls that his father never physically chastised his children and would make a fuss of them on the few times he was around. If Frank displeased him, he would not rebuke him to his face, but would write a letter. On one occasion when Frank was home on holiday from Eton during the winter, he had been out to buy some sacks of logs for the fire and had put them in the hall, intending to remove them later. Unfortunately, his father brought home some smart friends – something he did when he wanted to convey a happy family image – and he was appalled by the sight of logs in the main entrance. He wrote Frank the customary letter and left it on the hall table. Upon seeing it later, Frank knew what it was about and left it unopened where it remained for several weeks.

Apart from Sundays, the children saw little of their father. Frank recalls six-year-old Gale saying, "Wouldn't it be nice if we had a real Daddy!"

Frank remembers his father:

> My relationship with my father was a strange one as I first remember him when I was six, when I came home from school and saw this old man sitting in the chair who said to me, 'I'm your Daddy.'

From then on, he barely lived under the same roof as his family, but would expect us to be on parade if he had people he wanted us to meet. I think he was proud of his wife and family, but totally unsuited to either marriage or parenthood. He could be incredibly generous, but only with things he wanted you to have and not necessarily what you yourself desired. I can only remember about three occasions when he visited me at school to take me out for the day and only one occasion when he came without my mother; he arrived in his big American car with a young girl in tow; it was acutely embarrassing.

Plugge took every opportunity to draw as much as he could from the IBC. He made Ann a director at £20 per week as well as claiming for the servants. Until the company called a halt, he would put down all his purchases as expenses to the IBC. He was having trouble getting his money out of John Mills, and Bill Wood kept up the pressure for him. When Plugge was short of cash, the only one who suffered was Ann; he still lived off 'the fat of the land', and his generosity to his friends and acquaintances continued without hinder. Many times Ann suffered the embarrassment of the bailiffs entering the house and marking off pieces of furniture for removal to pay outstanding debts or Frank's school fees. Still, they had a television to brighten their evenings, a rarity in the early fifties.

Ann kept up a social round, which included taking the children to the parties of her friends' children. She also enjoyed the company of men and was still very attractive. Molly Williams, Emlyn's wife, remained close and did everything she could to help Ann. Their sons, Brook and Frank, had been at prep school together and were best friends.

The situation at the International Broadcasting Company is well described by Allen Stagg, who had joined the IBC from Radio Luxembourg in 1952:

> When I joined UPC,[1] as it was known then, the work carried out
> was mainly drama programmes for an independent producer,
> Harry Allan Towers.[2] These included series such as the *Black
> Museum,* introduced by Orson Welles, and *The Scarlet Pimpernel.*

---

[1] When the IBC reopened after the war, it used the name UPC (Universal Programmes Corporation, the pre-war subsidiary of IBC). However, when Allen Stagg joined in 1952 he engineered a change of name to IBC Studios, as he felt this to be more appropriate.

[2] Harry Alan Towers began his career at Radio Luxembourg at the age of fifteen. In 1939, when the station closed down, he wrote many scripts for the BBC. Among others, he created *Much Binding in the Marsh* and *March of the Movies.* He joined MGM as its radio adviser and started a transcription service, producing recorded programmes for Radio Luxembourg and the world. By 1951, he had 30 shows a week running on Luxembourg. He also created the National Radio Awards.

There were occasional music sessions for the small independent record labels and programmes for Radio Luxembourg. The people I remember at that time were Richard Meyer, John Terry, the manager, Tig Roe, a recording engineer, Bernard Marsden, a really clever technical engineer who kept the primitive equipment going (just!) and occasionally designed, built and stuck on a new part, breadboard fashion, with the warning "Don't Touch". There was also a handyman cum studio attendant called Paddy. I never knew his other name.

On the ground floor were the admin people, Captain Plugge, Bill Wood, Mrs Shaw and Miss Savage.

I was engaged to run Studio B, a small room on the second floor with quite basic facilities, which was used mainly for tape editing of the drama productions, which were recorded in Studio A on the first floor.

Studio A had a large control room with a partly raised floor to one side (which had been the control room pre-war or the main studio in number 37 Portland Place, which had been destroyed by a bomb during the war). This section was used as a machine room and for playing in sound effects. Staff was hired, unofficially, from the BBC to do this work, these specialists were organised by a wizard named David Law.

My main function was to edit the drama programmes as they were recorded. It was quite challenging work, as I would try to get ahead of the recording, so that I would be waiting for the next reel. As I finished the editing on a programme, I would make copies for the different countries who were taking the programmes; South Africa, Australia, New Zealand, etc, the programme then being 'tailored' to suit the requirements of each country.

The company then began carrying out recording for Pye, and soon after, Philips, and my workload escalated.

1955 saw the commencement of commercial television and quite suddenly all the studio staff left to join this new venture, leaving just Paddy and myself.

It is worth noting that the recording business at that time was completely different from today in that there were only three studios in London which were capable of professional music recording, EMI, Decca and IBC (as it was now called), and it was not possible to hire staff for this highly specialised work.

At about this time I became responsible for the management as well as the recording work. I had to get staff, but they were

158

nowhere to be found, so my solution was to train my own engineers. This took some time, but gradually I was able to hand over more and more recording assignments to the increasingly capable young engineers and concentrate more on the running and development of the studios.

The workload continued to build as I started to record classical music and this became an ever more important part of the studio's work.

There was an increasing demand to improve IBC's disc mastering facilities, but as always the fly in the ointment was Captain Plugge. I knew well that any request to invest money in the business was met with the same reply – "NO". He did not seem to appreciate the fact that we needed to improve our services to keep our clients happy, even though we were, at the time, very profitable. There were many arguments, but eventually, I managed to persuade him that he would be able to get even more money out of the studios.

Surprisingly, at this time, I was able to convince him that Studio A should be enlarged. Using the space taken up by the existing control room gave us an L-shaped room, a new control room being built at the opposite end of the studio, but at a higher level, so no floor space was lost.

Lenny did not limit the indulgence of his favourite pastime to Diana's Hunting Lodge. The time he spent in the office was erratic and there were often strange young ladies flitting around the building; "all of a kind", as Allen Stagg remarked.

Lenny took pleasure in parking his impressive Buick in front of the IBC offices in Portland Place. He had the habit of barging his way out of his parking space by means of the huge chrome bumpers: he would push any car in front forward and then reverse into the car behind, thus creating sufficient space to manoeuvre his mighty vehicle with the least use of the steering wheel. Few cars of today could take such mishandling.

In the late forties, Lenny had met a young woman from Alsace Lorraine. Her name has been forgotten, so for the sake of the story we will call her Nicole. Nicole was in her mid twenties and met Lenny when she was staying in London. She found his charm irresistible and they became close. Eventually, due to the death of her father, Nicole had to return to France. Lenny drove her to the airport. She was sitting next to him when he noticed her writing something on the back of an envelope. When she pressed it into his hand, he thought it was a thank-you note and tucked it into his pocket to read later. Having waved her off, he returned to London, unaware that he would never hear from her again.

At home, he took out the envelope. On the back, Nicole had written her will, leaving all her worldly goods to him. Lenny put the 'will' in his desk.

A few years later, he heard that she had died. He went to Paris to see his lawyer, Maitre Riche, who confirmed that under French law the will was legal. Thinking that it would be nice to have some memento of Nicole, he asked Riche to follow up with her family. An appointment was made and Riche and Lenny travelled down to Alsace together. Nicole's mother refused to meet this Englishman who had turned her daughter's head, and would deal only with Maitre Riche.

Lenny stayed in a local hotel to await the outcome of the negotiations. Riche, puffed up with pride, returned to the hotel to inform him that a settlement of £25,000 had been agreed. It was a very rich family.

Some memento! Riche was quite a gourmet and the two men celebrated with an immense dinner complemented with several bottles of the best wine. Lenny had the task of manoeuvring this rotund and very drunk lawyer to his room more than once during their stay.

Lenny realised that if he took this windfall into the UK he would be liable for a lot of income tax, so he decided upon Monaco as the best haven for his money. He would need a resident's permit, so he moved to Monte Carlo, that city which he knew and loved, to spend a year there in order to qualify. He found a small studio apartment in a block of flats called the Palais Victoria. There was to be a considerable delay before he received his inheritance, but he would be ready when it arrived.

In 1954, Frank, now seventeen, obtained his father's permission to spend a long vacation in France 'to improve his French'. He stayed in Paris in Boulevard Raspail with an old friend of Lenny, Max Brusset, a Deputy who was now Mayor of Royan, a post he held until 1958.

Frank found the visit anything but restful. Brusset was a 'ball of fire', rushing in and out all the time. His very attractive daughter, Dominique, was some compensation, although Frank decided not to risk a liaison. The *au pair* was also very pretty and carried less risk. Frank recalls being at a dinner party with Brusset who introduced him as the son of his very good friend *Capitaine* Plugge.

During the visit, Frank was taken to see Brusset's chateau. Whilst taking a walk with the family through the grounds, he noticed an odd concrete building, and when he asked what it was, he was told it was something to

Ann and Frank in the USA

Hamilton Place
after the bombing

Best friends Brook Williams and Frank – 1941

Frank in his favourite uniform

Ann and 'Black Jack'

Lee Bouvier and Frank
Central Park – 1942

Future First Lady

Jack Bouvier
and his daughter, Jackie,
East Hampton – 1942

Louvetot pylon destroyed in 1940

Louvetot damaged in 1944
by Allied incendiaries

1945 election

Lenny at Palm Beach
with friends

Ann with the twins
Gale and Greville

Allen Stagg, seen here in the control room.
He joined the IBC in 1952

Painting of Diana over Lenny's bed
Diana's Hunting Lodge

Gale and
Greville

Molly before her marriage
to Michael Parkin

Gale's wedding to Jonathan Benson in December 1964

Artist Lenny in Rome 1964-66

Lenny's studio in Rome

Lenny's artwork:

a figure

a painting in strong colours

a bronze

April Ashley, whom Lenny met in Rome.
They returned to London and often went
to the ballet together

I am the princess, you are the slave,
but what a beautiful evening
Love April

Anton Dolin
One of the many visitors
to Dolphin Square

Miss Finland visits
Diana's Hunting Lodge.
Note the mess of wires
and two of the many
telephones in the flat

Michael de Freitas
Michael X

Halé Kimga (Gale) and Hakim Jamal

Greville
and Lenny

Frank and Lenny

Greville watches over his sister's funeral pyre
in Trinidad – 1972

Ann and Lenny appear together
for social occasions

Lenny – the end of a great pioneer

Greville's lonely grave in Morocco
1973

Lenny signs off...

do with radio before the war. On next seeing his father, he mentioned the visit. Lenny scowled and told him the place he had visited was the Chateau d'Epone which he had purchased before the war, and that Brusset should have returned it to him when peace was declared. Frank asked him why he had not taken the case to court and Lenny replied that it would have cost too much money. He may also have known that the chateau needed extensive restoration, which was to cost Brusset a small fortune.

Although, Lenny did not smoke, drink or swear, one vice he did have was gambling, and so the Monte Carlo Casino was the ideal place to pass the time. He was short of cash as usual and was able to gamble only very moderately. He made friends with Errol Flynn who was living there whilst his wife, Patrice Wymore, was filming in London. Flynn, an addicted gambler and usually surrounded by a bevy of attractive women, was well known at the Casino. Lenny joined the crowd.

Lenny phoned Frank in Paris and suggested that he should come to Monte Carlo for a few days. Frank flew down immediately. He was underage, but Errol Flynn's influence got him into the Casino. Flynn would tell him where to place his chips on the roulette table, celebrating when he won but despondent when he lost.

Lenny eventually obtained his Monaco resident's permit in the mid fifties and was able to transfer his windfall into the safekeeping of the Bank of Precious Metals.

In 1955, Lenny's old friend, Bill Wood, retired from the London Transport Executive (formerly the Underground Group) after 42 years of service. Lenny made him General Manager of the IBC. Bill's main job was to act as a negotiator between the staff and Lenny, but Allen Stagg for one was aware of the close friendship that existed between them and therefore not sure whether to trust everything that Bill said. It was reminiscent of the situation that Bill was in with Lenny and Lord Ashfield all those years before – 'be careful what you say, he's a friend of the boss'. Despite this, Bill Wood understood Stagg's frustrations and helped him whenever he could.

As Stagg said in his account, he had trained some of the top recording engineers in the country: such names as Eric Tomlinson, who later recorded much of the music for the James Bond films, and Adrian Kerridge together with Dennis Preston, who were to set up CTS Studios. In all, he had supervised the training of around forty engineers. It was during his time at the IBC that Stagg first made the acquaintance of Isabella Wallich, the first female record producer. They worked with her for the next forty years.

161

Jackie Bouvier kept in touch with Ann and had visited in 1949. Over from the States again, with husband John Kennedy in October of 1955, the two women were not able to meet. Jackie sent a long letter in which she expressed her disappointment and affection:

> I just have to tell you how much we talk about you – Lee and I will never forget you and all the heavenly times we had together – and how gay and beautiful you always were. You sounded just the same on the phone and it kills me to think we now won't meet until next year. Jack was so looking forward to it. I've told him so much about you – Please forgive me Ann and realise how disappointed I was. How I should have loved to see Frankie again and the twins and Captain Plugge. If you ever come to the States please let me know.
> Loads and loads of love to you
> Jackie

The Kennedy family later unknowingly provided the name for a radio station. In 1963 Ronan O'Rahilly was planning the first offshore radio station and was looking for a name. Whilst flying to Dallas he happened to glance through an American magazine. On the centre pages was a photograph taken in the Oval Office of President John F. Kennedy with his young son and daughter. The image of John Junior crawling under his father's desk inspired O'Rahilly although it was the daughter whose name he used. Radio Caroline was born.

For several years, Lenny and Ann had been friends of Sir Bernard Docker, Chairman of Birmingham Small Arms (BSA), which owned Daimler. The Plugges often spent time in the South of France with Sir Bernard and his wife, Norah, on their yacht, the *MY Shemara*, built for Sir Bernard in 1938. At 212 feet long and powered by two 1,920-horsepower diesel engines, it dwarfed the *Lennyann*. The Shemara had a large crew, including a professional cook. Frank remembers the superb accommodation for guests; towels were provided for bathing, green for most of the guests and red for the Duke and Duchess of Windsor. During the Second World War, it had served as an anti-submarine training ship.

Sir Bernard was Norah's third husband; from lowly beginnings, she had married rich men who indulged her extravagant tastes. Her most notorious venture was to talk her husband into providing a new Daimler, but with a difference. The radiator, bumpers and fittings were gold-plated, and the upholstery was zebra skin. In 1955, the car was displayed at the London

Motor Show for all to admire. Lady Docker delighted in showing it off to the miners in Durham, who doffed their caps respectfully as she invited forty of them to spend some time on their yacht in the Mediterranean. All went well until it was discovered that Sir Bernard had not paid for the gold-plated Daimler out of his own pocket, but out of company funds. This would cost him the chairmanship of the company.

In April 1956, during the wedding of Prince Rainier and Grace Kelly, Norah was again in the headlines. Although she and her husband had been invited to the event, her son, Lance Callingham, had not. During dinner in the hotel, they shared a table with the Plugges and Bill Wood, who was there on his own with the object of spending some time with a lady friend. Norah quickly became tipsy. She was very upset about Lance not receiving an invitation and began to demonstrate her anger when the waiter offered her a bread roll. She retorted, "Take it to the Prince and tell him what he can do with it!" On the table were two small paper flags, one American and one Monegasque. Picking up the flag of Monaco, Norah tore it up and for some reason stuffed it into Bill Wood's hand. Instead of putting the pieces into his pocket, he dropped them onto the floor under the table where they were later found. When the news of Norah's actions was reported to the Prince, the Dockers' invitation was withdrawn and they were banned from Monte Carlo. Furthermore, because of the treaty between France and Monaco, the Prince was able to ban them from the whole Department of the Alps Maritime. This was absolute social disaster as it barred them from visiting all their favourite haunts of Cannes, Nice, and Juan-les-Pins. The nearest place they could moor their yacht was the then almost unknown fishing village of Saint Tropez.

Sir Bernard tried to win back a seat on the BSA board at a shareholders' meeting in December 1957. Plugge had purchased a very small number of BSA shares so that he could attend the meeting. Giving a brave speech in support of Bernard, he was greeted with shouts of "How many shares have you got, then?" Docker failed in his attempt by 78 votes to 26.

On returning to London, Frank was called up for National Service, which he spent with the Parachute Regiment in Suez and Cyprus. He returned to the UK in December 1956 and was stationed at Aldershot until his demob in the October. This posting meant that he was able to go to many of the important parties during the 1957 season. The tabloid press, with its avid readers, loved to publicise the escapades of the debutantes and their handsome young beaux, embroidering stories such as "Who smudged the Hon. Juno Wynn's lipstick?" Juno was the daughter of Denisa, Lady Newborough and claimed descent from a French king. The incident occurred at a Deb Ball and, apparently, when Juno arrived home with her lipstick smudged, she was "spanked with her mother's slipper". The *Daily Sketch* claimed that it was Frank who had done the deed, but he declared he would have been pleased to confirm it, "if only it were true".

Lady Newborough, Denisa, was a somewhat eccentric character who kept a hat shop opposite Claridges in Davies Street, Mayfair. The shop was in the basement and she lived in the three floors above. She kept her coronet on display in a case on a shelf, spent most of her time playing cards with friends, and considered customers a nuisance. Frank recalls that during his visits, the top flat above the shop seemed to have an amazing number of men coming and going. When this was commented upon, Denisa explained that her tenant was a nice girl who looked after herself, and that she left her to her own devices. Reputably, Denisa, was arrested for running a brothel during the war, but was let off. Her accent was mid-European, but she kept her origins to herself. Her father was, in fact, Lazar Braun of Subotica in Yugoslavia. Denisa had married Lord Newborough in 1939, following his divorce the previous year. He owned a large estate in Wales where he enjoyed firing cannon out to sea, until one day he shot through a yacht's sail, putting an end to this pastime.

In January 1958, Frank celebrated his twenty-first birthday with due accord at Lowndes Square. Peter Chambers of the *Evening Standard* reported it thus:

> The dancers cha-cha'd under sombre portraits of Louis XIV and the Spanish Infanta. By the fireplace stood an empty champagne bottle and a pair of high-heeled shoes belonging to Miss Felicity Drew.
>
> Sir John Rothenstein ate turkey and salad and admired the paintings. Miss Susan Hampshire samba-ed in her stockinged feet.
>
> Her ex-fiancé, Mr Brook Williams, son of actor Emlyn Williams, took his champagne on the run, in mid-foxtrot.
>
> "Is this a reconciliation?" I asked. "Anything can happen," replied Miss Hampshire.
>
> A man in a decorated waistcoat sauntered past, flicking his friends with a daffodil. Model Miss Ann Gyrsting sat on the stairs in a fur-topped sack. "It's blond fox-fur," she said. "Blond is the colour of this season." Lady Cecil Douglas told me that her daughter, Susan, who went to the United States to represent Britain at the international debutantes' ball, is finding everything gigantic, especially the men.
>
> "She's delighted to find so many men over six feet," she said.

Sir Jocelyn Lucas asked me to point him out the prettiest girl in the room. I chose Miss Veronica Belloc Lowndes, dark, long-lashed and velvety. She said her family owned Lowndes Square when it was nothing but grass. And she threw in for good measure: "Hilaire Belloc was my great-uncle."

At a party later that year, Jimmy Newton introduced Frank to a young art teacher called Molly, who invited him to the forthcoming New Year's Eve Chelsea Arts Ball, which at that time was held at the Royal Albert Hall. It was notorious for the decorated floats that paraded in competition, displaying the charms of many scantily clad young ladies. At the end of the evening, the floats were torn down and completely destroyed. Altogether a riotous evening.

Frank invited Molly, as his new girlfriend, to Lowndes Square to meet his mother, and his sister and brother, Gale and Greville. She was very impressed with the obvious grandeur in which they lived. Molly was vibrant, pretty, sexy and fun to be with. Frank revelled in her company, until one day he introduced her to his father. Molly found Lenny charming and treated him with respect. He found her fascinating, and a few days later, having found her number in his visitors' book, he phoned her. On the pretext that he would like to introduce her to a television producer friend of his who may be able to get her some work painting scenery, he invited her to dinner at his Dolphin Square apartment. She agreed. He picked her up in the Buick and whisked her off to Chelsea.

The television producer was very attentive, and even the presence of his wife did not stop him from making a pass at Molly and patting her knee under the table. After the couple left, Molly let fly at Lenny using the sort of language he had not heard since he canvassed the dockers at the last election campaign. She accused him of giving this producer the impression that she was a prostitute, and that the possibility of work was just an excuse. He had lured her there under false pretences.

To her horror, Lenny collapsed onto the floor in front of her. Molly's anger dissolved into fear. This distinguished businessman and ex-MP lay before her, seemingly suffering a heart attack and possibly dying. Little did she know that this was one of Lenny's ploys when things went against him. She prodded his apparently lifeless body with the toe of her shoe and softly called his name, whereupon he sprang to life, apologising for having frightened her. Getting to his knees, he threw his arms around her legs and burying his face in her skirt. In a muffled voice he said, "I would give you anything you asked for, anything. Just say you'll be mine; that's all I ask."

As usual, Lenny's magic charm worked. Although young enough to be his granddaughter Molly, found herself patting his bald head and saying, "There, there. There's nothing to cry about. I forgive you."

They never went out together. Lenny wanted to be there for her to come home to after going out with her other boyfriends, although he warned her about going to bed with them in case she caught some terrible disease. He told her it was better to sleep with only him and save herself for a future husband. He began to school her on how to go about getting that husband and make the best marriage. He advised her that the trick was to be brilliant in bed. Molly remembers him telling her:

> ...look at Mrs Simpson; the only way she got the Prince of Wales and nearly became queen was because she was so flabbergastingly good at cock sucking. Her skills in that direction tied the Duke of Windsor to her apron strings forever and if I got even one tenth that good at it, then I could make a fine match.[1]

Of course, it would take practice and lots of it. Molly believed this fatherly old gentleman, but did not necessarily relish the idea of practising on him, although practise she did. Here he was at nearly seventy being serviced regularly by a pretty girl who believed that 'Daddy' knew best. She had fallen into his trap. The 'warming up' technique had worked again.

The fridge in the flat was stocked with Krug champagne, caviar and smoked salmon. Molly liked the champagne but found the caviar revolting. Lenny also had a supply of sleeping pills, to ensure her a good night's rest. Molly awoke in the morning wondering what he had been up to while she was dead to the world. But he provided her with good champagne, top quality food, morning tea in bed and a fiver for her taxi to the school where she was teaching.

Molly eventually met and married Michael Parkin, an executive of NAAFI.[2] Ann was delighted to hold the wedding reception at Lowndes Square, with Molly spending her last night of freedom there. Michael Parkin became a television executive and later a gallery owner. Molly became a well-known author whose books were notorious for their humour and explicit sexual episodes. Frank says that some of the situations described rang a bell with him.

In 1958, the Plugge family motored down to Monte Carlo in the red Buick for a holiday, staying in the Palais Victoria. Returning the following year,

---

[1] *Moll: Making of Molly Parkin* (Victor Gollancz, London 1993).

[2] Navy, Army and Air Force Institutes.

166

they stayed at the prestigious Hermitage Hotel, where Lenny decided to hold a party. He sent out invitations to everyone he knew, whether they were likely to come or not. The idea was that in return he would receive invitations to their parties.

Frank married Gillian Westwood in November 1959, an occasion not ignored by Lady Newborough, who claimed that they had married secretly in Monte Carlo, unbeknown to the family. This was fiction; he married at the local registry office with the family in attendance. Lady Newborough went on to state that the news came as a considerable blow to many a Mayfair mother. Since Frank and his Rolls Royce had first made an impact on the 'deb' world, he had been regarded as one of the most eligible young men in town.

Greville was following the same education route as Frank: Eton and then university. He graduated from Oxford with a law degree, although he never put it to any use. Gale attended the Lycée in London, despite Lenny's wish that she should go to Heathfield, a school for 'nice girls'. Ann disagreed and arguments ensued, but she won in the end.

In 1960, Frank talked his father into giving him a position at the IBC. Lenny had not been in favour of this and neither had the staff, who did not want the boss's son in the office. Even so, Frank was found a job with Allen Stagg who was to train him. Stagg found Frank very pleasant, but probably not cut out to be a recording engineer, and Frank found that Portland Place was not the ideal building for a recording studio. The wooden floors creaked, and often he would have to screw down the offending boards to cure the problem. He left in 1962 when his father sold the company.

12
1962-1970
From Italy to Beverly Hills

Plugge sells the IBC
To Rome to paint and sculpt
Return to Diana's Hunting Lodge
The Plugge Patent Auto Circuit fails
Emigration to Los Angeles

As usual, Lenny needed more money; his inheritance from Nicole had all gone. He had by this time lost interest in the IBC and decided that its sale would raise a considerable sum. The Company was an attractive proposition for the potential buyer, particularly as it was housed in a prestigious building in a very desirable area of London. Unfortunately, the buyers that eventually acquired the company from Plugge were not interested in recording. The Berman brothers, owners of Commercial Industrial Services Limited, were financiers and interested only in asset stripping.

If Stagg thought Plugge had been tight with the finances, these two were even worse. Bromislav Berman was particularly unpleasant, although his brother Dr Joseph Berman was a little more amenable. Allen Stagg remembers:

> While it was difficult to deal with Captain Plugge, it was nothing
> compared to the people who took over the organisation. They were
> brothers named Berman who were completely impossible. They
> knew nothing of the business and had no interest in it. This was
> certainly the most unpleasant period of my whole career. As an
> example of their behaviour; their chauffeur was not allowed to
> have the keys for the petrol cap of the car. When fuel was needed
> he had to ask for the keys and was given enough money for two or
> three gallons, returning the keys immediately he had filled up.
>
> Thankfully their ownership did not last long, so the studios were
> able to recover from the damage caused by them fairly quickly.

IBC Studios was an independent company and, throughout the sixties until its closure in 1977, continued to attract the very best stars. Along with Decca and EMI, it was one of the 'big three' recording studios. Several top stars were able to use recording studios of their own choosing rather than those of the record companies to which they were contracted. Such groups as The Beatles, The Who, Status Quo and The Bee Gees frequented Studio A. The Rolling Stones laid down demo recordings in March 1964 for submission to record companies, but the IBC hierarchy was not impressed. Decca was, and The Rolling Stones won a recording contract.

Radio Luxembourg came into the picture again in the 1950s when the IBC was asked to record some programmes for Ross Radio Productions. One was *A Shilling for a Second*. Another was *Candid Mike*, the radio version of the later highly successful television show *Candid Camera*.

Bill Wood stayed on as director, and Henry Connell continued as Company Secretary. Allen Stagg was headhunted from the IBC in 1968 to take over the EMI Abbey Road studios.

To conclude the story of the IBC, in 1972 the Berman brothers sold the company to Eric Robinson, the well-known impresario. Finally, in 1977, the company was dissolved. Lenny Plugge's dream child had lasted forty-seven years.

Having sold the IBC in 1963 for approximately £120,000, Lenny was solvent again. He paid off his outstanding debts of £20,000 and decided to try out a system he had been working on for years. Prior to the war, he had employed a woman to sit night after night by the roulette wheel to record the numbers as they came up. Lenny had carefully integrated the information into a system to beat the roulette wheel.

Now ready to try out his system, he co-opted Frank and went to the Monte Carlo Casino. Frank read out the predicted winning numbers so that his father could gamble on them. Unfortunately, the system failed and a considerable amount of money went into the coffers of the Casino. He was not after all to be another 'man who broke the bank at Monte Carlo'.

Lenny was still spending most of his time at Diana's Hunting Lodge, his flat in Dolphin Square. Although little more than a bed-sit, the furnishings were sumptuous. From the visitors' book he kept, it is obvious that everyone who came to the apartment was very impressed and amazed by his ingenuity. He referred to it as his 'love nest'; one might say he had become the personification of the classic *roué*.

All the family visited, including Ann; the children popped in regularly, adding their glowing comments into the visitors' book. Many illustrious celebrities were entertained by Lenny, from the Sultan of Penang to

Annigoni, the artist who painted a well-known portrait of the Queen. Ballet dancers were regular visitors, as Lenny was very fond of the ballet; John Gilpin and Anton Dolin were just two. Frank describes his impression of the place:

It was a very small flat, the entrance hall was tiny, with a bathroom leading off; to the left was the sitting room. Every inch of the walls was covered in silk or paintings. If you opened a cupboard, the inside was also lined with silk. Each fitting was secured with gold plated screws. A double bed was in one corner, with a beautiful red velvet bedspread inset with tapestry panels. The tassels hanging around the bed operated the lights, the radio and television. The place was furnished with many small items in satin wood taken from Hamilton Place. He also had several of his own paintings and sculptures on display.

There was a large oil painting of a semi clad 'Diana' by Ansiaux mounted in the ceiling over bed. The artist described the picture thus:

Near the crystal lake, in a sun-kissed clearing of the singing forest, closely watched over by her favourite and faithful dog, Diana, exhausted after the extensive hunt, lays gently asleep and fervently dreams with exaltation of Love's passionate fulfilment.

Among those with whom he formed a special association was a woman named Erica. She and Lenny would write love poems to each other in the visitors' book. Hers were in French or German, his replies in English or French. One of Lenny's verses to 'My little Erica' went as follows:

May the roses speak the words I dare no longer say
Can they just reach your heart and my heart's thoughts convey
For hearts are tender souls that harbour joy and pain
Your little heart so loving, is sweet, is kind, is gay.
Basking in the sunshine, must never see the rain
My poor heart is broken and fast bleeding away.

Friends would visit often to enjoy the luxury and splendour of being surrounded by valuable oil paintings while being indulged with caviar and champagne. It is clear from the almost unintelligible scrawl of some that they had imbibed rather too well.

Lenny had a substantial collection of works of art housed at Lowndes Square. In 1964, aged seventy-five, he decided to take up art himself. He flew to Rome to stay at the Brazilian Embassy as the guest of the

Ambassador, Hugo Gouthier, while he studied painting and sculpture at the Accademia di Belli Arti.

At home, in London, Gale was getting married. Lenny attended the wedding on December 12th, 1964 at St Michael's Church, Chester Square. The groom, Jonathan Benson, was an assistant film director and had been a suitor of Deirdre, the woman who later became the wife of actor Corin Redgrave. Corin, brother of Vanessa Redgrave, was best man. Lenny gave his daughter a car as a wedding present: a Mini, which he had gift wrapped and parked on the pavement outside Lowndes Square. Unfortunately, Gale's marriage was not to be a happy one.

While in Italy, Lenny spent a year in Florence studying at the University, particularly focusing on a painting by Titian called 'The Venus of Urbino' as he was preparing to write a book on the subject. He believed he had the first of two versions of the painting in his collection, or 'The Leonard Plugge Foundation' as he liked to call it. His art collection decorated the walls of Lowndes Square and Diana's Hunting Lodge. Others he kept in a basement room at Dolphin Square, ostensibly a storeroom that he had converted into a library.

After his year in Florence, Lenny returned to Rome and rented a studio in Vialle Massini, where he lived and dressed the part, wearing a painter's smock and a Rembrandt-style hat. Carol and Pepe Lopez, artist friends, had invited Lenny to a soiree and it was here that he was introduced to April Ashley. April was a well-known transsexual, having had the operation in Morocco in the fifties. She was tall and attractive, and Lenny took an immediate liking to her. He told her all about his decision to become an artist and about his tower studio in Rome. While in the Eternal City, the two saw a lot of each other. They attended many fancy dress balls, which Lenny loved. He enjoyed dressing up as a cardinal, and was thrilled when women came up to him to be blessed.

April and Lenny regularly lunched at Piccolo Mondo where he would tell her of all his latest ideas to make himself rich again. At the restaurant one day, April introduced her friend, Sarah Churchill, to Lenny. During the conversation, Lenny told Sarah that people said he reminded them of her father, Winston. This did not go down well with Sarah and she told him what she thought.

Late in 1966, Lenny abandoned his artist life in Rome and returned to England. He was back at Diana's Hunting Lodge in Dolphin Square, entertaining ladies whenever he had the opportunity. The book on 'The Venus of Urbino' was never written.

April also returned to London, where she continued her friendship with Lenny. He often took her to the ballet, and April recalls the evening when, after visiting Covent Garden to see Fonteyn and Nureyev in *Giselle*, Lenny invited her back to Diana's Hunting Lodge. She politely declined and said that he had plenty of young girls to keep him happy, but Lenny persisted, telling her not to be worried as he was impotent. "There was something about him", wrote April, "that brought out my maternal instincts and I said 'yes'." She did not, however, fulfil any of his romantic wishes, but left a note in the visitors' book, written on a page of the theatre programme: "I am the Princess, you are the slave, but what is beautiful, Lenny? Love, April".

Lenny kept a box at Covent Garden, and he would bring flowers for throwing onto the stage at the end of the performance to show his appreciation. April recalls the time when he brought flowers from the gardens in Lowndes Square: he had pulled them up, still with clods of earth on the ends. When the ballerinas awaited their usual cascade of flowers from Lenny, they were greeted with missiles thumping onto the stage. They quickly learned to duck to avoid floral appreciations from Lenny's box. As he grew older, his strength and aim deteriorated and the bouquets sometimes landed in the orchestra pit.

Ann and Lenny continued to appear together socially, Ann playing the part of the attentive wife. One such occasion was when they held a small luncheon party at the Carlton Club of which Lenny had long been a member. The event was widely reported in the press, including an entry in the *Court Circular*. The guests at this 'small' luncheon were the First Secretary of the Turkish Embassy and Mme Akgun Kiciman, the French Military Attaché and Mme Jacques Barjou, Count and Countess Jean de Gennes, Mr and Mrs Vyner-Midgley, Miss Veronica Midgley, Miss Sheila Scott, Baron Clement Franckenstein, Mr Alan Clore, and Mr Frank Plugge. It was quite a turnout, considering that Lenny was next to broke. His finances were stretched to the very limit; the money from selling the IBC was gone and he resorted to selling furniture to pay the bills. He even surrendered an insurance policy for £2,000 in favour of the children to get some ready money.

Lenny was now living full time at Dolphin Square, and had rented a flat there for Ann. Frank and Gale were both married and Greville was living in Australia, so 15 Lowndes Square was unoccupied. Edward, the servant, had died and Plugge took on a live-in security man to protect the property from squatters or vandals. His name was Herbert James Mitchell, a

66-year-old ex-sergeant in the Scots Guards who described himself as a private investigator. Mitchell moved in with his wife and a man called Ernie who had Down's Syndrome.

This was the period when illegal gambling had taken off in London, and private houses were sometimes used as unlicensed casinos. To supplement her meagre income, Ann had occasionally let out part of Lowndes Square for *chemin de fer* parties arranged by Frank. Lenny did not become involved, but was happy for this to help the family income.

During the late sixties, Frank also held weekend poker sessions, and it was at one of these meetings that David Cammell was introduced to the house. Cammell was involved with the film industry and had recently earned a reasonable sum from writing a script. On his first evening, he was unlucky and went back the next evening to try to recoup his losses. But the cards were against him and he had to hand over the entire fee he had earned for the film script.

Cammell was preparing a film with American producer Sandy Lieberson, and wanted to shoot totally on location. The film was called *Performance* and was to star Mick Jagger, Anita Pallenberg, Michele Breton and James Fox. The script was written by David Cammell's brother Donald who also directed. Cammell was looking for a suitable empty house, and Number 15 Lowndes Square seemed an ideal location. Lenny Plugge jumped at the chance of making some money from the rental of the house, and agreed a sum with Sandy Lieberson.

One sticking point was the art collection, which Lenny insisted must be insured to the value of two million pounds. David Cammell looked at the collection and was not impressed; the paintings looked tired and some canvases were sagging. The 'Leonard Plugge Foundation' consisted of sixty paintings – some being copies rather than originals – by a variety of artists including Gainsborough, Raphael, Reynolds, Rubens, Titian and Veronese. Eventually a sum of one million pounds was agreed. To ensure no damage was done to the paintings, they were removed from the walls and carefully packed away.

Work began on building sets within the house, and Lowndes Square became a buzz of activity. It was so busy and noisy that Lady Robens, the wife of Lord Robens, Chairman of the National Coal Board, who resided in the Square, phoned David Cammell complaining about the ice cream vans being parked in the vicinity and the peace of the area being disturbed. "Don't they realise," she said, "that there are more titled people living in Lowndes Square than any other square except Eaton Square?"

Lady Robens then complained to the owners of the house, which turned out to be mortgaged up to the hilt to the Sun Life Insurance Company. Plugge had not mentioned this to Cammell or Lieberson and should not have rented the house out without the permission of Sun Life. This disclosure effectively put a halt to the filming, threatening the millions of dollars invested in the production. A senior QC, who was initially optimistic about resolving the problem quickly, was appointed to fight the case, but Sun Life refused to budge. After a lot of negotiation, an agreement was made out of court that filming could continue if Plugge gave up the lease. This played into Plugge's hands, as the lease was a full repairing one and was due to run out in a couple of years. Naturally, he agreed, and filming continued.

The film was described by Mick Jagger as being:

> about the perverted love affair between Homo Sapiens and Lady
> Violence. It is necessarily horrifying, paradoxical and absurd. To
> make such a film means accepting that the subject is loaded with
> every taboo in the book.

In the film, Number 15 Lowndes Square was to be the home of a rock star, Turner, played by Mick Jagger. In order to create the correct atmosphere, the house was decorated with hangings, covers and cushions from Morocco and the Hindu Kush area of Afghanistan. There was also a sumptuous bed festooned with cords and sashes, and a sunken bath inlaid with Persian tiles. The bath was to be used in a scene showing a *ménage à trois* with Jagger, Pallenberg and Breton, an arrangement that allegedly became fact during the course of the shooting.[1] The film contained violence, drug-taking and sex, and supposedly reflected the rock scene of the time. Drugs were openly used on set. The sex scenes were particularly explicit, including one where the cameraman crawled under the sheets with his 16mm camera while Jagger and Pallenberg embraced inches from his lens. Keith Richards, Pallenberg's boyfriend, got to hear about the authenticity of the scenes and apparently gave her a hard time when she returned home.

Lenny must have been shocked to the core at what was going on in his house; the pretty girls he could accept, but the swearing, the drugs and the violence would have been totally alien to him.

One weekend, while the crew were clearing up, they noticed a team of men carrying out packages and loading them into a van. Assuming the men were to do with Captain Plugge, they paid little attention. Later, Frank

---

[1] Article by Mick Brown in the *Telegraph Magazine*, dated June 3rd, 1995.

reported to his father that he had seen two of his paintings – the King and Queen of France by Pierre Mignard – in the window of an antiques shop in Kensington, owned by Charles Howard. Lenny was horrified. Frank said that he should inform the police immediately, but Lenny was against this idea, saying that he would sort it out himself.

Having finally recognised that he had probably been taken in by Mitchell, his caretaker, Lenny went to the police. Mitchell, on the run, was eventually arrested and held at Paddington Police Station. He was granted bail, and his lawyer phoned David Cammell, asking if he would put up the money. Cammell just laughed.

The ex-Scots Guard was brought to court, charged with stealing thirty-two paintings worth £100,000, a watch valued at £600, items of furniture and jewellery belonging to Ann, and with forging two cheques for £1,000 each. He also pleaded guilty to possessing a pistol without a licence. The defence gave Plugge a difficult time, dragging up cases where he had been sued for bank overdrafts and non-payment of bills. They also claimed that he employed Mitchell to frighten his creditors away from the house. Mitchell, who also used the name Walter George Waterhouse, was sentenced to two years.

When Mitchell went to prison, his wife moved out of the house, leaving Ernie, the man with Down's Syndrome, curled up in his lice-ridden blankets in the attic with a large Alsatian dog for company. The film crew were kind enough to clean him up and give him a new mattress.

During the making of the film, Lenny made the occasional visit, wearing his long fur-lined overcoat and escorted by two glamorous models. Even at eighty, he was still able to impress the ladies.

Lord and Lady Robens were compensated for their inconvenience by a holiday in the West Indies, courtesy of the film company.

During this time, Ann spent as much time as she could with Molly and Emlyn in Corfu. She loved the island, which was a haven of peace and security away from the stresses of London. Her numerous visits had made it possible for her to learn a little Greek, making her feel even more at home. Greville and Frank often visited her there.

For several years Lenny had been working on an invention that he felt sure would make him rich again. He had thought of the idea when driving around Europe and the States. In those days, it was quite a common occurrence for the car battery to go flat, or lose its charge. His idea was to

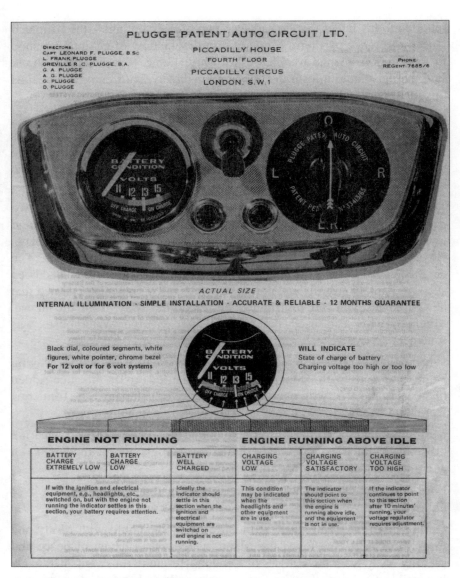

use two batteries with an automatic indication of when one was getting low, so that the driver could flick a switch to change over to the other battery that had been charged by the engine. In 1968, he took out patents in both England and France, and set up a company to market the unit. Plugge Patent Auto Circuit Limited had offices on the fourth floor of Piccadilly House, in the very centre of London. All the members of the family were listed as directors, including Lenny's grandson, Dominic.

PLUGGE PATENT AUTO CIRCUIT LTD

DIRECTORS.
CAPT LEONARD F. PLUGGE, B.Sc.
L. FRANK PLUGGE
GREVILLE R C. PLUGGE, B.A.
G. A. PLUGGE
A. G. PLUGGE
G. PLUGGE
D. PLUGGE

PICCADILLY HOUSE
FOURTH FLOOR

PICCADILLY CIRCUS
LONDON. S.W.1

PHONE:
REGENT 7685/6

IT IS IMPOSSIBLE TO INCUR A BREAKDOWN DUE TO A FLAT BATTERY OR A DEFECTIVE CHARGING SYSTEM OR A RELUCTANT STARTER IF YOUR CAR IS FITTED WITH THE PLUGGE PATENT AUTO CIRCUIT

The Plugge Patent Auto Circuit is a multiple compound of electric circuits patented over the world. It provides independent sources of electric power available at any time in case of necessity, or emergency. The numerous and various circuits available can be individually brought into action by the PPAC Master Switch.

The Plugge Patent Auto Circuit permits the energy to be electrically connected or else electrically disconnected, to or from, the Car's main circuit. The multiple electrical power brought to bear is most valuable should there be difficult starting in the morning or in winter or in freezing countries. All these choices of circuitry can be made instantaneously available by the Plugge Patent Auto Circuit's Master Switch situated on the dash in front of the driver's seat and at his easy reach.

The Instrument is fitted with coloured tell-tale lights, which indicate at a glance the operational position of the PPAC Master Switch, and the particular Circuit which is at that moment in use. At the same time the PPAC Battery Condition Indicator comes into action and the driver can read at a glance on the illuminated dial at the left of the panel the state of charge of Battery installation. The PPAC Battery Condition Indicator also gives a reading showing the operational state and behaviour of the car's charging circuit incorporating the Generator or the Alternator, and the general running condition of the whole Charging System of the Car.

The coloured tell-tale lights show continuously which circuits are in use, and which circuits are not in use. They also indicate by their absence and extinction when the electric energy is completely cut out of the Electric Circuit of the Car, such as it should be when the Car is out of use, parked or placed in it's Garage. In this latter Master Switch Position, there is no danger of the Battery loosing its charge, or of continuously discharging owing to the starting switch having been inadvertently left on, or a light or an electric circuit or a gadget having been forgotten. At any time, if desired, the PPAC Battery Condition Indicator, and the coloured tell-tale lights can be independently turned off by means of a small switch specially incorporated in the centre of the panel for that purpose.

The driver has the choice at all times of the various alternative independent sources of electrical energy. These provide the extra power available, and the supplementary electric storage space for the additional electric power that the Charging System of the Car accumulates for use in case of need and emergency.

The Plugge Patent Auto Circuit is indispensible for a Car equipped with an Alternator. In the case of an Alternator the rate of charge can be very high, but that high rate of charge cuts out automatically when the internal resistance of the Battery becomes too great for various reasons such as for instance on a long run, and the special high charging rate available is lost and wasted. Not so when the Plugge Patent Auto Circuit is installed. This extra stored electrical power comes into use if a defect arises in the Car's Charging System, caused for instance by a slipping belt or by carbonised brushes in a generator, suddenly reducing the rate of charge, or cutting out the charging process altogether.

The Instrument is robust, compact and self-contained. It can be fitted to any Car in a matter of an hour or so, depending on the make of the Car.

Although the Plugge Patent Auto Circuit is constructed primarily to be used with a 12 Volt system, as provided in most Cars, it can also be supplied for a 6 Volt system, or in fact for any other Voltages that may meet the demand for Heavy Lorries, Vans, Trucks, Buses, Coaches, Caravans, Trailers, Speed Boats, Motor Cruisers, Yachts or private Aeroplanes.

The Automobile Association's statistics show that their patrols encountered 1,430,428 motorcar breakdowns on the roads of Great Britain in 1967. Of these 37%, more than one half a million, or 1,500 broken down motorcars per day, were attributable to electrical failures, only 11% or some 150,000 were due to tyre trouble. Three electrical failures for each flat tyre. Only one motorist in four is a member of the A.A.

WHY DO YOU NEED ONE?

1. Because one of the most frequent causes of breakdowns today is a flat or worn out battery. Hardly surprising considering the ever increasing demands made on a battery today by all the equipment of modern motor cars — such as, double and quadruple head lights, fog lights, side lights, tail lights, parking lights, roof lights, map reading lights, boot lights, bonnet light, number plate light, reading gauges, electrically operated windows, electrically operated seat adjustments, cigarette lighter, screen wipers, electric horn, electric petrol pump, electric heater, electric heater blower, electric window screen heater, air conditioning installation, broadcast receiver, tape recorder, tape player, gramophone player, radio telephone, electric loud hailer, flashing lights, electric siren, electric gong, rotating lights, radar control, all this in addition to the primary purpose of a Battery namely the electric starter, the sparking plugs, the electric coil, the only three things for which the Battery was in the first instance provided for.

2. Because it pays to take care of your battery. The working life of a battery when neglected is considerably shortened and a replacement is an expensive item. The permanent presence of the PPAC circuitry gives a mental sensation of great safety and security.

3. Because fewer cars today have starting handles and a flat battery may leave you stranded. Especially in the case of a car fitted with automatic gears. In such case the car cannot be pushed to start the engine because the engine freewheels, and does not revolve.

WHAT DOES IT TELL YOU?

1. The state of charge of the battery. A well charged battery and the provision of the PPAC circuits helps you make a quick start.

It also means you can leave your sidelights on for long periods, all night in fact, without fear of a flat battery breakdown. The PPAC Battery Condition Indicator tells you the state of charge of your battery at a glance at any moment.

2. The charging voltage. It is harmful to charge a battery at too high a voltage as this shortens its life. If the battery is charged at too low a voltage it will eventually become flat. In both cases the PPAC Battery Condition Indicator warns you well in advance, giving you time to correct the fault before a breakdown occurs. If it does occur, the other circuits can be switched into use and the Car driven away.

FITTING INSTRUCTIONS

Connect as indicated by the lettering on the back panel of the PPAC instrument.

Use suitably heavy cables for connections and check that these electrical connections are secure and properly insulated.

There are four positions to the Plugge Patent Auto Circuit Master Switch, all indicated by the white arrow, and the coloured tell-tale lights.

Position R. Green Light only.

Position L. Red Light only.

Position LR. Both Red and Green Lights.

Position O. No Lights — This position is the Safety Position when the car is not in use.

The instrument is designed so that the pointer adjusts slowly, giving a clear and steady reading. It should not oscillate rapidly.

Lenny felt sure that the place to sell this invention was the United States. He circulated details to several of the car manufacturers there, including General Motors, Chrysler and Chevrolet, trying to persuade them to incorporate the device into their cars at the production stage. They were all very polite in their replies, but were not interested in taking up the idea. He wrote this report, published in *Newsweek* in 1969:

> PLUGGE ELECTRIC CIRCUIT: Motorists need no longer worry about flat batteries. The Automobile Association giving its statistics for the year 1967, states that 37% of calls for assistance from its members, came under electrical failures, against only 11% for flat tyres.
>
> Calls encountered amounted to 1,430,438 with a membership of 3,600,369 and these figures indicate that throughout Great Britain with a car population of 14 million road vehicles, electrically broken down motorcars were scattered at the consistent rate of over 6000 every day during 1967.
>
> The Plugge Circuit can be fitted to any car within an hour or so and it is claimed to make it impossible for your motorcar or motorboat to incur a breakdown due to a flat battery, a defective charging system or a reluctant starter. If incorporated at the factory at the negligible cost of a small royalty, export sales of any make adopting the circuit would double in a year.
>
> Captain Leonard Plugge the British Politician and Scientist is the inventor of this new dash-fitting device, with which certain Police cars are already equipped. Captain Plugge was the originator of the first car broadcast receiver in the world and also invented and developed the technique of the two-way Car Radio Telephone, now used by Police Forces in all countries.
>
> The instrument is marketed by the Plugge Patent Auto Circuit Co. Ltd. of Piccadilly House, Piccadilly Circus, London, England.

Lenny had great faith in this invention, and continued to put money into its development for many years. He became convinced that the huge United States market was closed to him because the Americans were against anything that was designed and developed outside their own country, a notable example being Concorde, first flown in the same year.

The Plugge Patent Auto Circuit would never be put into large-scale production: Lenny's dream of regaining his millionaire status faded as the years passed. Of his other inventions, Frank remembers the prototype of television glasses consisting of a hood made of cardboard, inside which was a maze of mirrors. The idea was to watch the television through the device, possibly to give a stereoscopic effect. It did not appear to be very effective; no drawings or details survive. In his *Who's Who* entry, Plugge mentions the invention of a stereoscopic cinematograph, but nothing further is known about this project.

By 1970, Lenny's financial affairs were going from bad to worse; he owed money everywhere and was struggling to avoid bankruptcy. His appearance was of a man very down at heel, and his friends and family could not help noticing his scuffed shoes and the food stains on his clothing. He seemed not to pay any heed to his dishevelled state. The dapper man of the House of Commons was no more.

Diana's Hunting Lodge was also showing signs of neglect. Frank noticed that the fridge was stacked with rotting smoked salmon and half-empty bottles of champagne. The wine glasses were greasy and bore lipstick stains. The electricity had been cut off and candles provided the only light. Lenny had reached the age of eighty and with wires trailing all over the flat, the inevitable accident happened: a candle set light to the silk drapes and the place caught fire. Much of the old gentleman's cherished love nest was destroyed or damaged. Fortunately, the twelve volumes of his leather bound press-cutting books, though scorched, were saved.

In May, Lenny decided to escape. He had made many friends around the world and had entertained them lavishly on their visits to England; he would now visit them and indulge himself in their hospitality. His first stop was Costa Rica, where his arrival was headline news in *La Prensa Libre*, which referred to him as the inventor of the metal aeroplane and the car telephone; as having the prettiest wife in London; as being a world famous sculptor and able to speak French, German and Italian. A full page gave details of his achievements, real and imaginary. Within two months, he had outstayed his welcome and he travelled to Jamaica where he lodged with the Nathans in St Anne's Bay before moving on to Beverley Hills in Los Angeles.

Meanwhile, back in London, sons Greville and Frank were endeavouring to resolve his financial affairs. There were the three apartments in Dolphin Square: Beattie 701 and 702 as well as Hood 902.[1] He also had three basement storerooms. When the family was not occupying the flats, they were sub-let. The brothers had to find the money for the rent, rates and electricity, and sort out their father's income tax problems.

---

[1] Dolphin Square was split up into a number of 'Houses' named after admirals, hence Beattie and Hood. Each House consisted of numbered apartments.

13

1971–1979
Double Tragedy

Trinidad – 1972
Morocco – 1973

Following the failure of her marriage to Jonathan Benson, Gale was feeling low and looking for new meaning. Rather naïve but very much a free spirit, she became involved with Black Power.

Vanessa and Corin Redgrave introduced her to the leader of the movement, Michael de Freitas, who was born in Trinidad, the son of a Portuguese planter and a black woman. He had come to London, married, and worked with Peter Rachman, the notorious slum landlord. In the early sixties, he became influenced by Malcolm X (Malcolm Little), the Muslim Black Power leader in the States who was murdered in 1965. De Freitas decided to take up the gauntlet in England and called himself Michael X. His pronouncement – that any white man seen with a black woman should be shot – earned him a year in prison under the new Race Relations Act. Soon after his release, he was accused of robbery but he jumped bail and went to Trinidad in 1970. He converted to Islam and changed his name to Michael Abdul Malik.

Gale was so impressed by Malik that she joined his Black Power group, which was based mainly around the West Indian community in Notting Hill. She also became strongly influenced by another Black Power leader, Allen Donaldson, an African American born in Boston in 1931. Donaldson claimed that his conversion to Islam by Malcolm X had cured him of his drug and alcohol addiction. Having changed his name to Hakim Jamal, he wrote a book recounting his experiences with Malcolm X, and extolling his virtues.

Hakim Jamal was an imposing, charismatic man, who exerted considerable influence over those who most admired him, especially women. He once arrived at the party of a well-known film director with Vanessa Redgrave on his arm, demonstrating her support for Black Power. The actress, Jean Seberg, had introduced Jamal to Vanessa, who then introduced him to her brother, Corin, and his wife, Deirdre. Vanessa had also become involved with the Black Panther movement and she told them that Jamal would be staying at her house while he was investigating the position of Black Power in England. Jamal was a very eloquent speaker; his hypnotic gaze convinced many people of the worthiness of his cause.

At the end of 1969, following a passionate affair with Jean Seberg, Hakim Jamal visited England for the second time. When Gale met him, she was swept off her feet by his 'swashbuckling' image and gold earring. She soon began worshipping him almost as if he were God. The trouble was that Malik – Michael X – actually believed himself to be God.

Jamal broke away from the Redgraves and, together with Gale, spent some months travelling abroad, particularly in Morocco. He was looking to return to a 'black' country.

In 1970, Gale went with Jamal to North America where they toured in a Volkswagen minibus. Jamal had abandoned his own family in California for this itinerant life with a middle-class English girl who was now his self-confessed slave. They spent about a year in this way before moving down to Guyana. After a month there, Jamal was asked to leave, so they moved on again.

Jamal was hoping to make more money from the sale of his Malcolm X book. The advances he had received from André Deutsch and his American publisher, Random House, had long gone and they were desperately short of cash. When they heard that Malik was in Trinidad they decided to visit him at his so-called agricultural commune at Christina Gardens, a private housing estate in Arima, near Port of Spain. They rented a small bungalow about a hundred yards from Malik's house.

In 1971, André Deutsch launched Jamal's book: *From the Dead Level: Malcolm X and Me*. Frank Plugge met him on that occasion, and Jamal told him that he was God.

Frank responded with, "Why shouldn't *I* be God? What makes *you* God?"

Jamal called Gale over to him and hypnotised her. She became as stiff as a board, whereupon he supported her across two chairs and appeared to 'levitate' her.

"Why does that make you God?" asked Frank.

"Can *you* do that?" countered Jamal.

Frank shook his head.

"That's why I am God," came Jamal's reply.

Frank found his arrogance too much to take, but Gale was totally bowled over by him. She changed her name to Halé Kimga (an anagram of Gale and Hakim) and took to wearing African-style clothes. She referred to herself as Hakim's 'handmaiden', so besotted was she with him. She sold almost all her possessions and even asked Frank to dispose of the ornate English escritoire given to her by her parents as a wedding present. Frank paid her £100 but kept the beautiful walnut box, just in case she came to her senses. She didn't.

Jamal acknowledged Malik as his master and therefore had to subdue his claim to be God when in his presence. But Gale believed that her lover was God and that he should make this known to Malik, which caused friction. Gale, despite having been so influenced by these people, was not really accepted. She did not fit in well at the commune and was caught up in a world where she did not belong.

Malik ruled by spreading fear and he developed the notion that the spilling of blood would keep the commune together. He regarded Gale with deep suspicion and took against her. In December 1971, she was sent on a begging mission to Guyana. While she was away, Malik summoned Stanley Abbott, who was in London, to come to the commune. Jamal wanted some help and sent to the States for one of his 'co-workers', an African American known as Kidogo (a contract killer whose real name was Marvin Deane). Both men came to Trinidad as instructed.

Unsuccessful in her mission, Gale returned in time for Christmas. Malik invited Edward Chadee, an Indian car salesman, for the New Year. Another Indian, a boy called Adolphus Parmassar, was also staying at the commune with Malik. Steve Yeates, a young Trinidadian and close associate of Malik, was also there.

On the evening of January 1st, 1972, Malik gathered five men together at his house: Steve Yeates, Stanley Abbott, Kidogo, Parmassar and Chadee. He drew them into a private meeting and put it to them that Halé (Gale) was the cause of Jamal's mental strain and that she must be got rid of. Chadee fearfully kept quiet. Abbott suggested giving her a plane ticket back to England, but he went along with Malik's plan. By the end of the meeting, the men understood that Yeates was to take Gale to the farm to fetch the milk while the other four were to dig a hole in some waste ground two hundred feet from the house. The hole, to be dug in forty-five minutes, was to be four feet square and four feet deep. Malik did not tell them who was to kill Gale or how it was to be done. Jamal was to be kept out of it; Malik himself would take him for a drive.

Early the following morning, as ordered, Yeates took Gale to the farm – and Abbott, Kidogo, Parmassar and Chadee collected tools for digging and went to the waste ground. Malik arrived in his car and showed them where the hole was to be dug, next to a manure heap. Back at the car, Malik called Abbott over and gave him specific instructions as to how Gale was to be killed. Yeates would bring her back from the farm, and Abbott was to drag her into the hole. Kidogo already had his instructions to stab her in the heart with his cutlass. Malik explained that he and Jamal would be going to see Abbott's mother and that if Abbott went against the plan, he and his mother would die. Malik left and the hole was dug.

Steve Yeates arrived with Gale and she was invited to see what the men were doing. When she asked what the hole was for, Abbott said it was for fresh matter to be decomposed. He said, "Come and look. Do you like it?" She said, "Yes. But why?" Abbott grabbed her and jumped with her into the hole. Kidogo leapt in and – with Abbott holding onto her as she struggled violently – he stabbed at her wildly with his cutlass making superficial wounds and a deep cut in her arm. Gale pleaded desperately to Yeates, who was watching, "Steve, what have I done to deserve this?" But he did nothing to save her. Abbott, in the chaos, cried out for someone to help. Yeates then jumped into the hole, took the cutlass from Kidogo and drove it through Gale's neck. She collapsed and the three men got themselves out of the hole. Her legs were still thrashing about as the men began filling the hole.

The five men returned to Malik's house, and then Kidogo went to Gale and Jamal's bungalow, opposite, and bundled up her clothes and papers. The plan was to make it look as if she had packed and left. On the Guanapo River bank, Yeates, Abbott, Kidogo and Chadee set fire to Gale's things. Anything that would not burn was buried.

The Christina Gardens commune, now including Indians Chadee and Parmassar who had been made lifelong members on the night of the murder, stayed together for a short time before it started to break up. Trina Simmonds, Steve Yeates's girlfriend, started receiving threatening phone calls warning her to keep her mouth shut. In mid January, she returned to London to live in hiding.

Hakim Jamal was not involved in the actual killing. He claimed that he and Gale had argued and she had gone off. No one queried this and she was not missed. Jamal and Kidogo left Trinidad on January 20th – eighteen days after the murder – and went back to Boston. Jamal was quoted as making sentimental remarks about Gale, such as: "She was perhaps one of the greatest women that ever lived. She ought to have a statue in Hyde Park."

Five weeks after Gale's murder, a second killing took place at the Christina Gardens commune. Michael Malik, aided by Stanley Abbott, brutally murdered a rebellious negro recruit named Joe Skerritt on the February 8th because he refused to assist in the raid of a police station for arms. Abbott forced him into a pit where Malik chopped him on the neck with a machete and then smashed his head with a stone. They buried his body where it fell, not far from where Gale lay, in the same piece of waste ground.

Steve Yeates, who had so coldly murdered Gale, could not comprehend this killing of a black man. Two days later – February 10th – he went on a trip to the Sans Souci beach with some of the others and went swimming in the dangerous waters. Some witnesses said he was trying to rescue a drowning woman. The police suspected Malik of murdering him, but had no evidence. However, suicide could not be ruled out. Although someone threw him a rope, he made no attempt to reach for it. With a grimace, interpreted by some as a smile, he disappeared beneath the waves.

Abbott helped Chadee and Parmassar to escape and then went to Tobago and stayed with relatives. On February 19th, Malik and his family left for Guyana. That evening, the empty Malik house went up in flames.

Arson was suspected. The Trinidad police were on the scene and, this being the home of Michael X, they made a search for guns. What they found was Skerritt's body. Two days later – on February 24th – they discovered Gale's body where it had lain for more than seven weeks. The following day, the police phoned Lenny in Beverley Hills with the news and asked for identifying features. Lenny, distraught, managed to contact Greville who was in Mexico.

In London, Ann had been dining out with Frank and his girlfriend, Sammy. Molly Williams, Ann's friend of forty-five years had died a couple of months before, in December. Molly had been a shoulder to cry on when things became too hard to bear. She and her husband, Emlyn, had paid for holidays so that Ann could enjoy a break in their house in Corfu. Emlyn and his son Brook were supportive, but her beloved Molly was gone. She was planning to go out to Emlyn's house in Corfu.

Ann, Frank and Sammy came home to a telephone call. It was from a newspaper claiming to have a report that Gale had been found murdered. The family had not even known that she was in Trinidad. A telegram also arrived from Lenny for Frank, telling him to expect terrible news. Frank immediately contacted Scotland Yard and the Foreign Office to try to find out more, but no one could give much information.

It took Greville two and a half days to travel from Mexico City to Trinidad. By the time he arrived, Abbott, Chadee and Parmasser had been arrested and were behinds bars in Port of Spain. Greville went to the mortuary to identify his twin sister. The body of the young woman was so decomposed that it was impossible to be certain, but a gold filling provided the vital clue. In London, Frank contacted Gale's dentist who confirmed that Gale did have such a filling. The Trinidad authorities arranged for the dentist to be flown over to give a positive identification. The autopsy revealed that there was earth in her lungs and intestines: she had been alive when she was buried.

Malik, in Guyana, heard that Skerritt's body had been found. With his beard shaved off and wearing new clothes, he checked into a hotel under yet another new name and stayed in his room for three days. Close to breakdown, he learned from the newspapers, brought to him by the maid, that Gale's body had been found. Abandoning the hotel room, he took a taxi to Mackenzie (now known as Linden), and from there he fled into the interior. After another three days on the run, he was found hiding in an open shelter, cold and exhausted, and was arrested at dawn for the murder of Skerritt and flown back to Trinidad.

Despite his distress, Greville held a press conference. He arranged for Gale's body to be cremated on March 4th on the beach at Trinidad, and her ashes scattered over the sea. The dentist, Roland Knight, was the only other white man at the cremation. Among her personal effects, which Greville sent to London, was one of the last letters she had received from Lenny. It contained a poem by Lamartine that he had translated:

> On these white pages, where my verses unfold,
> May oft a souvenir, perchance your heart recall.
> Your life also only pure white pages behold,
> With one word, happiness, I would cover them all.
> But the book of life is a volume all sublime,
> That we cannot open, or close just at our time,
> On the page where one loves, one would wish to linger,
> Yet the page where one dies hides beneath the finger.

Greville, in a letter to Lenny from Trinidad, put his feelings into words:

> The whole terrible tragedy makes me sick to the stomach every
> time I think of it and brings tears to my eyes. Sometimes I can't
> help thinking of it, when people around me are making small talk
> and being superficial and bourgeois, and I think how irrelevant
> and trivial what they are saying is in the light of the terrible death
> that ended the life of such a beautiful girl.

Greville felt very strongly about the part that Hakim Jamal had played, and wanted the police to bring him in for questioning. Although he accepted that Jamal was not involved in the actual killing, he considered him morally responsible. He could not stand the thought that Jamal might be sitting in hiding somewhere, smirking that he had got off scot-free. It profoundly angered him – but he was not to know that Hakim Jamal was soon to meet with rough justice.

In the month after Gale's body was found, Frank and his mother left for Corfu. The next day, Greville arrived back in London and, a week later, he joined the others in Corfu where he spent a few days with Ann. He planned to go to Morocco and then fly to California to see Lenny, but he was invited to go sailing with an old girlfriend, Angela, around the shores of Greece. He took up the offer, hoping that it would help to put the past events behind him. Later, he headed off to Morocco and Spain and then travelled to the USA to spend some time with Maidee Walker, a girl from a rich Texas oil family.

Greville and Frank frequently wrote to Lenny, keeping him abreast of the news – and Lenny replied in his large scrawling hand. There were still many things to be sorted out in London, particularly regarding the sale of the remaining paintings. Frank, who was living at 702 Dolphin Square, had his hands full, including paying the bills and sending Lenny money whenever he could. The case continued against Charles Howard, the antique dealer, who was claiming ownership of several of the stolen paintings. Lenny's solicitors were still putting the evidence together to prove they belonged to him. The paintings, in the meantime, were in the hands of the police. This lawsuit had been dragging on since 1969. When the hearing eventually came, it would be necessary for Lenny to return to London.

Frank and Greville visited Lenny in California in July of 1972 and were pleased to find him in good form and well accommodated. He was still living in Burton Way, Beverley Hills and had surrounded himself with a large group of friends. He had bought a second-hand Simca car that turned out to be a disaster, but he was able to get his money back and buy a Chevrolet.

The two brothers then returned to their mother in Corfu, Frank taking his young son Dominic with them this time. Greville took Maidee who, when they returned to London, shared a flat with him for a while, unbeknown to her parents.

186

Frank had various schemes for making money. One idea was to buy sets of military buttons, give them a polish and mount them on card with the regiment's name to sell them to American tourists. He also had a line in erotic jewellery. This consisted of a ring on which was mounted a couple making love, which he reproduced at a cheap price and sold at a goodly profit. Lenny had passed on his entrepreneurial skills.

Greville had obtained an apartment in Morocco at Essaouira, a small seaside resort, about 100 miles from Marrakech. Maidee visited whenever she could and several of his friends would spend holidays there.

In Trinidad, Adolphus Parmassar, the Indian boy, admitted his guilt and turned state witness in return for immunity. In the autumn of 1972, Malik and Abbott were tried and sentenced for the murder of Joseph Skerritt. Malik was condemned to death by hanging. Abbott was given twenty years. Both men appealed.

The trial for Gale's murder took place the following year. Malik, already condemned, was charged with Gale's murder but was not tried. With Parmassar as a witness for the state, Steve Yeates drowned and Kidogo still missing, only two men were left on the stand – Stanley Abbott, already sentenced to twenty years, and Edward Chadee, the Indian car salesman. Abbott, present at both murders, was the only one tried for both. Each man was found guilty and sentenced to death by hanging. The convictions were controversial because some saw them as being hinged on the suspect confession of Parmassar who may have distorted his testimony to help the police to get the convictions they were after. Chadee's sentence was later commuted to life imprisonment. Abbott was to wait a long time for his sentence to be carried out.

On May 2nd, 1973 – sixteen months to the day after Gale's murder – Hakim Jamal was shot dead in front of his family by a black gang in Boston.

*

In late June 1973, Greville and his friend Peter Headley arranged to drive down from London to Morocco for a short vacation. Another friend, John Rendell, lent them his Mercedes van equipped with mattresses in the back for sleeping nights on the journey. John was to follow a few days later in the comfort of Peter's 3.5 litre Jaguar.

Greville arrived in Algeciras with Peter on July 5th and sent postcards to his mother in Corfu and his father in California. On their arrival in Essaouira, they were invited to a party with friends a few miles away. The party went with a swing, with local wine and the customary smoking of cannabis. Peter decided to leave in the early hours, jumped into the Mercedes, and set off back to Essaouira, not realising that Greville was already bedded down in the back.

Peter was not certain of the route in the dark and missed the turnoff. Intending to go back, he made a U-turn, but made it too close to the top of a hill. A truck hit the van full on. Greville was killed outright. Peter was thrown out and suffered severe lacerations to the face and a fractured skull.

Frank was in London when he received news of the tragedy. He took the first available flight to Casablanca, hired a car, and drove the 270 miles non-stop to Essaouira.

Ann was in Corfu and Frank phoned Emlyn to tell her. He also phoned Maidee's mother who informed Maidee in Aspen who then rang Lenny with whom she was in regular contact. The shock was terrible; he felt that he no longer wished to live. The family was devastated. Letters of condolence flooded in from all over the world.

Frank attended the funeral, which took place at Essaouira in Morocco at 4 pm on Thursday July 12th. In a letter dated August 26th, Maidee told Ann of her great love for Greville and of how they were planning to get married in the autumn.

Shortly after returning from Morocco, Frank was driving through north London when he was stopped by the police for a driving offence. The police searched him and found a wallet with a small tablet of LSD tucked into one corner. Frank was appalled and explained that the wallet had been among his deceased brother's effects brought back from Morocco. Luckily, the police believed him and he was released.

Peter Headley, the driver, was given a three-month suspended sentence and a fine. He never really recovered from the experience and later took to heroin. He died in South Africa in 2005.

*

Malik, condemned for Skerritt's murder and charged with Gale's, maintained that he was innocent of both killings. After several appeals, the last of which was to the Privy Council in London, he was hanged in the Royal Gaol in central Port of Spain on May 16th, 1975 for the murder of

Joseph Skerritt. Many people called for a reprieve, including John Lennon who donated one of his pianos to raise money. At the proposed time of the execution, the British press resurrected the whole sorry story, and it appeared in most newspapers. Frank recalls:

> On the day he was to be executed, LBC held a phone-in to which I
> added my contribution that he should hang. Just before the
> execution hour the radio announcer stated that he was about to go
> into the execution chamber. I was driving my car somewhere in
> the country. I stopped and waited until the announcer told the
> listeners that Michael X was now dead. I drove off with a feeling
> of deep satisfaction.

It was now three years and four months since Gale's death.

Stanley Abbott spent six years in a death cell. He was finally hanged on April 27th, 1979 for his part in Gale's murder.

Of the seven men linked to Gale's murder – Malik, Jamal, Yeates, Abbott, Kidogo, Chadee and Parmassar – only three survived. The Indian boy, Adolphus Parmassar, turned state witness to escape trial. Edward Chadee, the Indian car salesman, had his death sentence reduced to life imprisonment. Kidogo was never found. The other four lost their lives: Steve Yeates, the one who had delivered the fatal stab wound to Gale, drowned; Michael Malik (Michael X) hanged for murdering Skerritt; Stanley Abbott was sentenced to twenty years for Skerritt's murder and hanged for his part in killing Gale; Hakim Jamal, suspected of being involved in the planning of his girlfriend's death, was himself murdered.

14

1977-1996
The Final Years

Plugge's final years in Los Angeles
Headlines and gossip
"A man before his time"

Money remained very much a problem for Lenny. He had succeeded in getting a UK state pension as well as a pension granted to ex-Members of Parliament who have fallen on hard times. Although officially he was an illegal immigrant in the USA, he somehow managed to obtain Medicaid and Medicare there. He continued to send letters to Frank asking for money, and Frank sent him what he could afford, as had Greville before his death.

In his frustration at being unable to market the Plugge Patent Auto Circuit, and his disappointment at not receiving any recognition from his own country for the work he had done in broadcasting and politics, Lenny wrote to Prince Philip. In an annex to his letter, he told of his career and his inventions, as well as all the members of the nobility he had had the pleasure of meeting, including the Prince himself and several of his relatives.

> Reveu-ing [sic] all these Great Personalities, I cannot help
> mentioning your charming and Regal Father, the late Prince
> Andrew of Greece, who should have been King and who carried
> in his charm of manner, his great intelligence, his "savoir faire",
> his Royal Outlook, all the makings of a King and of a Great and
> Noble King. He was very proud of his son, of you, and often
> spoke to me about you in the most glowing terms. How right he
> was as events have shown, for you must have inherited very many
> of his attributes, which coupled with your own very personal
> Charm you have become the Idol of the British People.

(13 March 1977)

No reply has been found.

Lenny's enduring charm and charisma, coupled with his English manners, endeared him to the Americans. He was looked upon as a lovable old eccentric and was invited to many parties. Several of the Consul Generals included him on their reception lists. On one occasion, the British Consul

190

was expecting a visit from Prince Charles, and Lenny was invited to his reception. He told the Prince that he had known his grandfather, Prince Andrew of Greece. Prince Charles was most interested and asked him what he was like. Lenny related a few reminiscences and anecdotes, much to the Prince's delight.

On special occasions, Lenny wore the various honours and medals he had gained during his life – but the ribbon of the *Legion d'Honneur* he wore in his buttonhole all the time. Living quietly in Los Angeles on his reputation and charm, he still had his moments. Alan Whicker – in one of his globe-trotting programmes, transmitted in 1980 by Yorkshire Television – interviewed him as a representative of the ex-pat community in Hollywood. Lenny sat on a park bench, dressed in his dark suit and overcoat, complete with cane and Homburg hat in the scorching Californian sun, the epitome of the English eccentric. Few people watching that programme would have known what the old man had given to broadcasting or that his name was known worldwide in the twenties, thirties and forties.

April Ashley had left Hay-on-Wye and was now living in California. She recalled having dinner with Lenny at Oscars on Sunset Boulevard, Los Angeles. The ailing entrepreneur's companion was a neighbour, Malcolm Peters, who watched over him.

In a letter to Olive Newton on January 4th, 1979, Lenny wrote, "I am so glad that you have seen darling Ann and that she's looking so well and happy and is as always so beautiful."

Shortly after this, in the autumn of 1980, Lenny suffered a severe stroke, which left him badly afflicted. He died of bronchopneumonia and heart disease on February 19th, 1981 at the age of 91 in the Memorial Hospital of Glendale, Los Angeles. Some accounts state that countesses and several of the Californian society ladies were at his bedside to mourn his passing. In fact, he died alone.

In interviews with the author, Lenny is remembered with affection.

Bill Wood:

> Poor old Lenny, you don't know how much I miss him. I loved him. Full of fantastic ideas. When it came to negotiation, Lenny never did any; I did the lot. No good at business at all. I did the negotiation with solicitors and everyone else. (1982)

Bob Danvers-Walker:

KW: Did you consider that Plugge could be the doyen of commercial radio?

BDW: Without question. He had no predecessor in Europe. He was an entrepreneur, a man before his time. He envisaged the possibility of another form of wireless and broadcasting.

KW: What would you say were his main attributes as a man?

BDW: In a business world? Being able to visualise a good thing. Able to communicate that. He projected that into their thinking as well. He wanted everybody to be his 'yes men'.

(January 30th, 1983)

Anne Neville O'Brien first met Lenny in her early twenties:

It was at his flat in Dolphin Square one summer evening in 1966. I was taken by a friend I had met at a party. Lenny was in his late seventies with a background of real achievement.

I recall signing the famous visitors' book full of comments from the many famous visitors who had also enjoyed the experience of Diana's Hunting Lodge.

We became friends and he introduced me to the sophisticated London of the mid sixties: the best theatres, restaurants and parties. Always in great form, he knew absolutely everyone. He took me to the ballet and threw flowers on to the stage at the end. He took me backstage to meet the stars like Margot Fonteyn. Mostly we met in small groups, but occasionally I was his lady for the evening. He taught me a great deal. I have nothing but good to say about him. He was an excellent host and a kind and undemanding friend. He always saw the best in people. Although he was short in stature, he had a most impressive manner.

He threw fabulous parties at his large Lowndes Square house. His topics of conversation were riveting. Lenny was very much a night man and very generous to all his friends. (2007)

Anne's husband – her boyfriend at the time – also remembers Lenny as personable and imposing despite his small stature.

April Ashley reminisces:

I have so many happy memories of Lenny. Such a sweet person. A wonderful, wonderful sweet eccentric. Kind, sweet beyond words. He was a darling, darling man; you could not help but love him. Everybody loved him. I never met anyone who disliked him.

(May 2nd, 2007)

Since Molly's death in December 1971, Ann had taken over as Emlyn Williams's dresser, and accompanied him on his trips abroad. Later, she moved into his apartment in Doverhouse Street in Chelsea, but the relationship was strictly platonic.

A few happy years followed for Ann, who enjoyed her two grandchildren, Dominic from Frank's marriage to Gillian, and Francesca from his later marriage to Jenny, which also ended in divorce.

In 1989, a book was published in America entitled *A Woman Named Jackie*. The author, C. David Heyman, relates an affair that took place in East Hampton between Jack Bouvier and the young wife of a British army officer stationed in Washington. Ann and the family read the serialisation in *The Sunday Times*. Although the woman in question was not named, they knew very well who she was.

The book went on to record the trip Jackie had made to London in 1949 when she visited her father's former sweetheart and the two children. Also mentioned is a letter sent by Jackie to her father, commenting that the twins looked remarkably like him. Bouvier's reply to his daughter, who was living in Paris at the time, said:

> You are dead right about the Plugge twins. They definitely could not be his, and there is no question about it.

This gave rise to the idea that Bouvier was the father of Gale and Greville.

The interest in the story escalated when researchers from *The Sunday Times* discovered the identity of the 'young wife of a British army officer', and named Ann in the following week's episode. The article included pictures of Lenny, Ann, Jack Bouvier, Michael X and Gale. The story was juiced up with a headline: TRAGIC SECRET OF JACKIE'S BRITISH BROTHER AND SISTER.

Aged eighty, Ann was then living alone in her Doverhouse Street apartment, Emlyn having died. She was besieged by reporters knocking at the door and shouting through the letterbox, making her life a misery. When was the pain going to stop? She had looked back on her affair with Jack Bouvier as a period in her life when she had been happy; now it was nothing but fuel for gossip. She had suffered the loss of two of her children in the most dreadful circumstances and yet here were people trying to bring back the past to her in the cruellest manner, just for a story.

In the States a few weeks later, *The Star*, with a standing nowhere near that of *The Sunday Times*, lead with a front page headline – MYSTERIOUS MURDER OF JACKIE ONASSIS' SECRET SISTER – again based on the book.

Ann, assisted by Frank, took immediate steps and raised an action against the author and *The Sunday Times* for libel. Heyman stated that he took the information from John H. Davis's book *The Kennedy Clan*, published earlier the same year.

The crux of the assumption had come from the statement made in Jack Bouvier's letter to Jackie in 1950. No one had thought to check the dates: Ann and Lenny returned to England from America in June 1943 and the twins were born on November 4th, 1944. The book was full of inaccuracies.

The Sunday Times made a financial settlement out of court and published an apology.

Ann died of leukaemia on July 18th, 1993.

In 1996, Davis followed up with a second book: *Jacqueline Bouvier – An Intimate Memoir*. Again, there were serious inaccuracies. The assertion that the twins were fathered by Bouvier was repeated. To set the facts right, Frank entered into correspondence with the author. He made various points: Plugge's rank and title was Captain, not Colonel; at the time of the affair, he was an MP and no longer in the services; he had never stayed in Washington, and if he had been working there, Ann and Frank would have been with him and not in New York.

Davis issued an apology to Frank and promised that all future printings of his book would be corrected. This last instance illustrates how the story of Captain Leonard Plugge has been plagued with errors and confusions since his death in 1981.

At last, this biography tells the real and true story of an extraordinary life. Plugge will be remembered chiefly for his considerable achievements in the development of commercial radio. Inspired by wireless at an early age, chance events like meeting Le Grand on his visit to Fécamp, and his friend Bill Wood demonstrating to him a radio that he had built from a kit, set him firmly on the road to becoming a highly respected authority on all aspects of broadcasting.

His continental trips gave him first-hand knowledge of the problems surrounding broadcasting in Europe, and meant that he became personally acquainted with the heads of most of the major radio stations. He thus became an important voice in the discussions on the control of allotted wavelengths. His profound enthusiasm for the development and structuring of international broadcasting rivalled that of the more conventional John Reith.

The establishment of the IBC was the first challenge to the monopoly of the British Broadcasting Corporation, the livelier programmes from Radio Normandy being a particularly popular alternative to the BBC's rather staid weekend fare.

Aside from his broadcasting ventures, Lenny's ability as an inventor was demonstrated in the development of the car phone, road markings and the Plugge Patent Auto Circuit. As Bob Danvers-Walker said. "He was an entrepreneur, a man before his time."

Plugge was a man of immense energy, great enthusiasm and dedication. Regardless of his obvious failings, his irrepressible personality and charm ensured that his many friends regarded him with great affection. The suffering caused by the tragedies in his later life can only be imagined.

Regarding his successes in the development of commercial broadcasting, it was left to France and the USA to show appreciation, the former by awarding him the *Croix de Chevalier de la Legion d'Honneur*, and the latter by the bronze medallion presented by the NBC. Here at home he will always be remembered as, in the words of Seán Street,[1] "the true founding father of British commercial radio".

---

[1] *Crossing The Ether: Pre-War Public Service Radio and Commercial Competition in the UK* by Seán Street (John Libbey Publishing 2006).

APPENDIX A – IBC Station Data

Illustrating the build up of the stations where IBC had input and many of the changes of wavelengths

Times are approximate; this information is intended as a guide only. IBC speakers moved around between stations regularly; moves for short periods are not necessarily shown.

Summer time changes are ignored for the purpose of these listings.

Main sources of information are from IBC News Sheets, plus information provided from personal records of IBC staff.

SPEAKERS

E.E. Allen
Godfrey Bowen
W. Brown-Constable
A. Campbell
Nancy Crown
J.W. Cummins
Henry Cuthbertson
David Davies
Thorp Devereux
C.A. Dick
Norman Evans
J.L.R. Fellowes
H.V. Gee

S.H. Gordon-Box
H.K. Hitchcock
C.P. Hope
Ralph Hurcombe
William Evelyn Kingwell
Frank Lamping
Kenneth Maconochie
Benjy McNab
F. Miklavcic
P. Miklavcic
Ian Newman
E.J. Osterman
Roy Plomley

Tom Ronald
Allan Rose
John Selby
Faith Shipway
Max Stanniforth
W. Stewart-Saunders
John Sullivan
Bob Danvers-Walker
Stephen Williams
Graham Wilson
Hilary Wontner

Wavelength / Power		Dates	Days	Start Time		Speaker

FRANCE

RADIO FÉCAMP (Fécamp)

Wavelength / Power		Dates	Days	Start Time		Speaker
246m	0.5Kw	6 Sep 31	Sun	22.30	(2 hrs)	Kingwell
~	~	15 Nov 31	Sun	22.30	(3 hrs)	Kingwell
~	~	22 Nov 31	Sun	23.00	(2 hrs)	Kingwell
~	~	29 Nov 31	Sun	22.30	(3 hrs)	Kingwel
~	~	6 Dec 31	Sun	22.30	(1½ hrs)	Kingwell
~	~	19, 20 Dec 31	Sat & Sun	19.00	(1 hr)	Stanniforth & Kingwell
				22.30	(3½ hrs)	
~	~	27 Dec 31 to 24 Jan 32	Sun	18.30	(1½ hrs)	Stanniforth
				22.30	(4½ hrs)	

FRANCE cont.

RADIO NORMANDY (Fécamp)

Wavelength / Power		Dates	Days	Start Time	Speaker
~	10Kw	30 Jan 32	Sat	00.00 (3 hrs)	Stanniforth
~	~	31 Jan-14 Feb 32	Sun	18.30 (1½ hrs)	Stanniforth
				22.30 (½ hr)	
		20 Feb 32	Sat	03.00 First *Grand Goodnight*	Stanniforth
~	~	21 Feb 32	Sun	18.30 (1½ hrs)	Stanniforth & Williams
				21.30 (5½ hrs)	
~	~	27 Feb 32	Sat	00.00 (3 hrs)	
~	~	29 Feb-4 Mar 32	M-Fri	12.00 (1 hr)	Stanniforth & Williams
223m	~	5 Jun 32	Sun	14.00 (1 hr)	Stanniforth & Williams
				23.00 (2 hrs)	
226m	20Kw	2 Apr 33	Sun	16.00 (11 hrs)	Danvers-Walker,
~	~	From 3 Apr 33	M-Sat	17.00 (10 hrs)	McNab & Lamping
200m	~	21&28 Jan 34	Sun	08.45 (5¼ hrs)	Ronald, McNab,
~	~	22 Jan-3 Feb 34	M-Sat	11.00 (1 hr)	Sullivan & Stanniforth
				15.30 (2½ hrs)	
				22.00 (4 hrs)	
206m	~	From 4 Feb 34	Sun	08.45 (5¼ hrs)	Ronald, McNab,
~	~	From 5 Feb 34	M-Sat	11.00 (1 hr)	Sullivan & Stanniforth
				15.30 (2½ hrs)	
				22.00 (4 hrs)	
269.5m	~	From 14 Apr 35	Sun	08.15 (3¾ hrs)	Danvers-Walker,
				14.00 (5 hrs)	Campbell & Osterman
				21.30 (3½ hrs)	
~	~	From 15 Apr 35	M-Sat	08.15 (½ hrs)	
				16.30 (1½)	
				23.00 (2 hrs)	
~	~	From 21 Jul 35	Sun	08.00 (4 hrs)	Danvers-Walker,
				14.00 (5 hrs)	Osterman & McNab
				21.30 (4½ hrs)	
~	~	22-27 Jul 35	M-Sat	08.00 (1 hr)	
				16.30 (1½ hrs)	
				23.00 (3 hrs)	
~	~	From 19 Aug 35	M-sat	As above	Danvers-Walker,
					Osterman & Cummins

RADIO NORMANDY (Louvetot)

Wavelength / Power		Dates	Days	Start Time	Speaker
212.6m	~	27 Mar 38		*Programmes continued with very*	
274m	~	25 Dec 38		*similar timings. Speakers varied.*	

Wavelength / Power		Dates	Days	Start Time		Speaker
RADIO PARIS (Paris)						
1725m	75Kw	29 Nov 31	Sun	23.00	(1 hr)	
~	~	6 Nov 32	Sun	13.00	(1 hr)	
				15.00	(1 hr)	
~	~	2 Apr 33	Sun	14.00	(2 hrs)	Ronald
				17.30	(½ hr)	
~	~	16 Apr 33	Sun	15.00	(2 hrs)	Ronald & Williams
~	~	30 Apr 33	Sun	15.00	(2 hrs)	Ronald & Williams
				18.30	(½ hr)	
~	~	7 May 33	Sun	17.00	(2 hrs)	Williams
~	~	14 & 21 May 33	Sun	14.00	(5 hrs)	Williams
~	~	4 & 11 Jun 33	Sun	14.00	(1 hr)	Williams
				18.00	(1 hr)	
				22.00	(½ hr)	
~	~	18 Jun 33	Sun	14.30	(½ hr)	Brown-Constable
				22.30	(½ hr)	
~	~	25 Jun & 2 Jul 33	Sun	17.30	(½ hr)	Brown-Constable
				22.30	(½ hr)	
~	~	16 & 23 Jul 33	Sun	22.30	(½ hr)	Williams
~	~	30 Jul 33	Sun	13.30	(5½ hrs)	McNab
				22.30	(½ hr)	
~	~	6-27 Aug 33	Sun	22.30	(¾ hr)	Williams
~	~	3 Sep-5 Nov 33	Sun	13.30	(2 hrs)	Ronald, Shipway & Dick
~	~	12-26 Nov 33	Sun	13.30	(2¾ hrs)	McNab & Dick
POSTE PARISIEN (Paris)						
328m	60Kw	17 Dec 33	Sun	22.30	(½ hr)	
~	~	24 Dec 33	Sun	18.15	(½ hr)	
~	~	31 Dec 33	Sun	18.00	(¾ hr)	
~	~	7 Jan 34	Sun	18.15	(½ hr)	
				22.30	(1 hr)	
~	~	14 Jan 34	Sun	18.00	(¾ hr)	
				22.30	(1 hr)	
312m	~	21 Jan 34	Sun	17.30	(1¼ hrs)	Ronald
~	~	28 Jan 34	Sun	18.15	(½ hr)	Ronald
				22.30	(1 hr)	
~	~	4 Feb 34	Sun	17.45	(1 hr)	Ronald
				22.30	(1 hr)	
~	~	From 11 Feb 34	Sun	17.00	(1¾ hrs)	Ronald
				22.30	(1 hr)	
~	~	18 Mar 34	Sun	17.00	(1¾ hrs)	Ronald
				22.30	(1 hr)	

Wavelength / Power		Dates	Days	Start Time	Speaker
				FRANCE POSTE PARISIEN cont.	
~	~	25 Mar 34	Sun	17.00 (1¾ hrs)	Ronald
				22.30 (½ hr)	
				Sunday broadcasts continued at similar times.	
				McNab took over as Speaker on 20 May 34	
	100Kw	20 May 34	Sun	17.30 (1 hr)	McNab
				22.30 (1 hr)	
~	~	24 Jun 34	Sun	17.30 (1 hr)	McNab
				22.30 (1 hr)	
~	~	25-30 Jun 34	M-Sat	22.30 (½ hr)	McNab & Hope
~	~	30 Sep 34	Sun	17.00 (2hrs)	Sullivan
				22.30 (1¼ hrs)	
~	~	From 28 Oct 34	Sun	16.30 (2½ hrs)	Sullivan
				22.30 (1¼ hrs)	
~	~	29 Oct 34	M-Sat	22.30 (½ hr)	
		6&15 Nov 34		*No broadcasts*	
~	~	From 12 Nov 34	M-Sat	22.30 (1¼ hrs)	Sullivan
~	~	From 24 Feb 35	Sun	17.00 (2 hrs)	Sullivan
				22.30 (1½ hrs)	
~	~	15 Mar 36	Sun	~	Danvers-Walker
~	~	29 Nov 36	Sun	~	Plomley
~	~	25 Apr 37	Sun	~	Sullivan
~	~	20 Jun 37	Sun	18.00 (1 hr)	Sullivan
				22.30 (½ hr)	
~	60Kw	15 Aug 37	Sun		Sullivan
~	~	*From 24 Apr 38	Sun	09.00 (2 hrs)	Sullivan
				16.45 (2¼ hrs)	
				21.00 (2 hrs)	
~	~	25-30 Apr 38	M-Sat	09.00 (2 hrs)	
~	60Kw	6-11 Jun 38	M-Sat	09.00 (2 hrs)	Sullivan
				22.30 (½ hr)	
~	~	20-25 Jun 38	M-Th,Sat	09.00 (2 hrs)	Rose
				22.30 (½ hr)	
~	~	24 Jun 38	Friday	09.00 (2 hrs)	
~	~	*From 4 Jul 38	M, W, Sat	9.00 (2 hrs)	Rose
				22.30 (½ hr)	
~	~	*From 7 Jul 38	Th, Fri	09.00 (2 hrs)	
				Similar timings continued	
				until close down in 1939	Rose

Wavelength / Power		Dates	Days	Start Time		Speaker
RADIO TOULOUSE (Toulouse)						
385m	8Kw	From 18 Oct 31	Sun	22.40	(½ hr)	
~	~	From 2 Apr 33	Sun	17.30	(½ hr)	Brown-Constable
				21.30	(1½ hrs)	
~	~	From 3 Apr 33	M-W F,St	22.30	(½ hr)	
~	~	6 Apr 33	Thur	22.30	(1 hr)	
~	~	From 16 Apr 33	Sun	18.30	(½ hr)	Brown-Constable
				22.30	(1½ hrs)	
~	~	17-22 Apr 33	M-W F,St	23.30	(½ hr)	
~	~	From 20 Apr 33	Thur	23.00	(1 hr)	
~	~	8-13 May 33	M-Sat	23.30	(½ hr)	Brown-Constable
RADIO TOULOUSE (St Agnan)						
~	~	17-22 Jul 33	M-Sat	*No Broadcast*		
~	~	23 Jul 33	Sun	18.30	(½ hr)	Ronald
				22.30	(1½ hrs)	
~	~	24-29 Jul 33	M-Sat	23.30	(½ hr)	Ronald
~	~	30 Jul-5 Aug 33	Sun-Sat	*Broadcasts suspended*		
RADIO CÔTE D'AZUR (Juan-les-Pins)						
249.6m	10Kw	2 Apr 33	Sun	21.30	(1½ hrs)	Hitchcock
~	~	3-8 Apr 33	M-Sat	23.00	(1 hr)	
~	~	16 Apr 33	Sun	22.30	(½ hr)	Hitchcock
				00.00	(½ hr)	
~	~	From 17 Apr 33	M-Sat	00.00	(1 hr)	
~	~	From 23 Apr 33	Sun	22.30	(2½ hrs)	Hitchcock
~	~	From 11 Jun 33	Sun	22.30	(2½ hrs)	Hitchcock
~	~	12 Jun 33	*All weekday programmes cancelled*			
222.6m	~	21 Jan 34	Sun	22.30	(2½ hrs)	
240m	~	From 11 Feb 34	Sun	22.30	(2½ hrs)	
235.1m	~	From 21 Jun 36	Sun	22.30	(2½ hrs)	
~	~	6 Dec 36	Sun	17.00	(1¼ hrs)	
				22.30	(1 hr)	
~	~	4 Apr 37	Sun	16.00	(1½ hrs)	
				21.30	(1 hr)	
RADIO MÉDITERRANÉE (Juan-les-Pins)						
~	27Kw	18 Apr 37 to 30 Jan 38	Sun	22.30	(2½ hr)	

YUGOSLAVIA

RADIO LJUBLJANA

Wavelength / Power		Dates	Days	Start Time	Speaker
574.7m	7Kw	From 5 Apr 33	Wed	17.00 (½ hr)	Miklavcic, P
~	~	From 5 Jul 33	Wed	17.30 (½ hr)	Miklavcic, P
~	~	From 26 Jul 33	Wed	21.30 (½ hr)	Miklavcic, P
~	~	From 17 Oct 33	Tue	21.30 (½ hr)	Miklavcic, P
569m	~	From 16 Jan 34	Tue	21.30 (½ hr)	Miklavcic, P
~	~	8 Feb 36	Sat	*Broadcasts suspended*	
~	~	From 20 Mar 36	Fri	21.30 (½ hr)	
~	~	From 24 Apr 36	Fri	22.30 (½ hr)	
~	~	From 9 Oct 36	Fri	21.30 (½ hr)	Miklavcic, F
~	~	From 23 Apr 37	Fri	22.30 (½ hr)	Miklavcic, F
~	~	From 30 May 37	Sun	23.30 (½ hr)	Miklavcic, F
~	~	11 Jun 37	Fri	21.30 (½ hr)	Miklavcic, F
~	~	From 25 Jun 37	Fri	22.30 (½ hr)	Miklavcic, F
~	~	From 15 Oct 37	Fri	21.30 (½ hr)	Miklavcic, F
~	~	From 15 Apr 38	Fri	22.30 (½ hr)	Miklavcic, F
~	~	26 Aug 38	Fri	22.15 (½ hr)	Miklavcic, F
~	~	From 9 Sep 38	Fri	22.30 (½ hr)	Miklavcic, F
~	~	18 Nov 38	Fri	22.15 (½ hr)	Miklavcic, F
~	~	2 Dec 38	Fri	21.20 (½ hr)	Miklavcic, F
~	~	9 Dec 38	Fri	21.30 (½ hr)	Miklavcic, F
~	~	7 Apr 39	Fri	*No Broadcast*	

IRELAND

RADIO ATHLONE (Eire)

Wavelength / Power		Dates	Days	Start Time	Speaker
413m	60Kw	From 11 Sep 33	M-Sat	21.30 (1 hr)	Hope
224m	1Kw	*Relayed by Dublin*			
217m	1Kw	*Relayed by Cork*			
		From 19 Nov 33	Sun	13.00 (3 hrs)	Hope
531m	60Kw	14 Jan 34	Sun	*No Broadcast*	
241.9m	1Kw				
222m	1Kw				
~	~	15-20 Jan 34	M-Sat	21.30 (1 hr)	Hope
~	~	21 Jan 34	Sun	13.00 (3 hrs)	Hope
~	~	From 22 Jan 34	M-Sat	21.30 (1 hr)	
~	~	From 26 May 34		*Broadcasts suspended*	

Wavelength / Power		Dates	Days	Start Time		Speaker

SPAIN

EAQ (SW) (Aranjuez)
30m	20Kw	1-7 Oct 33	Sun-Sat	01.00	(½ hr)	Gordon-Box
~	~	8-14 Oct 33	Sun-Sat	00.00	(½ hr)	Gordon-Box
~	~	19-25 Nov 33	Sun-Sat	00.00	(½ hr)	Danvers-Walker
~	~	From 4 Mar 34	Sun & Sat	00.00	(½ hr)	Danvers-Walker
~	~	27 May 34	Sun,T,T,Sat	01.00	(½ hr)	Danvers-Walker
~	~	16 Sep 34	Sun,T,T,Sat	00.00	(½ hr)	Gordon-Box

EAQ (SW) (Madrid)
30m	20Kw	23 Sep 34	Sun,T,T,Sat	00.00	(½ hr)	Gordon-Box
~	~	10 Mar 35	Sun only	00.00	(½ hr)	Gordon-Box
~	~	4 Aug 35	Sun only	00.00	(½ hr)	Allen
~	30.43Kw	27 Dec 36	Sun only	00.00	(½ hr)	Allen
~	31.65Kw	25 Apr 37	Sun only	00.00	(½ hr)	Allen
~	~	24 Oct 37	Sun only	*Broadcasts suspended*		

UNION RADIO (Madrid)
424m	15Kw	1 Oct 33	Sun	02.00	(1 hr)	Gordon-Box & Danvers-Walker
~	~	8 Oct 33	Sun	01.00	(1 hr)	Gordon-Box & Danvers-Walker
~	~	From 10 Oct 33	Tu & Th	01.00	(1 hr)	
293m	15Kw	14 Jan 34	Sun			Gordon-Box & Danvers-Walker
274m	~	21 Jan 34	Sun			Gordon-Box & Danvers-Walker
~	~	28 Feb 35	Thur	01.00	(1 hr)	*Last broadcast*

RADIO SAN SEBASTIAN
453m	0.6Kw	From 11 Dec 33	Mon	01.00	(1 hr)	Gordon-Box & Danvers-Walker
~	1Kw	11 Jan 34	Th			Gordon-Box & Danvers-Walker
238m	~	22 Jan 34	Mon			Gordon-Box & Danvers-Walker
~	~	25 Feb 35	Mon	01.00	(1 hr)	*Last broadcast*

RADIO BARCELONA
252m	1Kw	From 13 Dec 33	W, Sat	01.00	(1 hr)	Gordon-Box & Danvers-Walker
274m	8Kw	11 Jan 34	Thur			Gordon-Box & Danvers-Walker
377m	~	24 Jan 34	Wed			Gordon-Box & Danvers-Walker
~	~	2 Mar 35	Sat	01.00	(1 hr)	*Last broadcast*

RADIO VALENCIA
267m	1.5Kw	From 15 Dec 33	Fri	01.00	(1 hr)	Gordon-Box & Danvers-Walker
352.9m	2Kw	11 Jan 34	Thur			Gordon-Box & Danvers-Walker
		24 Feb 35	Sun	01.00	(1 hr)	*Last broadcast*

Wavelength / Power		Dates	Days	Start Time	Speaker

ITALY

RADIO ROME

Wavelength / Power		Dates	Days	Start Time	
420.8m	50Kw	From 16 Sep 34	Sun	20.00 (½ hr)	*Trial*
~	~	From 7 Oct 34	Sun	19.15 (½ hr)	*Trial*
~	~	28 Oct 34	Sun	19.00 (½ hr)	*Last broadcast*

Appendix B – IBC Postwar

Popular Artists

Chris Barber	Gracie Fields	Johnny Ray
Shirley Bassey	Judy Garland	The Rolling Stones
The Beatles	Edmond Hockridge	Mike Sammes
Acker Bilk	Peter Knight	Ann Shelton
Petula Clark	Cleo Laine	Dorothy Squires
Russ Conway	Julie London	Cyril Stapleton
John Dankworth	Norman Luboff	Wally Stott
Lonnie Donegan	Jane Mansfield	Frankie Vaughan
Diana Dors	Bill McGuffie	The Who
Robert Farnon	Max Miller	
Adam Faith	Nana Mouskouri	

Classical Artists

Julian Bream	Leon Goossens	Max Steiner
Frank Cordell	Leslie Jones	Sidney Torch
Colin Davis	Muir Mathieson	John Williams
Geraint Evans	Peter Pears	
Sir Eugene Goossens	Stanford Robinson	

Orchestras

Ambrosian Singers	New Philharmonia
English Chamber Orchestra	Pro Arte
Hallé Orchestra	Royal Danish Orchestra
London Symphony Orchestra	Royal Philharmonic Orchestra
London Philharmonic Orchestra	

Facilities

Studio A – up to 40 musicians	Technical Department
Studio B – up to 10 musicians	General Office
Assembly Room (editing, etc)	Two acoustic echo chambers
Two master disc cutting rooms	Two echo plates

In-house Recording Equipment

Ampex 300/3s	EMI BTR 1s	Mobile equipment
Ampex 300/2s	EMI BTR 2s	Lyrec Disc Cutting
Ampex 350/2s	EMI TR90s	Neurmann Disc Cutting

Bibliography

ASHLEY, April & FALLOWELL, D:
  April Ashley's Odyssey (London: Jonathan Cape, 1982)

BOYLE, Andrew:
  Only the Wind will Listen (London: Hutchinson, 1972

BRIGGS, Asa:
  The History of Broadcasting in the United Kingdom – Volume 1: *The Birth of Broadcasting* (London: Oxford University Press, 1961)

BRIGGS, Asa:
  The History of Broadcasting in the United Kingdom Volume 2: *The Golden Age of Wireless* (London: Oxford University Press, 1965)

BRIGGS, Asa:
  The History of Broadcasting in the United Kingdom Volume 3: *The War of Words* (London: Oxford University Press, 1970

BRIGGS, Susan:
  Those Radio Times (London: Weidenfeld and Nicolson, 1981

CRABTREE, R.:
  The Luxury Yacht – From Steam to Diesel (David & Charles, 1973)

DAVIS, John H:
  Jacqueline Bouvier – An Intimate Memoir
  (New York: John Wiley, 1996)

DAVIS, John H:
  The Kennedy Clan (London: Sidgwick & Jackson, 1985)

DEAN, Sir Maurice:
  Royal Air Force and Two World Wars (London: Cassell, 1979)

DONOVAN, Paul:
  The Radio Companion (London: Harper Collins, 1991)

GIFFORD, Denis:
  The Golden Age of Radio (London: Batsford, 1985)

GILBERT, Martin:
  Churchill: A Life (London: Heinemann, 1991)

GILBERT, Martin:
  Never Despair: Winston Churchill 1945-1965 (London: Heinemann, 1988)

GUINNESS,
  Jon and Catherine: *The House of Mitford* (London: Hutchinson, 1984)

HERSH, Seymour M:
  The Dark Side of Camelot (New York: Little, Brown & Co. 1997)

HEYMAN, C. David:
  A Woman Named Jackie (London: Heinemann, 1989)

IBC:
This is the I.B.C. (London: International Broadcasting Company, 1939)

KAMM, Antony and BAIRD, Malcolm:
John Logie Baird – A Life (National Museum of Scotland Publishing, 2002)

LEMAITRE, Jean:
Allo! Allo! Ici Radio Normandie (Paris: Durand et Fils, 1984)

LEWIS, Cecil A.:
Never Look Back (London: Hutchinson, 1974)

LEWIS, Peter:
The 50s (London: Heinemann, 1978)

MATTHEW, C.:
A Different World – Stories of Great Hotels (London: Paddington Press, 1976)

McARTHUR, Tom and WADDELL, Peter:
The Secret Life of John Logie Baird (London: Hutchinson, 1986. Reprinted by Orkney Press in 1990 as Vision Warrior: The Hidden Achievement of John Logie Baird)

NAIPUL, V.S:
'Michael X and the Black Power Killings in Trinidad' in *The Return of Eva Peron with The Killings in Trinidad* (London: André Deutsch, 1980)

NICHOLSON, T.R.:
The Age of Motoring Adventure 1897-1939 (London: Cassell, 1972)

NOBBS, George: *The Wireless Stars* (Norwich: Wensum Books, 1972)

PARKIN, Molly: *The Making of Molly Parkin* (London: Victor Gollancz, 1993)

PIDGEON, Geoffrey:
The Secret Wireless War (UPSO, 2003)

PLOMLEY, Roy:
Days Seemed Longer: Early Years of a Broadcaster (London: Eyre Methuen, 1980)

REDGRAVE, Dierdre:
To be a Redgrave: The Inside Story of a Marriage (London: Robson Books, 1983)

SMITH, Anthony:
British Broadcasting (Newton Abbot: David & Charles, 1974)

WEST, W.J:
Truth Betrayed (London: Duckworth, 1987)

WILSON, Colin and SEAMAN, Donald:
Encyclopaedia of Modern Murder 1962-82 (London: Arthur Barker, 1983)

Index

2LO: 24, 25, 28, 32, 34, 38, 65
3AR: 91
3LO: 91
6BM: 29
Abbott, Stanley: 182, 183, 184, 185, 187, 189
Accademia di Belli Arti: 171
Adam (servant): 142
Aeronautical Committee: 150
Aeronautical Society, Royal: 19, 121, 142
Aether I (Paige): 34
Aether II (Packard): 42, 43, 44, 45, 47, 51, 56, 61, 64
Aether III (Standard): 62, 63, 64, 65, 68
Aether IV (SS1): 87
Aether V (SS1): 87
Aether VI (SS1): 87, 100, 103, 106, 123
Airtime: 128
Aldiss, Barry: 10
Alfonso, King: 36
Alfred, Mr: 70
Alfredo: 119
Allen E.E.: 197, 203
Allen, W.E.D.: 109
Ambrosian Singers: 204
Anderson, Sir John: 126
Andrew of Greece, Prince: 190, 191
Angela (friend): 186
Annersley, Lord: 120
Annigoni, Pietro: 170
Ansiaux: 170
Aquitania: 101
Arnold, Tommy: 155
Arvad, Inga Marie: 139
Ashfield, Grace: 20
Ashfield, Lord: 20, 21, 69, 103, 161
Ashfield, Miriam: 20
Ashley, April: 171, 172, 191, 192
Asquith, Lord: 147
Auchincloss, Hugh: 141
Auntie Diana [Stanniforth]: 85
Auntie Muriel: 84
Australian Broadcasting Company: 91
Auto: 37, 38
Autocar, The: 38, 101
Automobile Association: 34, 178
Baird Televisor: 32
Baird, John Logie: 32, 75
Bajer, Peter Paul: 145
Balkans: 43, 44, 45, 50, 61
Barber, Chris: 204
Barjou, Mme Jacques: 172

Baruch, Bernard: 138, 139
Bassey, Shirley: 204
Batchelor, Horace: 10
Batey, Mr: 107
BBC (British Broadcasting Company): 10, 11, 23, 24, 25, 27, 28, 29, 30, 32, 37, 40, 42
BBC (British Broadcasting Corporation): 9, 64, 66, 69, 80, 83, 87, 88, 89, 90, 95, 96, 97, 98, 106, 108, 109, 110, 112, 116, 118, 119, 124, 127, 128, 129, 131, 135, 142, 150, 152, 153, 158, 195
Beal, Gilbert: 120
Beardmores of Coatbridge: 23
Beatles, The: 169, 204
Beaverbrook, Lord: 151
Bebis: 58
Beddington, Mrs Claude: 20, 103
Bee Gees, The: 169
BEF (British Expeditionary Force): 130, 131
Belfast Telegraph: 113
Belles of Normandy: 120
Belloc, Hilaire: 165
Benedictine: 71, 72, 76, 134
Benson, Gale (Nee Plugge): 171, 172, 180-189, 193
Benson, Jonathan: 171, 180
Berman, Bromislav: 168
Berman, Dr Joseph: 168
Bibo, Irving: 77
Biggs (Le Grand): 83, 92
Bilk, Acker: 204
Birdwood, Field Marshall Lord: 130
Bishop of Durham: 93
Black Museum: 157
Black Power: 180, 181
Blériot, Louis: 66
Blighty magazine: 131
Bloch, Marie Louis: 100
Blue Danube, The: 48
Bottomley, Arthur: 140, 150
Bouvier family: 140
Bouvier, Jack: 139, 140, 142, 143, 145, 193, 194
Bouvier, Jackie: 140, 141, 145, 162, 193, 194
Bouvier, John Vernou: 140
Bouvier, Lee: 140, 141, 145, 162
Bowen, Godfrey: 197
Bowlly, Al: 114
Braun, Lazar: 164
Bream, Julian: 204
Breton, Michele: 173, 174
Bristol Brabazon: 20

207

British Gazette, The: 40
British Worker, The: 40
Broadcast Over Britain: 89
Broadcast Records: 82
Broadcasting Act, 1990 : 9
Broadcasting House: 69, 118
Bromley, Mr: 120
Brother, can you spare a dime?: 103
Brown and Starr: 118
Brown, Mick: 174
Brown-Constable, W.: 197, 199, 201
Brusset, Marie: 137
Brusset, Max: 134, 136, 137, 138, 160, 161
BSA (Birmingham Small Arms): 162, 163
Buckingham, Earl of (Robert Hobart): 120
Burgess cartoon: 119
Burgess, Guy: 127
Burrows, Arthur: 23, 29
Busby, George: 131, 135
Butler, Rab: 142
Callingham, Lance: 163
Cammell, David: 173, 174, 175
Cammell, Donald: 173
Campbell Steven, The Reverend: 112
Campbell, A.: 197, 198
Campbell, Nina: 155
Canadian Broadcasting Corporation: 105
Candid Camera: 169
Candid Mike: 169
Cannes: 28, 116, 120, 124, 127, 136, 138, 154, 163
Cantor, Eddie: 103
Capital Radio: 9
Capitol: 10
Carlton Club: 172
Caudebec Chateau: 125, 126
Caudebec-en-Caux: 124
Celebrity Concert: 98
Cercle: 155
Chadee, Edward: 182, 183, 184, 185, 187, 189
Chamberlain, Neville: 124
Chambers, Peter: 164
Champness, Mrs: 64
Charles, Prince : 191
Chase: 17, 147
Chateau d'Epone: 137, 161
Chatham Observer: 117
Chenhalls, Alfred: 144
Children's Hour (BBC): 83
Christian Peace Movement: 129
Christian Science Monitor: 37
Christina Gardens: 142, 181, 183, 184
Churchill, Randolph: 142

Churchill, Sarah: 171
Churchill, Winston: 40, 138, 144, 151, 152
Churchill's Bodyguard: 144
Citizen Kane: 102
Claridges: 164
Clark, Petula: 204
Classic Beauty Preparations: 81
Clews, Henry: 120
Clore, Alan: 172
Clum: 146
CNR (Canadian National Railways): 42
Compagnie Francais de Radiophonie, La: 70
Compagnie Luxembourgoise de Radio Diffusion: 113, 114
Concours d'Elegance: 100, 154
Connell, Horace: 64, 169
Conrad, Con: 77
Conservative [Party]: 90, 105, 106, 107, 117, 118, 138, 139, 151
Conservative Association, Rochester and Chatham Joint : 105, 117, 118
Conway, Russ: 204
Cordell, Frank: 204
Cottesmore School: 148
Court Circular: 172
Cripps, Stafford: 112, 151
Crofton, Bill: 91, 92
Cross, Cynthis: 42
Crossing The Ether: Pre-War Public Service Radio and Commercial Competition in the UK: 195
Crown, Nancy: 197
CTS Studios: 161
Cummins, J.W.: 197, 198
Cunningham, Marquis: 121
Cunningham-Reid, Captain A.S.: 139
Cuthbertson, Henry: 197
Daily Express: 101
Daily Mail: 66, 67, 75
Daily Mirror: 117
Daily Sketch: 164
Daily Telegraph, The: 74
Daisy Bell: 107
Dan Dare, Pilot of the Future, The Adventures of: 10
Dankworth, John: 204
Danvers-Walker, Bob: 87, 91, 92, 94, 131, 135, 192, 195, 197, 198, 200, 203
Dark Side of Camelot, The: 139
Daventry: 35, 36, 57, 96
Davies, David: 135, 197
Davies, Sir Alfred: 105
Davis, Colin: 204

Davis, John H.: 194
Davis, Marion: 102
Days Seemed Longer: 118, 136
de Freitas, Michael (Malik): 180
de Gaulle, General Charles: 142
de Gennes, Count and Countess Jean: 172
de Groot's Orchestra: 27
de Losinga: 77
Deane, Bill: 124, 147
Deane, Marvin (Kidogo): 182
Decca: 10, 158, 168, 169
Deutsch, André: 181
Devereux, Thorp: 197
Diana's Hunting Lodge: 153, 159, 169, 171, 172,
    179, 192
Dick, C.A.: 197, 199
Dobson, Cowan: 118
Docker, Lady Norah: 162, 163
Docker, Mrs B.: 120
Docker, Sir Bernard: 162, 163
Dockyard Committee: 150
Dodd, Ashley: 120
Dolin, Anton: 170
Dolphin Square: 153, 155, 165, 169, 171, 172,
    179, 186, 192
Donaldson, Allen (Hakim Jamal): 180
Donegan, Lonnie: 204
Donner, Mrs Gerald: 120
Doran, E: 90
Dorothy: 15, 44, 49, 60, 61
Dors, Diana: 204
Douglas, Lady Cecil: 164
Douglas, Susan: 164
Drew, Felicity: 164
Dunstan, Eric: 96
EAQ Aranjuez: 82, 94, 97, 203
EAQ Madrid: 104, 203
East Hampton: 139, 140, 193
Eckersley, Frances: 128
Eckersley, Peter: 23, 109, 128
Edgar, Molly: 120
Edward (servant): 156, 172
Edward VIII, King : 117
Egan, Patrick: 101
Egyptian Gazette, The: 126
Eiffel Tower station: 31, 32, 33, 37, 38, 44
Elizabeth II, Queen: 170
Elizabeth, Princess: 121
Elizabeth, Queen (Queen Mother): 127
EMI: 152, 158, 168, 169
Empire Broadcasting: 44
English Chamber Orchestra: 204

ENSA (Entertainments National Service
    Association): 144, 152
Entre Rios Railway Company: 74
Era, The: 86
Erica: 170
Ernie: 173, 175
Ethel: 44, 57, 58
Evans, Captain Arthur: 115
Evans, Geraint: 204
Evans, Norman: 197
Evening News: 66, 67
Evening Standard: 164
Everett, Geoffrey: 153
Faith, Adam: 204
Farnon, Robert: 204
Fécamp: 71, 73, 75, 76, 77, 78, 80, 81, 83, 85,
    87, 91, 92, 93, 95, 115, 116, 120, 124, 130,
    131, 134, 135, 137, 194, 197, 198
Fellowes, J.L.R.: 197
Fenwick, Gordon: 67
Fields, Gracie: 96, 204
Fletcher, Harry: 119
Florence: 44, 50, 61
Flotsam and Jetsam: 96
Flynn, Errol: 161
Fonteyn, Margot: 172, 192
Forester Agar, Mrs: 120
Fox, James: 173
Fragson, Harry: 65
Franckenstein, Baron Clement: 172
From the Dead Level: Malcolm X and Me: 181
Frost, George: 33
Gainsborough, Thomas: 173
Gaitskell, Hugh: 40, 41, 106
Gamlin, Lionel: 98
Gardner, G.H.: 33
Garland, Judy: 204
Garnier, Pierre: 83
Garrison Club: 155
Gaumont-British Picture Corporation: 75, 88, 93
GDER (Groupement pour le Developpement des
    Emissions Radiophoniques): 31
Gee, H.V.: 197
General Strike (1926): 40, 75
George V, King: 107
George VI, King: 127
Gibbard, May: 147
Gilpin, John: 170
Gipsy Band: 119
Giselle: 172
Glossary of Aeronautical Terms: 19
Goff, Sir Park: 105
Golding, Mr: 120

Goldsmith, Major and Mrs Frank: 120
Gonat, Jacques: 70
Goodnight Melody, The: 95, 113
Goodnight Waltz, The: 77
Goossens, Leon: 204
Goossens, Sir Eugene: 204
Gordon-Box, S.H.: 104, 197, 203
Gouthier, Hugo: 170
Gramophone magazine: 106
Grand Goodnight, The: 77
Griffith, Maurice: 135
Grisewood, Freddy: 96, 98
Guinness Book of Firsts: 62
Guschiner, Herbert: 120
Gyrsting, Ann: 164
Halé Kimga (Gale Benson): 182
Hallé Orchestra: 204
Hamilton Place: 120, 121, 123, 137, 141, 145,
    146, 153, 154, 155, 170
Hampshire, Susan: 164
Happy Listening: 133, 150
Hargreaves, Jack: 119
Harmsworth, Harold (Lord Rothermere): 66
Harris Brand, R: 107
Headley, Peter: 187, 188
Hearst, William Randolph: 102
Heath, Neville: 147
Henley's: 86
Henson, Leslie: 155
Henson, Nicky: 155
Herald Broadcasting Station: 91
Hersh, Seymour: 139
Heyman, C. David: 193, 194
Hibberd, Stuart: 96, 98
Hilliam, B.C.: 96
Hitchcock, H.K.: 197, 201
Hitler, Adolf: 109, 139
HMV (His Master's Voice): 67, 82
Hoare, Oliver: 128
Hoare, Samuel: 128
Hobart, Robert (Earl of Buckingham): 120
Hockridge, Edmond: 204
Holloway, Godfrey: 135
Hope, C.P.: 197, 200, 202
House of Commons: 90, 108, 109, 113, 128,
    142, 146, 152, 179
Howard, Charles: 175, 186
Howard, Leslie: 144
Hulton, Lady: 120
Hurcombe, Ralph: 135, 197
Hylton, Jack: 68
IBA (International Broadcasting Association): 9

IBC (International Broadcasting Company): 13,
    69, 70, 73, 75, 76, 80, 82, 83, 86, 87, 90-95,
    97, 98, 104, 108, 113-116, 118, 119, 124,
    129, 130, 131, 133-136, 138, 145, 151, 154,
    155, 157-159, 161, 167-169, 172, 195
IBC Studios: 168
In Town Tonight: 106
Incorporated Society of British Advertisers: 110
Inter Allied Aeronautical Commission of Control:
    19
International Broadcasting Bureau: 29
International Broadcasting Union: 90, 109
It's Time to Say Goodnight: 114
ITV (Independent Television): 9
Jackson, Jack: 10
Jacqueline Bouvier – An Intimate Memoir: 194
Jagger, Mick: 173, 174
Jamal, Hakim: 180, 181, 182, 183, 186, 187,
    189
James Bond: 161
James, Mildred: 44, 61, 64
Joan and O'Shea: 120
Johnson, Amy: 88
Joint Broadcasting Committee: 129
Jones, Leslie: 204
Josef, Grand Duke Franz: 123
Joyce, William (Lord Haw Haw): 114, 128, 152
Juan-les-Pins: 82, 91, 97, 129, 163, 201
KDKA station, Pittsburgh: 27
Keep the Home Fires Burning: 135
Keith, Mrs Alan (Baroness Fern Andra): 102, 103
Kelly, Grace: 163
Kennedy Clan, The: 194
Kennedy family: 162
Kennedy, Bobby: 145
Kennedy, Caroline: 162
Kennedy, John F. (Jack): 139, 145, 162
Kennedy, John Jr: 162
Kent Messenger: 119
Kern, Jerome: 103
Kerridge, Adrian: 161
Kiciman, Mme Akgun: 172
Kidogo (Marvin Deane): 182, 183, 187, 189
Kingwell, William: 73, 74, 76, 197
Knight, Peter: 204
Knight, Roland: 185
L'Auto Italiana: 37
La Prensa Libre: 179
La Vie Automobile: 37
Labour [Party]: 74, 106, 107, 112, 149, 151, 152
Laine, Cleo: 204
Lamartine: 185
Lamping, Frank: 197

Lasata: 140
Law, David: 158
LBC: 9
Le Grand family: 130
Le Grand, Alexander: 72
Le Grand, Fernand: 72, 73, 79, 83, 92, 125, 134, 137, 194
League of Nations: 105, 107
League of Ovaltineys: 10
Lee, Janet: 140
Legion d'Honneur: 118, 191, 195
Lemaître, Francine: 72, 79, 83
Lennon, John: 189
Lennyann: 116, 124, 138, 151, 162
Leonard, Albert: 69, 75
Leopold de Rothschild, Mrs: 121
Les Ambassadeurs: 155
Lewis, Cecil A.: 23, 24
Lewis, Ted: 77
Liddell, Alvar: 98
Lieberson, Sandy: 173, 174
Light Programme: 9
Little Miss Bouncer: 96
London Motor Show: 162
London Philharmonic Orchestra: 204
London Symphony Orchestra: 204
London, Julie: 204
Lopez, Carol and Pepe: 171
Lord Haw Haw (William Joyce): 114, 128, 152
Lost Chord, The: 57
Louis XIV: 164
Louis XVI: 122
Louvetot: 124, 130, 137, 151, 198
Love's Old Sweet Song: 68
Lowndes Square: 155, 156, 164, 165, 166, 170, 171, 172, 173, 174, 192
Lowndes, Veronica Belloc: 165
Luboff, Norman: 204
Lucas, Sir Jocelyn: 165
Lucerne Agreement: 91, 95
Luxmore, Mr Justice: 114
Lyons, Sir Henry: 115
M.P. Pederson Engineering Company: 41
Ma Normandie: 77
MacDonald, Malcolm: 107
MacDonald, Ramsay: 74, 107
Mackenzie, Sir Compton: 106
Maconochie, Kenneth: 197
Mainland, Leslie: 67
Malandain, René: 79, 83
Malcolm X: 180, 181
Malik, Abdul (Michael X): 180, 181, 182, 183, 184, 185, 187, 188, 189, 193

Mandel, Georges: 125, 134
Mansfield, Jane: 204
March of the Movies: 157
Marconi Company: 23, 33, 48, 66
Marconiphone Super 8: 64
Margaret, Princess: 121
Marsden, Bernard: 158
Marshall Field store, Chicago: 32
Martin, Mrs: 142
Marx, Groucho: 103
Marx, Harpo: 103
Matheson, Hilda: 129
Mathieson, Muir: 204
Maxwell, Charles: 131, 135
McCulloch, Derek (Uncle Mac): 83, 96
McEachern, Malcolm: 96
McGuffie, Bill: 204
McNab, Benjy: 91, 93, 96, 197, 198, 199, 200
McNab, Flossie: 91
Melba, Dame Nellie: 66
Meyer, Richard 'Dickie': 69, 77, 93, 113, 135, 136, 158
MGM (Metro-Goldwyn-Mayer): 157
Michael X (Abdul Malik): 180, 181, 182, 183, 184, 185, 187, 188, 189, 193
Michelle, Cynthia: 42
Midgley, Veronica: 172
Mignard, Pierre: 175
Miklavcic, F.: 197, 202
Miklavcic, P.: 197, 202
Miller, Max: 204
Mills, John: 155, 157
Milroy Club: 155
Mitchell, Herbert James: 172, 173, 175
Modern Wireless: 25, 36
Moll: Making of Molly Parkin: 166
Monson, Tony: 155
Monte Carlo: 28, 115, 120, 160, 161, 163, 166, 167, 169
Moon, Miranda: 155
Moore-Brabazon, John: 20
Morden, Grant: 68
Morden, Pat: 68
Morden, Peggy: 68
Morrison, Herbert: 152
Mosley, Oswald: 109, 128
Moss, Don: 10
Motor: 37
Mountbatten, Lady Louis: 121, 130
Mouskouri, Nana: 204
Much Binding in the Marsh: 157
Muckleston, Ann. See Plugge, Ann
Muckleston, Frederick: 100

211

Muckleston, Mildred: 100, 118, 153
Murray, Pete: 10
Mussibini, George: 74, 75
MY Shemara: 162
Myfanwy: 44, 58, 61
NAAFI (Navy, Army and Air Force Institutes):
    166
Nathans: 179
National Coal Board: 173
National Radio Awards: 157
NBBS (New British Broadcasting Station): 128,
    129
NBC (National Broadcasting Company): 116,
    195
New Philharmonia: 204
New Shell Book of Firsts: 33, 62
New York World Telegram: 103
Newborough, Juno: 163, 164
Newborough, Lady Denisa: 163, 164, 167
Newborough, Lord: 164
Newman, Ian: 197
Newsweek: 178
Newton, Jimmy: 153, 165
Newton, Mrs Clarence: 120
Newton, Olive: 117, 153, 155, 191
Nicole: 159, 160, 168
Noble & Hoares: 17
Noble, Ray: 114
NPA (Newspaper Proprietors' Association): 87,
    88, 89, 90
Nureyev, Rudolf: 172
Nursery Corner (R. Normandy): 83, 84, 91
O'Moilley-Keys, Mrs: 120
O'Rahilly, Ronan: 162
Obelensky, Prince and Princess: 103
O'Brien, Anne Neville: 192
Ogilvie, Lieutenant Colonel: 19
Oldacre, Mrs: 42, 44, 61, 69
Olivier, Sir Laurence: 148
Olivier, Tarquin: 148
Olympia Motor Show: 33
Onassis, Jackie: 145, 193
Orr-Lewis, Lady: 120
Osterman, E.J.: 197, 198
Ostrer, Isodore: 75
Other Department If You Please, The: 65
Ovaltine: 10
Packard (Aether II): 15, 43, 44, 48, 50, 56, 58,
    60, 64
Paddy (IBC studio attendant): 158
Paige Tourer (Aether I): 33, 37, 43
Pall Mall Place: 21, 22, 25, 104
Pallenberg, Anita: 173, 174

Parkin, Michael: 166
Parkin, Molly: 165, 166
Parliamentary and Scientific Committee: 142,
    150
Parmassar, Adolphus: 182, 183, 184, 187, 189
Pathé Newsreels: 135
Patton, General: 152
Payne, Jack: 96
Pears, Peter: 204
Pellenc, Monsieur: 125
Performance: 173
Peters, Malcolm: 191
Petra: 143, 144
Philip, Prince: 190
Philips: 158
Pick, Frank: 21
Plomley, Roy: 77, 118, 119, 120, 135, 136, 197,
    200
Plugge Patent Auto Circuit: 175-178, 190, 195
Plugge Snr, Frank: 17, 18
Plugge Wilhelmina (Mina): 17, 18, 63, 64, 142,
    146, 147
Plugge, Ann: 100, 101, 102, 103, 106, 107, 115,
    116, 117, 118, 120, 122, 123, 124, 127, 137,
    138, 139, 140, 141, 142, 143, 144, 145, 146,
    147, 148, 149, 150, 153, 154, 155, 157, 162,
    166, 169, 172, 173, 175, 184, 186, 188, 193,
    194
Plugge, Christina: 17
Plugge, Colonel Arthur: 19
Plugge, Dominic: 176, 186, 193
Plugge, Frank [cousin]: 18
Plugge, Gale: 147, 156, 165, 167, 171
Plugge, Greville: 147, 165, 167, 172, 175, 179,
    184-188, 190, 193
Plugge, L. Frank: 8, 103, 117, 118, 121, 124,
    137, 138, 139, 140, 141, 142, 143, 144, 145,
    146, 147, 148, 154, 155, 156, 157, 160, 161,
    162, 163, 164, 165, 166, 167, 169, 170, 172,
    173, 174, 175, 178, 179, 181, 182, 184, 185,
    186, 187, 188, 189, 190, 193, 194
Plugge, Mary: 18
Poet's Corner: 74
Portland Place: 92, 118, 130, 133, 136, 145,
    146, 151, 154, 155, 158, 159, 167
Post Office: 24, 30, 33, 41, 48, 89, 109, 128
Poste Parisien: 82, 83, 91, 95, 97, 98, 104, 135,
    136, 199, 200
Potter, Gillie: 96
Powell, Colonel Clifford: 152
Preston, Dennis: 161
Prince of Wales: 62, 166
Privat, Monsieur: 31, 32, 37, 38, 44

Pro Arte: 204
PTT (Posté, Télégraphés et Téléphonés): 38, 72, 125
Purbrick, Reginald: 120
Pye Radio Ltd: 158
Radio Amateur: 37
Radio Athlone: 104, 202
Radio Barcelona: 64, 104, 203
Radio Belge: 38, 46
Radio Caroline: 9, 162
Radio Celebrities cigarette card series: 96
Radio Clyde: 9
Radio Cork: 104
Radio Côte d'Azur (Juan-les-Pins): 82, 97, 104, 201
Radio Dublin: 104
Radio Express: 37
Radio Fécamp: 71, 73, 78, 137, 197
Radio Fraternité: 151
Radio Iberia, Madrid: 36
Radio International: 93, 131, 134, 135
Radio International Publicity Services Ltd: 42, 44, 69
Radio Klub Zagreb: 59
Radio Ljubljana: 129, 202
Radio Luxembourg: 9, 10, 89, 90, 94, 95, 97, 98, 106, 113, 114, 124, 129, 151-153, 157, 158, 169
Radio Luxembourg (Advertising) Limited: 153
Radio Méditerranée: 201
Radio Moscow: 95
Radio Normandie: 75, 85
Radio Normandy: 13, 71-94, 96, 97, 98, 104, 108, 109, 115, 116, 119, 120, 124, 128, 130, 135, 137, 150, 151, 153, 195, 198
Radio Normandy Calling: 119, 120
Radio Paris: 30, 31, 38, 70, 82, 87, 90, 92, 93, 95, 199
Radio Pictorial: 96, 97, 98, 106, 113, 114, 120
Radio Popularisation (La RP): 31
Radio Publicity: 90, 95, 114
Radio Publicity (London) Ltd: 70, 93, 95, 98, 113, 114
Radio Publicity (Universal) Ltd: 114
Radio Publicity Limited: 70
Radio Rome: 204
Radio San Sebastian: 104, 203
Radio Society of Great Britain (RSGB): 24, 28, 30
Radio Sport: 37
Radio Supplement, The: 28, 29, 37, 42
Radio Times, The: 25, 90, 97, 98
Radio Times, The Foreign: 29

Radio Toulouse: 70, 82, 87, 201
Radio Valencia: 104, 203
Radio Vienna: 48
Radiodiffusion-Télévision Française (ORTF): 151
Radiola: 30
Radio-Meccano-Phone: 31
Radiotjanst Aktiebolaget: 41
Radiovox. See Pierre Garnier
Radziwill, John: 155
Radziwill, Prince Stanislaw: 145
Radziwill, Princess: 145
Rainier, Prince: 163
Raphael: 173
Ray, Johnny: 204
RCA (Radio Corporation of America): 101, 153
Redgrave, Corin: 171, 180
Redgrave, Deirdre: 171, 180
Redgrave, Vanessa: 171, 180
Rediffusion, La: 125
Reith, John Charles Walsham: 11, 23, 24, 30, 40, 74, 87, 89, 194
Remy: 77
Rendell, John: 187
Renis face cream: 81, 82
Repton, Mr and Mrs George: 120
Rex Lodge: 104, 146
Reynolds, Joshua: 173
Richard Meyer Associates Limited: 136
Richards, Keith: 174
Riche, Maitre: 160
Rigg, Nancy: 100
RNVR (Royal Naval Volunteer Reserve): 40
Robens, Lady: 173, 174, 175
Robens, Lord: 173, 175
Robins, Harold K.: 129
Robinson, Eric: 169
Robinson, Roland: 139
Robinson, Stanford: 204
Robson, May: 102
Rockefeller: 103
Roe, Tig: 158
Rogers, William: 121
Rolling Stones, The: 169, 204
Ronald, Tom: 87, 91, 95, 118, 119, 135, 197, 198, 199, 200, 201
Roosevelt, Franklin D.: 138
Rose, Allan: 197, 200
Ross Radio Productions: 169
Rothenstein, John: 164
Rothschild, Lionel: 122
Roy, Harry: 155
Royal Danish Orchestra: 204
Royal Philharmonic Orchestra: 204

RSGB. See Radio Society of Great Britain
Rubens, Peter Paul: 173
Rutherford, Captain D'Arcy: 120
Sagfragi, Prince: 103
Salisbury, Lord: 66
Sammes, Mike: 204
Sammy: 184
Sanderson, Lady: 120
Sanderson, Sir Frank: 115, 120
Savage, Miss: 158
Savoie, Monsieur: 71, 72
Savoy Band: 35
Savoy Orpheans: 47
Scarlet Pimpernel, The: 157
Schwaiger, Dr: 49
Scott, Sheila: 172
Scott-Taggart, John: 21
Seberg, Jean: 180, 181
Selborne Society: 38, 62
Selby, John: 115, 116, 197
Selfridge, Gordon: 32
Selfridges: 32, 37
Sempill, Baron: 19, 117
Serpa Pinto: 143
Shanks, George: 42, 69, 80, 93, 115, 125,
    134-136, 138, 144
Shaw, Mrs: 158
Shaw, Mrs Connie F.: 120
Shaw, Percy: 127
Shelton, Ann: 204
Shilling for a Second, A: 169
Shipway, Faith: 197, 199
Short Aviation: 20
Short History of the Radziwill Family: 145
Short Sunderland flying boat: 20, 145
Short, Oswald: 20, 117, 145
Short, Vi: 117, 145
Simmonds, Trina: 183
Simpson, Mrs: 166
Skerritt, Joe: 184, 185, 187, 188, 189
Slavik, Captain Antony: 48
Slessor, Philip: 119, 131, 135
Smith, Valentine: 66, 67, 68, 75, 88
Sneider, Captain: 52, 54
Societé des Amis des Concert Artistiques de la
    Tour Eiffel: 31
South African Wireless Weekly, The: 36
Southwestern Bell Telephone Company: 154
Spink and Son Ltd: 82
Squires, Dorothy: 204
SS Royal Thames: 115
SS1: 86, 87, 101, 102, 106, 107, 123
Stage Door Canteen: 151

Stagg, Allen: 157, 159, 161, 167, 168, 169
Standard Cars: 62
Standard Telephone nine-valve superhet: 62
Standard YR51 (Aether III): 62, 64
Stanniforth, Diana: 83
Stanniforth, Max: 74, 75, 76, 77, 79, 81, 83, 85,
    86, 87, 91, 197, 198
Stanniforth, Rosamund Ann: 83, 85, 91
Stapleton, Cyril: 204
Star, The: 193
Status Quo: 169
Steiner, Max: 204
Stella: 68
Stevens, Greville: 100, 147
Stewart-Saunders, W.: 197
Stone, Christopher: 106
Stott, Wally: 204
Strangers All: 102
Street, Seán: 11, 195
Sullivan, John: 197, 198, 200
Sultan of Penang: 169
Sun Life Insurance Company: 174
Sunday Dispatch: 66, 67
Sunday Express: 88
Sunday Referee, The: 70, 74, 75, 87, 88, 90, 93
Sunday Times, The: 193, 194
Sutton Courtney: 147, 148
Sutton, Nanny: 147
Svoboda: 48
Swallow Coachbuilding of Coventry: 86
SY Ceto: 66, 67, 68, 75, 91
T.S.F.: 37
Tate MP, Mrs: 139
Taylor, Peter: 115
Telegraph & Telephone: 37
Telegraph Magazine: 174
Terry, John: 158
There is a Green Hill: 57
Thomas, Dylan: 74
Thompson, Walter: 144
Thorpe, Jeremy: 64
Thought for Today: 93
Thurston, Captain: 19
Titian: 171, 173
Tocan, Dudley: 120
Tomlinson, Eric: 161
Tommy's Half Hour: 135
Tommy's Quarter Hour: 135
Torch, Sydney: 204
Towers, Harry Allan: 157
Townsend, George: 101
Truth Betrayed: 128
Tryon, Major: 108

Turkish Embassy, First Secretary of: 172
Ullswater Committee: 109, 112, 127
Uncle Eric Fogg: 84
Uncle Harry: 84
Uncle Mac (Derek McCulloch): 83, 96
Uncle Pierre (Garnier): 83
Uncle Stephen (Williams): 84
Underground Group: 20, 21, 24, 30, 42, 61, 68,
   69, 104, 161
Union Radio Madrid: 36, 37, 94, 104, 203
United Nations: 150, 151
Universal Programmes Corporation: 104, 105,
   118, 157
Van Cleef and Arpels: 115
Van Dyck, Mynheer: 67
Van Soust, Monsieur: 46
Vansittart, Sir Robert: 124
Vaughan, Frankie: 204
Venus of Urbino, The: 171
Veronese: 173
Vidor, Charles: 102
Vienna, City of My Dreams: 48
Violette, Roland: 79, 83
Voice of America: 151
Von Westerman, Dr: 46
Vyner-Midgley, Mr and Mrs: 172
W.D. & H.O. Wills: 96
Walker, Maidee: 186, 187, 188
Wallich, Isabella: 161
Wallis, Keith: 8, 10, 11
Ward and Draper: 119
Waterhouse, Walter George: 175
Watson, Colonel: 152
Weldon, Maisie: 119
Welles, Orson: 102, 157
Wellington, Duke of : 121
West, W.J.: 128
Western Electric: 34, 37, 41, 44, 48
Westminster, Dukes of : 121
Westwood, Gillian: 167, 193
Whicker, Alan: 191
White, Claude Graham: 20
White, W.G.: 67
Whiteley, William: 65
Whiteleys of Bayswater: 65
Who, The: 169, 204
Who's Who: 178
William the Conqueror: 76
Williams, Alan: 148
Williams, Arthur: 63, 64
Williams, Brook: 146, 148, 157, 164, 184
Williams, Emlyn: 146, 155, 164, 175, 184, 188,
   193

Williams, John: 204
Williams, Molly: 146, 147, 157, 175, 184, 193
Williams, Stephen: 67, 68, 74, 75, 78, 79, 81,
   82, 83, 85, 86, 87, 92, 93, 95, 114, 129, 152,
   153, 197, 198, 199
Wilson, Aubyn: 69
Wilson, Bonita: 155
Wilson, Graham: 197
Windsor, Duchess of: 162
Windsor, Duke of: 124, 162, 166
Winter, Bonita: 84
Winter, Marius B.: 118
Wireless Constructor, The: 36
Wireless Publicity Ltd (Canada): 114
Wireless Weekly: 25, 29, 36
Wolkowsky and Grand: 120
Woman Named Jackie, A: 193
Wontner, Hilary: 197
Wood, Bill: 21, 22, 25, 34, 61, 103, 104, 120,
   121, 123, 141, 151, 157, 158, 161, 163, 169,
   191, 194
Wood, General Sir Kingsley: 90
Wood, Joan: 123, 124
Wood, Leo: 77
Woodall, Ivy: 64, 65
Woodall, Thomas: 65
Wooley Hart, Mrs: 120
Workers' Challenge: 129
World War I: 20, 77, 138
World War II: 145, 162
Writtle: 23, 66
Wymore, Patrice: 161
Yeates, Steve: 182, 183, 184, 187, 189
York, Duchess of: 121
York, Duke of: 117, 121
Yorkshire Television: 191
Young, Joe: 119
Ziegfeld, Flo: 103
Zographes, Mr N.: 120

215

Kelly Publications – Mass Media Titles

Baird Album
JOHN LOGIE BAIRD A Pictorial Record of Early Television
Development 1924-1938.
Introduction by Professor R.W. Burns. Foreword by Dr Graham Winbolt.
KP 2001. ISBN 1-903053-10-2.
vii + 72 pages of illustrations. 9¾ x 12 inches. Paperback.
Following a visit in 1989 to view the collection of historical documents put together by the Plessey Company at Ilford, Dr Winbolt was presented with various items, including an album of photographs relating to the early development of television, most of them of John Logie Baird and his pioneering work in the field. Having treasured the album for a decade or so, Dr Winbolt decided that the contents should be published and this book is the result. It is a faithful reproduction, with over 80 illustrations presented in the same order as they appeared in the original album with the captions virtually unaltered. Many of the photographs are rare and have never been published elsewhere. This edition is limited to 500 copies and will not be reprinted. **£14.95**

Baird Facsimile Reprint
THE BAIRD 'TELEVISOR' Seeing by Wireless.
With an Introduction by Ray Herbert.
KP 2005. ISBN 1-903053-21-8.
Consists of card folder (10¾ x 7¼) with inner pockets containing:
1.) 8-page Introduction by Ray Herbert.
2.) 8-page facsimile of the first promotional brochure on the Baird Televisor. There are four illustrations – the one on the front being reproduced on the card folder.
   'This little booklet tells how, after many years of pioneer work, the baffling problem was solved at last' **£10.00**

Baird Television Ltd. Facsimile reprint
THE BAIRD 'TELEVISOR' (Disc Model)
Reprint of this 1931 instruction booklet. KP 2001.
8 pages. Grey printed wraps. 5 half-tone illustrations and 7 diagrams.
This high quality facsimile is limited to 250 copies and will not be reprinted. **£5.00**

Currie (Tony)
A CONCISE HISTORY OF BRITISH TELEVISION 1930-2000
70 Years of Key Developments.
Foreword by Peter Fiddick.
KP 2004. Second Edition (Revised and Enlarged) ISBN 1-903053-17-X.
128 pages. Paperback. Over 80 illustrations.
Enlarged and updated version of the series of articles published in
1995/96 in the Journal of the Royal Television Society. (A companion to
Seán Street's A CONCISE HISTORY OF BRITISH RADIO 1922-2002')
£9.95

Currie (Tony)
THE RADIO TIMES STORY
Foreword by John Peel. Cover by George Mackie
KP 2001. ISBN 1-903053-09-9.
260 pages. 11 x 8½ inches. Paperback.
Over 600 illustrations, including 12 pages of colour.
The author's fascination with Radio Times began when he was four, and
he has been a collector ever since. Over the years he has become the
foremost expert on the magazine's history and content, and this book is
packed with information about the development of the world's oldest
listing magazine over the 78 years of its existence, as well as many
amusing anecdotes. In addition to telling the fascinating story of the
magazine, the book is also a social history of British broadcasting.
Profusely illustrated, this is an impressive volume packed with
information and nostalgia. **£18.95**

Dinsdale (Alfred) Facsimile Reprint
TELEVISION Seeing by Wire or Wireless.
KP 2000. ISBN 1-903053-05-6.
62 pages. Stiff wraps with dust wrapper. In pictorial slipcase, special to
this reprint. 12 full-page plates (6 diagrams; 6 half-tones).
Facsimile reprint of the original edition, published in November 1926.
This was the first book in English devoted entirely to the subject of
television, and describing a successful system of television (Baird's).
Copies of the first edition have fetched up to $4,800 at auction in recent
years. This facsimile edition is limited to 250 copies, and will very likely
become a collector's item itself. **£15.00**

Howett (Dicky)
TELEVISION INNOVATIONS
50 Technological Developments. A personal selection
KP 2005. ISBN 1-903053-22-6.
128 pages. 9½ x 8 inches. Paperback. Over 130 half-tone illustrations.
Designed as a media primer, this book charts for the first time, 50 key television innovations, including the development of zoom lenses, telerecording, outside broadcasting, video tape, electronic image tubes and studio pedestals. The author also presents a concise history of several mechanical television systems, featuring the innovations of Baird and Nipkow, as well as the work of many television equipment manufacturers including, RCA, Houston-Feerless, Philips, Sony, Ampex and Vinten. The photographs, many never before published, have been especially sourced for this unique book **£14.95**

Jones (Ian) MORNING GLORY
A History of British Breakfast Television
KP 2004. ISBN 1-903053-20-X.
256 pages. Paperback 9¼ x 6 inches (23.4cm x 15.6cm)
With 20 caricature drawings and cover by Graham Kibble-White. (The cover is a tribute to the TV Times cover for the launch of Breakfast Television).
The first book to tell the full story of British breakfast television from its inception in 1983. This lively account carries the reader from the beginnings of the BBC's Breakfast Time, through the rise and fall of TV-am, the launch of GMTV, the early success and later difficulties of The Big Breakfast, the problems of Rise, etc, right up to January 2004 **£16.95**

Street (Seán)
A CONCISE HISTORY OF BRITISH RADIO 1922-2002
Preface by Piers Plowright.
KP 2005. Reprinted with minor corrections. ISBN 1-903053-14-5.
156 pages. Paperback. 85 illustrations.
Seán Street, broadcaster, poet and historian, is Professor of Radio in the Bournemouth Media School at Bournemouth University, the first person to hold such a post in this country. Issued as a companion to Tony Currie's A CONCISE HISTORY OF BRITISH TELEVISION, this informative and entertaining book is a completely original publication. To quote from Piers Plowright's Preface it is: a coherent and dramatic sweep from the first scientifically-based attempts to send sound messages

over distance to the rich and sometimes rude complexity of 21st century digital broadcasting... The style is crisp, clear and often witty. Perhaps uniquely in a study of radio history this excellent book recognises the importance of the various commercial radio stations, pre-war as well as post-war, balanced against those of the BBC. **£10.95**

White (Leonard)
ARMCHAIR THEATRE The Lost Years
With forewords by Honor Blackman and Allan Prior.
KP 2003. ISBN 1-903053-18-8.
280 pages. 9¾ x 8 inches. Paperback. Over 130 half-tone illustrations.
The first book to give a comprehensive account of the later years of this important television drama series. A seminal part of the history of ITV drama, Leonard White's book covers the richly creative period 1963-69 during which he produced more than 175 single teleplays. This is a valuable addition to the history of television, with full credits to the many famous talents who made Armchair Theatre the much respected and successful drama anthology it was. Includes a chapter on the early days of THE AVENGERS. **£17.95**

FORTHCOMING: Spring/Summer 2008
Shubik (Irene)
PLAY FOR TODAY: The evolution of television drama
Reprint of this important work by the award-winning drama producer.

Kelly Books Ltd: *www.kellybooks.net*